That Great Sanity

Critical Essays on
May Sarton

Edited by
Susan Swartzlander and Marilyn R. Mumford

Ann Arbor

THE UNIVERSITY OF MICHIGAN PRESS

Copyright © by the University of Michigan 1992
All rights reserved
Published in the United States of America by
The University of Michigan Press
Manufactured in the United States of America

1995 1994 1993 1992   4 3 2 1

Library of Congress Cataloging-in-Publication Data

That great sanity : critical essays on May Sarton / edited by Susan
   Swartzlander and Marilyn R. Mumford.
      p.   cm.
   Includes bibliographical references.
   ISBN 0-472-10259-1 (alk. paper)
   1. Sarton, May, 1912–   —Criticism and interpretation.
   I. Swartzlander, Susan, 1958–   . II. Mumford, Marilyn R., 1934–
   PS3537.A832Z89 1992
   811'.52—dc20   92-36711
                                                              CIP

A CIP catalogue record for this book is available from the British Library.

Her work speaks to readers and audiences with such immediacy, sympathy, and power that thousands of women and men count themselves "friends of the work." For helping us to understand what it means to be "fully human," we dedicate this book to May Sarton with affection and respect.

Acknowledgments

The editors acknowledge the generous support of Bucknell University and Grand Valley State University; in particular, we would like to thank our deans, Eugenia P. Gerdes and Forrest Armstrong, and our department chairs, Robert L. Taylor, Jr., and Milton Ford, for their strong support of our work. Many colleagues and friends supported this project in its early stages; we note particularly Patricia B. Adams, Harry J. Berman, Susan Bowers, Tirzah Gerstein, Dorothy M. Healy (deceased), Jean Leslie, Phyllis Mannocchi, Valerie Miner, Roger Platizky, Liana Sakelliou-Schultz, and Susan Sherman. Several students at Grand Valley and at Bucknell helped to prepare the manuscript: Jennifer Blaker, Alex Buccino, Stacey Hollenbeck, Heather Klare, Cindy Long, Jillian Myrom, Gema Sanchez-Perez, Mary Schoonover, Thomas Stone, Amanda Swarr, and Angelique Trombino-Butler. For her valuable help, we thank Frances Kelleher. Judith Mage supplied enthusiasm and moral support in generous measure. For three years, we called on Nancy Weyant's superb bibliographic skills, and she always triumphed over the perversities of data bases. Finally, we want to thank LeAnn Fields, our editor at the University of Michigan Press, for her unfailing insight and helpful guidance as this book made its way through the editorial process.

Daniels. Reprinted by permission of Pantheon Books, a division of Random House, Inc.

May Sarton for permission to quote from unpublished letters in the Berg Collection, New York Public Library. Quotations are from an August 16, 1940 letter to Margaret Foote Hawley and from a December 29, 1929 letter to Sarton's parents.

W. W. Norton & Company, Inc. for quotations from *After the Stroke: A Journal by May Sarton*, copyright © 1988 by May Sarton; *At Seventy: A Journal by May Sarton*, copyright © 1984 by May Sarton; *The Education of Harriet Hatfield*, copyright © 1989 by May Sarton; *The House by the Sea: A Journal by May Sarton*, copyright © 1977 by May Sarton; *Journal of a Solitude*, copyright © 1973 by May Sarton; *Mrs. Stevens Hears the Mermaids Singing*, copyright © 1965 by May Sarton; *Recovering: A Journal by May Sarton*, copyright © 1980 by May Sarton; and for lines from the poem "Salt Lick," which appeared in *The Silence Now: New and Uncollected Earlier Poems*, by May Sarton, copyright © 1988 by May Sarton; *The Small Room*, by May Sarton, copyright © 1976 by May Sarton. Reprinted by permission of W. W. Norton & Company, Inc.

Every effort has been made to trace the ownership of all copyrighted material in this book and to obtain permission for its use.

Contents

Introduction:
In Our Mothers' Gardens

Maureen Teresa McCarthy

In her critical introduction to *Mrs. Stevens Hears the Mermaids Singing*, Carolyn Heilbrun states that, for May Sarton,

> ... there has been little organized acclamation, no academic attention, indifference on the part of the critical establishment. (Sarton 1974, ix–x)

Heilbrun's introduction to *Mrs. Stevens* was written more than fifteen years ago, and, as yet, Sarton has still received little serious academic consideration. In her recent *Writing a Woman's Life* (1988), Heilbrun states that: "May Sarton's fame is greater now that she is seventy-five than it has ever been" (127). Yet fame is certainly not synonymous with critical attention; fame may, in fact, contribute to critical oblivion. Sarton's work at present exists in a near vacuum; there is little literary or critical acknowledgment of her writing. Only one book-length study of her work has been completed, and the number of articles in academic journals is limited.

The few books in print about her consider May Sarton, the woman, as much as they do the work. The first, *May Sarton, Woman and Poet* (1982), is a compilation of articles and reviews edited by Constance Hunting. The second, *May Sarton, A Self-Portrait* (1982), is actually a transcript of a film made about Sarton and her work in 1979. The third is Agnes Sibley's volume, in the Twayne United States Authors Series, that considers her work only up until 1972. Elizabeth Evans has recently published a new volume on Sarton in the Twayne series, and scholars in various fields have begun to recognize Sarton's contribution to American letters. As Nancy Weyant documents in the bibliographic essay that concludes this volume, scholarly interest in Sarton is developing, but Elizabeth Evans's *May Sarton Revisited* is the only sustained consideration of her work yet to be completed.

The MLA Bibliography lists a total of nineteen references to Sarton during the last fifty years. Three of those are books noted above, one is a dissertation; three are in Japanese publications (Sarton spent some time in Japan), and four are chapters in books on another writer or topic. One is a compilation of letters Sarton received from readers. The remaining seven are articles published in *Frontiers, Women and Literature, Contempora, Critique,* and *Southwest Review.* Most of these consider Sarton as an example of the woman who ages with dignity while continuing to work.

The *Reader's Guide* lists several articles on Sarton within the last fifteen years, in publications such as *Ms., Vogue, New York Times Magazine,* and *House and Garden.* She is most frequently figured here as a survivor, a diarist or journal keeper, and a garden/nature writer.

Yet another version of Sarton the writer is constructed by Gale Research Company, which collates the reviews an author's work has generated. The Gale publications, which include *Contemporary Authors, Dictionary of Literary Biography, Contemporary Literary Criticism,* and *Something About the Author,* initially considered Sarton in 1962. At that time, Sarton was a serious writer who had been publishing for almost twenty-five years. She merited one-and-a-half columns of notice in *Contemporary Authors, New Revisions Series.* That edition stressed that her father was a noted historian of science, perhaps as evidence of her credibility as a writer. The reference was dropped from succeeding editions.

By 1975, Sarton rated five columns containing eight reviews in volume 4 of *Contemporary Literary Criticism.* However, she was still considered to be simply "queen of a small, well-ordered country," as James Dickey described her (*CLC* 470). All eight reviews were, at the least, condescending, with Dickey's among the more favorable. The 1980 edition of *CLC* also featured five columns and eight reviews, although at least two of them were positive, and the tone was less condescending than in the previous edition.

Volume 49 of *Contemporary Literary Criticism, 1988,* accorded Sarton thirty-five columns, twenty-nine reviews, and a picture. In this, the most recent edition, the reviews are generally favorable, even celebratory, and few of the original notices are included. However, all of the Gale publications generally consider Sarton a minor writer, the author of women's books that concentrate on "the feminine world of family and home" (313), as Elizabeth Janeway described Sarton's work in the 1988 *CLC.* Gale also notes that Sarton is a writer of children's books, and several reviews figure her as such.

The Gale treatment of Sarton attests that her work has merited increasing attention by reviewers and, presumably, from readers. Almost all of Sarton's work is currently in print, both in hard and soft cover editions.

Sarton's career has not been without a certain amount of professional recognition and a degree of acclaim. By 1960, she had been awarded the prestigious Guggenheim Fellowship, she was elected an honorary member of Phi Beta Kappa, and she had been elected a Fellow of the American Academy of Arts and Sciences. But professional recognition is not necessarily critical consideration. At fifty years of age, she was clearly an established writer and just as clearly ignored by the critical establishment. During the entire decade of the 1960s, there was not a single article on her cited in MLA.

Currently, Sarton is still generally overlooked by the academy, as evidenced by MLA. She may well be better known than she ever has been, but for years she was virtually unknown. However, there does seem to be an undercurrent of recognition, and it may be this to which Heilbrun is referring when she notes that Sarton is more famous at 75 than she has ever been. Allusions to Sarton and quotations from her work appear in various recent academic publications.

She is, for example, included in the *Norton Reader*, 6th edition, 1984. This anthology, which concentrates on expository prose, places Sarton in the section on "Personal Reports, Journals." Norton has not, however, placed Sarton in any edition of the *Anthology of American Literature*, although she is included in the *Norton Anthology of Literature by Women* (1985), edited by Gilbert and Gubar. That volume, and the Prentice-Hall *Women in Literature: Life Stages through Stories, Poems, and Plays* (1988), edited by Sandra Eagleton, both include selections from *Mrs. Stevens Hears the Mermaids Singing*, configuring Sarton as the elderly writer. Further, Gilbert and Gubar cite Sarton's work in several chapters of *No Man's Land, Volume 1, The War of the Words* (1988).

These inclusions are comparatively recent, all occurring in the mid- to late 1980s, and follow publication of Sarton's journal, *At Seventy* (1984), in which she acknowledges herself as "old." In that work, it is apparent that Sarton's idea of old is not at all the construction of old in our culture. In reply to the question of why is it good to be old, Sarton answers: "'Because I am more myself than I have ever been. There is less conflict. I am happier, more balanced, and ... more powerful'" (10). Aging women in our society are not commonly thought of as powerful.

And that, precisely, may be Sarton's triumph, for herself and her readers: her insistence upon her powerful self, work, discipline; the ability to shape one's life; the persistence of her career; the validity of choices; her essential survival.

Sarton's determined perseverance may also have been her downfall, in the sense of her exile from the literary canon. For the modernist author traditionally has no second act; "he" works hard, writes well, and drinks himself into oblivion at an early age. Sarton continually has chosen to do her own work as she understands it. She has always marched to the beat of a different drummer, in defiance of a culture that has increasingly demanded conformity while espousing individuality.

Despite claims to objectivity, the literary canon, as Jane Tompkins argues in *Sensational Designs* (1985), has tended to reflect "all those historical circumstances by which literary values are supposed to remain unaffected" (187). Thus, in the postwar decade of the 1950s, the canon espoused writers such as Hemingway, Fitzgerald, and Faulkner, who gave us the lost generation, scarred by war and technology.

That generation of postwar writers whom we have termed modernist reflected the extreme disorientation of a world invaded by the machine, a world very far from the garden. Irving Howe explained, in *The Decline of the New* (1963),

> ... the modern writer can no longer accept the claims of the world. If he tries to acquiesce in the norms of the audience, he finds himself depressed and outraged. The usual morality seems counterfeit; taste, a genteel indulgence; tradition, a wearisome fetter. It becomes a condition of being a writer that he rebel, ... against received opinions, ... against the received ways of doing the writer's work. (4)

Alone in her garden, the garden whose care she had learned from her mother, Sarton did not conform at all to the constraints of rebellion and despair. In works such as *The Bridge of Years* (1946), *The Single Hound* (1938), and "In Time Like Air" (1953), she expressed her belief in the power of family life, friendship, and decent human behavior to resist the dehumanization of the modern world.

She did receive a certain amount of recognition for this work, for it was in this decade that she was awarded the Donnelly Fellowship and the Guggenheim. She was also elected to honorary Phi Beta Kappa and to the American Academy of Arts and Sciences.

But critical attention continued to elude her, as she herself expressed in *Plant Dreaming Deep* (1968), one of her early journals. She also indicates her awareness of the canon constraints that she had ignored.

I believe that eventually my work will be seen as a whole, all the poems and all the novels, as the expression of a vision of life which, though unfashionable all the way, has validity. (Sarton 1968, 90–91)

Plant Dreaming Deep was issued in 1968, midway through one of her most productive decades. During that time she published three volumes of poetry, six novels, and the journal. Critical reaction continued to be slight, although her work was reviewed regularly.

And she continued to publish regularly. Early in the 1970s her work again elicited some recognition. Dawn Anderson's essay on Sarton's women appeared in *Images of Women in Fiction,* the 1972 collection from Bowling Green edited by Susan Koppelman Cornillon. The following year, Anderson chaired an MLA seminar that considered ten papers on Sarton's work. In 1974, Heilbrun's laudatory introduction prefaced the reissue of *Mrs. Stevens Hears the Mermaids Singing.* And, in 1979, the film *World of Light: A Portrait of May Sarton* was released.

But, again, the literary-critical establishment was virtually silent on Sarton's work. By the end of the 1970s, modernism had given way to postmodernism, and Sarton was still outside the constraints of the canon. In *Cultural Politics in Contemporary America* (1989), Todd Gitlin interpreted the current standard.

"Postmodernism" usually refers to a certain constellation of styles and tones in cultural works: pastiche; blankness; a sense of exhaustion; a mixture of levels, forms, styles; a relish for copies and repetition; a knowingness that dissolves commitment into irony; acute self-consciousness about the formal, constructed nature of the work; pleasure in the play of surfaces; a rejection of history. (Angus and Jhally, 1989, 347)

Writers such as Burroughs, Kozinsky, Hawkes, Fowles, Mailer, and Barthelme reflected this vision of the world, while Sarton persisted in her personal expression of commitment, energy, light, and tradition. She confronted her own vision of the artist as single woman and of the single woman as outside the culture.

Thus, Sarton's work conflicted with the tenets of modernism and postmodernism, and with the tenets of an emerging feminism as well. The second wave of feminist writing, which crested in the 1970s, was characterized by such writers as Millett, Greer, Janeway, Moers, Piercy, Roiphe,

Jong, Sexton, and Plath. All of these writers documented and validated
female experience, but their work frequently reflected traditional male terms
and accepted male standards. That is, a woman's right to live her own life
often meant the right to live as a man and write like a man. A life free
from the constraints of children, home, family, and commitment was celebrated. Sarton, whose work embraced tradition, home, family, discipline,
and heritage, was acknowledged, if at all, as marginal.

Even though Sarton recently has achieved a certain amount of recognition, her work as a whole still has not been accorded serious critical
analysis, even by feminist scholars. The current allusions figure her primarily
as the aged writer, the survivor, and do not deal with the richness and
subtlety of her approach to the human situation.

I suggest that this has as much to do with the critical frame of reference
as it does with Sarton's work. As Blanche Gelfant states in *Women Writing
in America* (1984),

> . . . I saw how pervasively I deal, as a critic, with violence, uncertainty,
> and nihilistic visions of life, and with the writer's quest for a language
> consonant with an American landscape that is always being discovered
> or created, that is always new. (1)

Sarton has never expressed a violent, uncertain, nihilistic vision of life,
although she certainly is aware of the violence and uncertainty in life.
Obviously, Gelfant is a product of the modernist-postmodernist canon,
which, as Tompkins demonstrates, commonly has institutionalized certain
values and ignored others. Critics who have been trained to think in those
terms are often unable to appreciate other visions as of equal value; one
may be either better or worse, but certainly not different. Difference has
virtually guaranteed exile from the canon of American literature.

The constraints of the canon do, in fact, reveal themselves in considering
Sarton's career (or lack of one). As a writer who ignored the accepted vision
of modernism and postmodernism, Sarton has been ignored by the academic
arbiters of the canon.

The professional recognition first accorded Sarton, the Guggenheim,
Phi Beta Kappa, and so forth, culminated in 1959, with no critical follow-
up. The second wave of attention accorded her work crested in the early
1970s, with Heilbrun's introduction to *Mrs. Stevens*. Again, further critical
attention did not materialize. The current allusions to Sarton may be seen

as the third crest, with the question of critical consideration largely yet to be addressed.

However, this line of thought can itself be seen as a perpetuation of the critical tradition that has ignored Sarton. The idea of opening the canon, of admitting others, is, in a traditional sense, a patriarchal construct, predicated on the binary of good/bad, either/or, as evidenced by literary standards. For admission still implies exclusivity. Of course, as Tompkins articulates in *Sensational Designs,*

> ... I do not wish to be understood as claiming that there is no such thing as value or that value judgments cannot or should not be made.... The point is not that these discriminations are baseless; the point is that the grounds on which we make them are not absolute and unchanging but contingent and variable. (193)

The contingencies and variables that have led to Sarton's exclusion from the canon also reflect feminist theory as it has evolved from an insistence on women's writing as being "just as good" as male writing, to an affirmation of the unique possibilities inherent in a woman-centered text. This reflection is also an interesting parallel to Sarton's career.

Feminist criticism is now a viable, respected methodology within the academy, but it has only recently come of age, as Elaine Showalter demonstrates in her collection of essays, *The New Feminist Criticism: Essays on Women, Literature, and Theory* (1985). Within the literary-critical establishment, early feminism was, in Freudian terms, noted for rebellion and aggression. Feminist criticism at that time concentrated on documenting the extent to which women had been excluded from the canon. It also insisted that there were many women writers who deserved canonization, whose work was good literature, equal to the work of canonized males. The concepts of "good" or "literature" had not been questioned to the degree that they are at present.

In the sense that established literary criticism could be seen as the law of the father, then the woman writer and the woman critic found herself in a peculiarly awkward position. Gilbert and Gubar illustrate this problem in *The War of the Words* (1988), volume 1 of *No Man's Land: The Place of the Woman Writer in the Twentieth Century.* This awkward position is demonstrated particularly well in the chapter "'Forward into the Past': The Female Affiliation Complex." If the woman writer were to embrace the prevailing standards of modernism and postmodernism, she essentially would betray herself. In accepting male standards of literature and criticism she would, in a Freudian sense, mature into normative behavior, but at the price of disassociation with the mother and her matrilineal heritage. It is only in working through what Gilbert and Gubar call the affiliation complex that the woman writer can affirm matrilineage.

The development of feminist criticism, as well as that of the feminist artist, can also be traced through these stages. Early feminist critics validated the law of the father with their rebellion against it, for rebellion posits itself against an established authority. It is only recently, as feminist criticism has abandoned the masculine definition and become woman-centered, that feminist critics have developed the confidence to affirm woman writers on their own terms. As Gilbert and Gubar maintain, women writers have ceased their struggle to possess the father and have turned to the mother as the source of affirmation and identity.

Sarton, then, has always been in a peculiar situation. She has inhabited a room of her own and has acknowledged her debt to her mother, both literally and literarily. Early commentary on her work thus reproached her for her emphasis on domesticity, as Elizabeth Janeway did in the *New York Times Book Review* (September 8, 1957).

> This is not a "woman's novel," a lending library favorite; it is much too precisely observed, truly told and serious minded. But it is limited to much the same material as these contrivances, the feminine world of family and home. (*CLC* 1988, 313)

The feminine world of family and home is now accorded as much validity as the masculine world of bulls and barrooms. The "private lives of one half of humanity," in Carolyn Kizer's words, are no longer "the world's best-kept secret" (from section 3 of "Pro Femina," in Kizer's *Mermaids in the Basement* [1963]). The (largely) feminine concerns of family, home, motherhood and daughterhood are now acknowledged and celebrated.

Texts such as Adrienne Rich, *Of Woman Born: Motherhood as Experience and Institution* (1976); Nancy Friday, *My Mother, My Self: The Daughter's Search for Identity* (1977); Jean Baker Miller, *Toward a New Psychology of Women* (1976); Nancy Chodorow, *The Reproduction of Mothering: Psychoanalysis and the Sociology of Gender* (1978); and Alice Walker, *In Search of Our Mothers' Gardens: Womanist Prose* (1983) affirm the maternal heritage. Women writers have always known the importance of the mother, though previously that insight was trivialized or ignored, as in the critical response to Sarton.

Sarton however, refused to trivialize or ignore her heritage and especially her matrilineage. In prose, poetry, and journal she celebrated the connections and affirmations that link mothers and daughters, friends and lovers, sisters, aunts, cousins. Her affirmation of community is unequaled in American letters, and, very possibly, in the life of the American artist.

For the American artist has, according to Harold Bloom, often acted in accordance with the constraints of the biological family, as we have understood and accepted those constraints. In other words, the sons have been driven to rebel against the fathers. The question, then, becomes one of nature or nurture. Is that rebellion natural, innate, or is it learned behavior?

Sarton would probably maintain that it is simply a cultural construct, one that she has repeatedly challenged. Sarton's relationship with her mother was warm and affectionate, and, in fact, she was delighted to publish a selection of her mother's letters to her. Throughout the introduction of *Letters to May* (1986), she celebrates the love she shared with her mother.

> And here . . . is my mother, writing to me whom she called her "dearest friend." Always . . . she treated me as a person in my own right, . . . She set me free . . . she was always honest with me. . . . The chance to publish a selection of her letters to me is one of the happiest events of my life. (xii)

Sarton and her mother enjoyed the special affection of a devoted mother and daughter, but Eleanor Mabel Sarton's letters to her daughter reveal that they shared a great deal more. They both possessed an intellectual curiosity and an artistic awareness that challenged and stimulated them. Sarton felt no need to rebel against her mother; rather, she affirmed her strength through her relationship with her mother.

Letters to May contains numerous references to people Sarton was to cherish all her life. Marie Closset, S. S. Koteliansky, Eva Le Gallienne, Muriel Rukeyser, and many others live on those pages. Friendship was not limited by age or generation; it was shared, as was experience. As her mother's daughter, as an outsider, a woman of European birth, May Sarton continually validated literary sisterhood. In her words, she was always in search of " . . . that great sanity, that sun, the feminine power." In the poem "My Sisters, O My Sisters," the first part of which concludes with the line just quoted, Sarton invokes Anna de Noailles, Dorothy Wordsworth, Emily

Dickinson, Sappho, George Sand, Madame de Staël, and Madame de Sévigné. Thus, she perpetuates the tradition of literary women documented by Ellen Moers, Patricia Meyer Spacks, Nina Auerbach, and all those writing women who lived and wrote before us.

In that poem and in numerous other works, Sarton acknowledged her literary ancestors; she welcomed rather than rejected. But while she was affirming the significance of a female tradition, she was also living a life based on close friendships and support. In the film *World of Light: A Portrait of May Sarton,* she says:

> I often think of that beautiful sentence from Yeats: "Think where man's glory most begins and ends and say my glory was I had such friends." And I feel it deeply because I was very lucky . . . in the people who came into my life. (Simpson and Wheelock 1982, 21)

She acknowledges Marie Closset, the Julian Huxleys, Elizabeth Bowen, Virginia Woolf, Eva Le Gallienne, all of whom have had a profound influence on her life and work. The poem "Because What I Want Most is Permanence" was written for Elizabeth Bowen, "Letter from Chicago" for Virginia Woolf, "A Hard Death" for her mother.

The sisterhood of literary women was not limited by friendship, nationality, race, or generation; rather, it was a sisterhood of the spirit, of "strange monsters" as Sarton said. Nor was this sisterhood a new development in letters; it is a long-established tradition. Like much of women's work, it has simply been ignored.

As literary woman, then, Sarton existed in contradiction to the terms of the academy. Her exile from critical attention was further insured by the fact that she affirmed her heritage as international, interracial, and unlimited by oceans or the boundaries drawn by men. The pages of her journals are filled with references to artists, writers, philosophers, scientists, intellectuals, and kindred spirits from all over the world. She repeatedly expresses her concern, sorrow, and awareness of the human condition in Ireland, Asia, Ethiopia, wherever there is suffering on this troubled earth.

Her vision, too, sees all the globe; her art encompasses our shared humanity. Her love for the play of light has been linked to the Dutch masters, her concern with family to Jane Austen. She herself has written of her European sensibility, of her English garden lore, of her love for Japanese stillness. She has never limited herself to being an American.

She has thought always in terms of a human sensibility, rather than

simply an American one, and that, too, may have contributed to her exile
from the canon of American letters. For American literature has, by definition, insisted on a distinctly American essence, the pure voice of the
nation. Even though the melting pot has been recognized as myth, the
national literature has been judged on its expression of "Americanness," as
Nina Baym explains in her essay, "Melodramas of Beset Manhood: How
Theories of American Fiction Exclude Women Authors" (1981). Literary
excellence, in the American academy, has come to be evaluated in terms of
"most American," however that may be defined in a particular era. Generally,
the definition has also included white and male; it has never stressed our
common humanity.

But Sarton has always dared to insist upon the human ties among us
all, passengers on spaceship earth. Her friendships have spanned races, generations, and gender lines as well. She has claimed many men as kindred
spirits, as friends of the heart. Thus she found herself in conflict with the
tenets of the newly developing feminism, for she could not espouse sepa-
ratism, whether of race, creed, or gender.

As she has written so often in her journals, Sarton has been an outsider
in every sense of the word. She has tasted of the forbidden fruit of knowledge,
yet she has lived in a garden of her own making. Alone in New Hampshire
or on the coast of Maine, her spirit has flourished as in a city upon a hill,
a city of sisterly and brotherly love. She has realized the tenets of the
American Adam, a new man in a new world, but, as Eve, she has been
invisible. Her invisibility, I think, has resulted precisely from her individuality, which may indeed be the essence of her own Americanness. But are
we prepared to accept her, as she is, as she has chosen to be?

If, as I am positing, feminist criticism has worked through the affiliation
complex and has empowered itself to go, as Alice Walker tells us, "in search
of our mothers' gardens," are we prepared to embrace the women we find
there? The lost mother "must," of course, be motherly, loving, nurturing,
supportive, and proud of her daughters (and of her sons). She must also be
strong, determined, and intent upon her own creative vision, whether it be
a garden, a quilt, or a poem. And she must not be dependent upon a man
to approve her work; as bearer of the creative spirit she must simply keep
on working.

May Sarton has been cultivating her garden and writing her books all
through the years. She has willingly nurtured the spark of creativity, passed
down to her from her mother and grandmothers, from her father and
grandfathers as well. In her affirmation of our shared humanity and innate

complexity, she has had the courage to embrace us all. But May Sarton is not a mother; she is, she says, a woman who loves women, a woman for whom the muse is feminine.

The allusions to her work are curiously silent on this point. As stated previously, she is most often configured as the survivor, the aged writer. Even the references to *Mrs. Stevens Hears the Mermaids Singing,* in which she explicitly depicts lesbian love, invoke Hilary Stevens as the writer who endures. This silence may be another indication of the resolution of the affiliation complex, for, in refusing to categorize Sarton as a lesbian writer, we are freed to embrace the lesbian in ourselves. Adrienne Rich explains, in *On Lies, Secrets, and Silence* (1979):

> And I believe it is the lesbian in every woman who is compelled by female energy, who gravitates toward strong women, who seeks a literature that will express that energy and strength. It is the lesbian in us who drives us to feel imaginatively, render in language, grasp, the full connection between woman and woman. It is the lesbian in us who is creative, for the dutiful daughter of the fathers in us is only a hack. (200–201)

Some feminists, Rich goes on to explain, have been afraid that they would be discredited if they were perceived as "woman centered," or labeled as lesbian. It is a fear that Sarton faced, a reality she confronted. Contracts were withdrawn, offers canceled after the publication of *Mrs. Stevens.* But Sarton has continued writing, teaching, living, creating "womanist" prose, as Alice Walker would say, all her life.

May Sarton has given us the gift of herself, in prose, poetry, the garden, the creation of her life and work. She has, in her words, sent love "forward into the past" ("Letter from Chicago," last line), and handed on the spark of woman's creative power. She has recorded her persistence, her solitude, her rage, her love of women, and, yes, her love for men. All those emotions and situations have been "forbidden" to women but, by virtue of her courage, are forbidden no longer.

Predecessors and Contemporaries

Poets and Friends:
The Correspondence of May Sarton
and Louise Bogan

Elizabeth Evans

On September 4, 1962, May Sarton wrote from her home (then in Nelson, New Hampshire) to her friend, the poet Louise Bogan:

> We have known each other now for quite some time. It began when I wrote you in 1944[1] (I think) and asked you to read poems at the Public Library in N.Y. and you said you could not appear in public—that is how long ago it was! ... It is the poet whom I love, as you know. So we entered a friendship, begun as more than that on my side, but fruitful and dear at any rate for many a year since then.

The correspondence between May Sarton and Louise Bogan is extensive. The Berg Collection in the New York Public Library lists forty-one folders containing the Bogan correspondence to Sarton—136 autograph letters signed, 31 typed letters signed, 35 postal cards. The Frost Library at Amherst College houses the papers of Louise Bogan, among them 176 letters from May Sarton, as well as postal cards (which were frequent when Sarton was abroad), Christmas and birthday cards. The correspondence between these two poets and friends was intense, especially from 1953 to 1956, when letters were frequent and relatively long. During this time, both poets fostered the correspondence, Bogan often ending a letter with the request that Sarton write to her. On occasion, Sarton included new poems or revisions of poems; in subsequent letters, Bogan usually commented on these poems with helpful suggestions. During the 1950s (the eleven letters presented here come from that decade), May Sarton was consciously developing as a poet. She admired Bogan and the status she had already attained: Bogan was an accomplished poet and the poetry critic for the *New Yorker* (a position of particular influence, power, and prestige). The letters between Sarton and

Bogan (when read in their entirety) show many interests that the two poets shared. The letters reveal, too, the differences in their ages, their temperaments, their obligations to family and to work, and their quite different experiences in the creative process. As one would expect, these letters also relate daily activities, concrete details the biographer must have and concrete details the reader enjoys.

Until the entire correspondence is annotated and published, interim excursions into the letters of Bogan and Sarton are useful. One such excursion was made in 1973, when Ruth Limmer published *What the Woman Lived: Selected Letters of Louise Bogan, 1920–1970,* providing a rich sample from the more than one thousand letters available at the time of Bogan's death. The volume includes thirty-six letters to May Sarton—almost all of which were published with excisions that Limmer justifies in her introduction. Limmer characterizes Louise Bogan as "tough and vulnerable, sharp-tongued and generous, intemperate and serene, wildly prejudiced and wholly fair" (ix).[2]

This essay complements one portion of *What the Woman Lived* by presenting eleven letters May Sarton wrote to Louise Bogan. Sarton's letters show that she was generous, concerned about social and political issues, driven to work, and forced to balance her domestic responsibilities with her professional life. This sample of Sarton's letters to Bogan suggests the complex nature of their friendship. Bogan was fifteen years Sarton's senior, twice married, the mother of one child. Sarton was the daughter of remarkable parents (her mother was an artist, her father an internationally renowned scholar of the history of science) who welcomed the professional association that friendship with Bogan represented.

During this time, Sarton, already a widely published poet, was developing and sharpening her skills. In the letters at hand, she occasionally questions her poetic talent, but never does she doubt her role as a poet. By the mid-1950s, Sarton had also published four novels; during the time these eleven letters span, she was hard at work on the novel *Faithful Are the Wounds* (1955). Since Sarton refers to this novel in some of the letters I include, a brief background is useful.

Sarton was planning this novel as early as November 1952 when she mentioned to a friend (the artist, William Theo Brown) that it would concern the way Matty's (F. O. Matthiessen) suicide affected a group of people who knew him well. One of Sarton's most successful novels, *Faithful Are the Wounds* explores the life and influence of Edward Cavan, a character based on Matthiessen—a distinguished Harvard professor who committed suicide in 1950. This work began, Sarton has said, as a political novel exploring the dilemma that a liberal person faces within a conservative community. While the novel does present the political issue, it came to center on other concerns—primarily on a man who found true communication of his passionately held views difficult, at times impossible. This shift in focus, Sarton has said, was far more compatible to her talents as a novelist, and the novel stands as an achievement in Sarton's work.

In her Pulitzer-prize-winning biography, *Louise Bogan, A Portrait,* Elizabeth Frank discussed the personal relationship between Bogan and Sarton, casting Sarton as pupil and Bogan as mentor.[3] To an extent this was the case, as it would have been for most younger poets at the time.[4] Professionally, Bogan was a lyric poet of the first order and, in addition, enjoyed a long tenure as poetry critic for the *New Yorker,* where, through reviews and articles, she judged much contemporary poetry. Personally, as Frank describes the relationship, "Sarton was in love with her [Bogan], and desired an *amitié amoureuse,* of which Bogan knew herself, for many reasons to be incapable" (Frank 1985, 353). Nevertheless, these letters suggest that the friendship, especially in the mid-1950s, was close. If Bogan did not choose to enter the relation Sarton may have desired, neither did Bogan discourage the correspondence. Indeed, letters and visits continued.

The eleven letters published here were written between 1953 and 1955. Any selection from such a large number of letters necessitates omissions; however, these letters do suggest the richness of the correspondence. They reflect Sarton's personality and document her various roles as mature writer, as daughter to a now widowed father, and as writer and traveler and friend. (A frequent traveler, Sarton often wrote from the West Coast, from New Mexico, and from Europe; Bogan—with a few exceptions—traveled only in the Northeast.) Readers of Sarton's journals will recognize familiar topics in these letters: Sarton driving herself to exhaustion, analyzing the actions that result in temper and tears, relating the public and private concerns that engage her energy. The two poets exchanged holiday gifts, and, though more visits were planned than took place, the two did meet in New York as well as in Massachusetts, especially when Bogan vacationed at Swampscott.

Anecdotes about mutual friends enrich the letters. For example, it is interesting to know that Louise Bogan met Sylvia Beach, describing the owner of Shakespeare & Company as "the J. Joyce woman . . . small and bitter-sweet, and an American." And both poets could, in spite of their difficulties from health or work, exhibit the saving grace of the smile and take quick pleasure in the absurd.

The Sarton letters are preceded by a brief headnote as needed. I have retained abbreviations and spellings except for obvious hand or typing errors that I have silently corrected.

[The letter dated 13 November 1953 gives an interesting account about Dylan Thomas's death and Sarton's moving reflections on Virginia Woolf.]

13 November 1953   14 Wright Street [Cambridge]
Dear Louise, it was good to hear. I always have a queer sense of suspension, of not having really landed, when I have been away and seen people until I hear something. I expect you are now beautiful and orderly and wonderfully clean after the upheaval, with the books back (I do hope the walls are the same color?) and the fish floating in his place. But it is an earthquake and must at some points have seemed hardly worth it. Anyway, now I think of you at peace—

It was a shock about Dylan Thomas.[1] I shall always remember the flood of relief I felt when I first read "October Morning" and "Fern Hill" and "Do Not Go Gentle into That Good Night," as if a long starvation were at an end. It is cruel that he should go, but it is, I suspect, the Dionysian fate, the exalted feverish climb that cannot make a natural end. How mysterious—these angels and self-destroyers who appear now and then. But something has gone out of our world now forever and it does chill one to the bone. Also I get scared because such deaths make one feel responsible, I mean responsible for one's own future—to have more time is such a responsibility. To use it well, to keep on growing, to be implacably self-demanding and self-critical. Given less to begin with, we must become more (but I am talking of myself not of you, of course)—what if Yeats had died at forty? Or Marianne Moore? I like best to think of poetry as a long life with the best at the end.

I finished Viola Meynell's novel[2] and shall send it along after the

---

1. Dylan Thomas died on 9 November 1953 in New York City at thirty-nine. The *New York Times* obituary (10 November 1953) noted that he "had intended, before returning to England from this last tour, to work with Stravinsky on the libretto of an opera. It is likely that by his death the world lost a masterpiece." Ironically, Sarton's friend, William Theo Brown, was with the Stravinskys when the news of Thomas's death reached them.

2. The novel Sarton refers to is Viola Meynell, *A Girl Adoring* (London: E. Arnold, 1927). Prolific in the teens and 1920s, Meynell published novels, volumes of verse, a volume of short stories, and an account of her parents' friendship with poet Francis Thompson. As

week-end. A strange, to me, not altogether successful novel—have you read it recently? I got fascinated by Gilda and the subterranean life of her love affair and felt a bit cheated when all that simply dropped out. And I was very much interested in the whole approach to character, entirely (so it seems) by analysis, a very daring thing to bring off so well. Morely is wonderfully real, the girl too. But as a whole it seemed to me almost like an excuse for some wonderfully keen perceptions and almost *statements* about relationships rather than making them happen for the reader. It has a sheen about it, but to me not quite a real sheen. Probably this is all quite a false view of mine—I read so badly when I am writing. Every book presents a series of private questions, every book one reads I mean. So pay no attention.

Nov. 14th

I got interrupted. I keep thinking about your book,[3] I mean the prose one you are writing now—I keep thinking of the form of it, not exactly autobiography you said, but I guess things that do not get said in the same way in poems, which can so rarely suggest the process of growth, one by one. It is very exciting to consider what you may be saying or not saying—when I saw you I was at the extreme downward curve about my novel and now I think I am slowly moving upward, at least I have a little more confidence now. And it begins to come alive. It was for a time, simply hard labor with no joy in it, but I do believe it was chiefly that I was dead tired. I cannot bear to waste time being tired, yet it is what I do so much of the time. I have come to believe that one creates time very much as one creates a work of art and that having no time (which is what makes fatigue) is all in one's own mind. This sounds quite crazy, but I'm sure you know what I mean. The difficulty with being a writer is that one is torn between life and work, all the time having to *preserve* oneself for work— then seeing that this is all wrong and work is made of life, an endless pendulum swing. The trick must be to learn this way with time which I believe you have—I felt it very tangibly when I walked into the room

---

Elizabeth Frank notes, Meynell was Bogan's "favorite English novelist, whose intuitions about emotion and its relation to the facts of behavior she considered unparalleled in their exactness and delicacy" (Frank 1985, 89).

3. Louise Bogan did not bring the autobiographical work to completion. The material appeared posthumously as *Journey Around My Room: The Autobiography of Louise Bogan, A Mosaic* by Ruth Limmer (New York: Viking, 1980).

and during the hours I was there. Time, which had been boxed, began to flow.

Tell me how you are—Did you see the excerpts from V. Woolf's journal in *Harper's Bazaar*? So moving and painful—*& yet* there to be read then—at hairdressers by people who do not care—[4]

[The poems Bogan had referred to appear in Sarton's fourth book, *The Land of Silence and Other Poems* (1953).]

Jan. 6th, 1954   14 Wright Street [Cambridge]
Dear Louise,

I'm overwhelmed by your kindness in taking the time and trouble to write me this letter about the book.[1] It is one of the deep events of my life. In fact, I do not quite know how to tell you what it was like, except that in all these years I have had very little criticism from anyone I trusted, almost none. So you can imagine, I hope, and perhaps you did such a kindness because you *have* imagined.

You are quite right about too many poems. The trouble is that it's six years work and they pile up, but that is no excuse for having permitted an overweight and I'll remember next time. I did want the book to be the whole person, not just one facet—but each section might well be three or four or five in all.

I have read and reread your sentence about "an impulse toward literature." I think I could understand this better if some day when we meet you told me a couple of the poems which exemplify this danger. I'm sure you are right about the effect, but I wonder whether the cause is not a matter of a kind of language rather than an impulse. I think I can say honestly that no poem in the book was written without a real experience back of it and the necessity to write it.

---

4. The November 1953 issue of *Harper's Bazaar* features a strange combination of articles in the "Fiction and Features" section—Charles Boyer and Mary Martin, Julie Harris and the Cat Girl, Margot Fonteyn and Rocky Marciano, Drama at Edinburgh, as well as poems by William Jay Smith and Babette Deutsch. In addition, forty-six selections from Virginia Woolf's diary (1940–41) were printed along with a photograph of Woolf. Opposite the photograph, the first diary entry begins: "These moments of despair."

1. The *Land of Silence and Other Poems* (1953) was dedicated to the memory of Mabel Sarton, who had died in 1950. The memorial poem, "The First Autumn," is one of several poems Sarton has written on her mother's death. The volume has six (untitled) sections, a total of sixty-six poems.

Possibly there is a key for me in what you say about being able to be
"colloquial" and "formal" at the same time. I wonder if "The Swans,"
for instance, is one of those you mean. Probably "Roses" (which I
would take out now) is and possibly the "Villanelle for Fireworks."
I wanted "the noble tone" in "The Swans" because of the birds they
are, but in the other two I think I begin to sense what you mean. I
am also very much aware of what your exclamation point after "stop"
in the sentence "say what you mean and then stop!" implies—the
tendency to overstate, or rather to make a statement which the poem
suggests anyway. I think this comes from the French in me, a desire
for absolute clarity, but it can take one right outside poetry into another
sphere. I was very pleased, however, that you liked "Take Anguish for
Companion" all of which is such a statement.

I do agree about Ruth Pitter.[2] Was much disappointed in her last
book, *The Ermine*. She is an old friend of mine and I loved her poems
before I ever knew her. She will, I think, live for a very few pure
poems, and these of a kind rare in our time, absolutely transparent
acts of the spirit. But she has not grown as a poet since she joined
the Anglican Church (I wonder why). It has made her more traditional
in a deadly sense than before and has not done what it might have
done i.e., to transpose her minor key into a major, and communicate
joy.

I don't know whether this letter of yours crossed mine with the
passage from De Selincourt but it was most interesting to see how
closely you, he, and Auden agree about the poetry of women.[3]

I take "prune" to heart, and also "be brave," good devices for the
new year.

Incidentally (this is gossip) Babette Deutsch was furious with me
about "Poets and the Rain" because I had seemed to place Yeats, Pitter,
and Rukeyser in one bracket.[4] I did not mean to do this,—I had simply

2. Ruth Pitter (1897–), an English poet, published *The Ermine: Poems, 1942–1952*
(London: Cresset Press, 1953). The volume won the Heinemann Foundation award. May
Sarton and Ruth Pitter had an interesting correspondence, especially during World War II,
when Sarton sent her many relief parcels. Pitter's letters describe the upheaval and trauma
the war caused her family and her business.

3. Basil De Selincourt (1876–1966) lived in England and was a friend Sarton saw on
her visits there. The letter Sarton sent Bogan with the passage by De Selincourt apparently
has not survived.

4. "Poets and the Rain" appears in section 6 of *The Land of Silence*. Although Sarton

been reading them the days preceding the poem and I do not really think the poem implies equality of importance (or only in a temporary almost accidental sense). B[abette] D[eutsch] wrote a very patronizing carping review (with some truth in it, though) of the book,[5] but I did not mind as she went on in the next P. to praise Garrigue to the skies. So I took what she said about me with several grains of salutary salt. Of course she is a serious critic, but I do not believe she gets to the heart of the matter as you do.

I'm glad you liked the box—it seems rather small for note paper??? I had thought of clips, erasers, that sort of thing.

Well, this letter is long enough. Forgive the typewriter but I learned to write by hand in mittens at an open air school and it is, hence, still hard labor. The typewriter saved my life.

I am coming to New York for a couple of nights the 22nd and 23rd of this month and hope to see you. I'll write a p.c. when I know about possible times—I am waiting to hear from a French girl whose family I promised that I would look up (I can't get this sentence straight—grammatically). She is elusive, doesn't write to them and hasn't answered various queries, but I must wait another week and give her a chance before making any other plans. It is rather a nuisance altogether.[6]

How good about *The Collected Poems!*[7]

Bless you again for taking time and trouble over the poems I just can't put what I feel about that into words.

June 17th 1954   14 Wright Street [Cambridge]
Darling, how lovely, how unexpected to have your long letter yesterday when I had paid no attention to *le Cheri* at all when I heard him

---

does not name Yeats, Pitter, or Rukeyser, it is possible to see imagery that suggests each poet.

5. In an omnibus review, Deutsch covered poetry volumes by Warren, Santayana, Bogardus, MacNeice, Sarton, Garrigue, Roethke, and Shapiro. Deutsch found a balance or counterbalance between volumes and paired them—Sarton and Garrigue, for example, were "at opposite poles."

6. In a subsequent letter, Sarton reports the moving conversation she had with this young French woman, whose traumatic childhood plagued her adult life and threatened her future as a concert pianist. Sarton advised the woman and mediated between her and the parents.

7. With Cecil Hemley as editor, Louise Bogan published *Collected Poems, 1923-1953* (New York: Noonday Press, 1954). (See Frank 1985, 352-62.)

whistling down the street. Somehow I felt all the locks and doors opening inside me and I could breathe again—it is wonderful that you are really going to be air-cooled in a kind of creme-de-menthe world of your own in the middle of the heat; my only objection is that you put poems (among the things you will do) in parentheses and everything else in the clear and, as you know, I think it should be the other way around.

I feel pleasantly demoralized by not having the book [*Faithful Are the Wounds*] round my neck—really it is astonishing, the relief. I am so full of ideas about fun things to do that I can hardly wait to get up, but I shan't begin anything new for a few days. I heard yesterday that Bollingen is doing a huge definitive Valéry in translation in many vols. and is looking for translators for the poems, so I thought I would try a few.[1] Did you ever finish *Palmes?* Didn't you once say that you had made a translation? I would so love to see it sometime if so. Then I think I'll feel out a chapter or two about *The Fur Person,* a children's book which I'll only do if it turns out to be as easy as pie.[2] I am sure it is one of those hit-or-miss things. This will include finishing a poem about the puss which begins

"He's Tom
At home;
Jones is his hospital name."

This masterpiece was begun a year ago and never finished!

---

1. Bogan and Sarton did jointly undertake the translation of some Valéry poems for the project the Bollingen Foundation sponsored. Bogan conferred at least once with people at the Foundation who indicated their delight in Sarton's ability to capture the French translation. Their efforts were "rejected when the Bollingen editors decided to publish the French text alongside a literal translation, but the results of several months of companionable collaboration eventually found their way to *Poetry Metamorphosis,* and the *Hudson Review*" (Frank 1985, 357).

2. *The Fur Person* (dedicated to Judith Matlack) was first published in 1957 by Holt, Rinehart and Winston with illustrations by David Canright. In 1978, Norton reissued this book with a new preface by Sarton, in which she gives the charming account of Vera and Vladimir Nabokov's subletting of 9 Maynard Place, then the house of May Sarton and Judith Matlack. The Nabokovs welcomed the cat, Tom Jones, "as a cherished paying guest during their stay" (8). *The Fur Person,* a Norton paperback in 1983, continues to amuse and delight "the fervent lovers and austere scholars whom Baudelaire called the particular friends of cats" (7).

I do hope I can see the summer apartment with the slipcovers on before I go. It will depend on whether Rinehart wants to see me as Katherine will do the proof on the last piece and send it.[3] And it would have to be between July 20th and 30th, a rather tight squeeze just before I fly.

It is a happy thing when people's lives come out right in the end like Edmund's, and his work on Israel sounds very fascinating, I must say.[4] I liked specially the vegetable garden—*potager*—I liked the "elevenses" too. How wonderful to have a wife to bring one cups of tea.

How fine about Maidie's trip to the West, and also that the book is *selling*. In fact, as you see, your letter made me happy.[5]

We are taking a day off and going in town to see the Boston Art festival, really a wonderful thing with tents up all over the Public Gardens and a great variety of "art" hung up in them. The fun about it is the people who come to look, people who never go into a gallery or a museum. They gave a free performance of Figaro, Frost read poems to 5,000 the other night, and now there is a free performance of "Ah, Wilderness." It is all quite gay and such an unexpectedly warm and folksy thing for Boston to put on.

Yesterday afternoon we had a tea to send off a very old friend who is moving to Cal. She remains a Communist (at about 75) which seems feeble-minded, but somehow endearing just the same. I went to school with her children and the gathering was mostly part of the old class so we brought out old photographs of the 5th grade Greek play[6] and got quite hysterical with laughter remembering things Miss Edgett the math teacher said such as, "You can't almost catch a train" etc. and we kept off politics which is just as well, as this gentle, vague, blue-eyed old lady becomes like a rabid witch at the mention of politics, a

---

3. Sarton probably refers to *Faithful Are the Wounds*, which Rinehart published in 1955.

4. In a letter dated 14 June 1954, Bogan spoke of her visit with Edmund Wilson and his fourth wife, Elena (see *What the Woman Lived*, 288–89). For a further discussion of Wilson and Bogan, see Frank 1985, 288–90, 325.

5. Mathilde (Maidie) Alexander was Bogan's daughter (and only child) by her first husband, Curt Alexander.

6. In part 2 of *I Knew a Phoenix*, Sarton fondly recounts early episodes at Shady Hill School, the Cooperative Open Air School in Cambridge. A photograph comes at the beginning of this section with the caption: "In the fourth grade we were Greeks, a year I remember with particular happiness." In this letter to Bogan, Sarton inadvertently says it was the fifth grade.

rather frightening transformation. . . . [Ellipsis added] The occasion was partly to give her a really quite large check which we had collected.

It is a most beautiful clear day, temperature 60—but so much better than heat which I guess we'll have at any moment. How good that you got the dress you wanted before the heat arrived to make shopping Hell and trying-on so sticky.

I forgot to say that when Evie Ames[7] came to lunch last week (she wrote the pigeon book, you know) she looked at everything in this house so attentively that it made me terribly happy—she really "tried on" the house as if it were a dress and noticed everything. Most Americans would, I believe, just see its shabbiness and all that we do not *have*, but it is a dear house and someday you really must see it. Just now a bit of gloom as Judy[8] decided to invest in a sale of storm windows, that silvery kind which is easily changed to screens in the summer, very practical and I am sorry to say, rather ugly. The facade has been, in my view, ruined, by this screen door. I gave a muted warning, but in vain. I did love the front door before and now it is utterly hideous. Very sad. But perhaps eventually it can be painted or removed.

I really must stop talking—

[p.s.] Here is the Phi B.K. citation (I don't get really initiated until next March): "M.S. a courageously individual contributor to the spirit of truth through her teaching as Briggs-Copeland instructor at Harvard and Radcliffe,[9] through her work in behalf of the poetic mind in all parts of the United States, and especially through her own distinguished prose and evocative and exquisite poetry."

(One could do without the last two adjectives, I think.)

[The letter from Sarton to Bogan dated 27 June 1954 comes during the period when these two women wrote frequently. During a two-week period in June, each wrote to the other five times. Thus, the letter and postal cards often answer many points in the previous correspondence. In her 21 June 1954 letter, Bogan asks if Sarton had seen Nan Fairbrother's

---

7. Evelyn Ames, a poet, whose interests included natural history and birds.

8. Judith Matlack (1898–1982), with whom Sarton lived for many years in Cambridge.

9. May Sarton was Briggs-Copeland Instructor of English Composition at Harvard from 1949 to 1952.

book, *An English Year.* Before Sarton answers, she borrows that title from
the lending library and then comments on it in her letter of 27 June. (She
found the four long rambling essays Fairbrother developed around the four
seasons "not quite good enough.")

I have deleted the name of the lover Sarton mentions. The restoration of
better relationships among the people involved is the point, not the identification of those people.]

Sunday, June 27th, 1954   14 Wright Street
   Dear Louise, I have made lists of the things to tell you all these
days, rather full days with no time for a real letter. But now it is
Sunday and we have just talked on the phone—so lovely always to hear
your voice whose timbre I sometimes forget in between. I was much
interested in your last card, but now realize that I misunderstood what
you said about making a *précis*—you meant, I take it, in a letter—the
whole question of when one is ready to begin to write is so very
fascinating, too soon, or too late, both fatal—the moment when it is
all in the air just within reach and one must *seize* it before it becomes
too clear or vanishes. I think the real problem with a novel is that
this process goes on over such a long period of time and one keeps
losing "the right moment"; all is dispersed at one moment, or over-
formulated the next. Well, I do not have to consider novels for a long
time to come, thank heavens. At the moment I never want to write
another. It will have to be a very strong compulsion and a real fountain-
jet of inspiration so that it could be written *d'un trait* and not a
patchwork quilt like this one.
   Yesterday I had a terrific day—it was rather a help to decide suddenly
that I must have flowers again and I made such a magnificent bunch
for my Chinese jar of three huge white peonies, with little red scars
in their centers, three most subtle carnations of a kind of *vin rose* color,
and two sweet williams left over from an old bunch, also winey. I
keep going downstairs to look at this presence. Judy is away and I
find it absolutely intoxicating to be alone here—accompanied by the
Fur Person, of course, who wakes me every morning at five by coming
and laying his paws on my face very gently and purring very loudly
(this means he wants to go out). I am just bursting with happiness for
some reason—well, one reason is that [---- ------], the girl with whom
I had such a strange and terrifying love affair, has been here for a week.
I made no moves as I felt it might be really too painful (specially for

her) but finally on the last day she appeared at the door and we had a long
clarifying, three-hour talk which was a real blessing. I shall go away with
a very much lighter heart as a consequence. Nothing is solved, or ever
will be, but we have perhaps reached a place where love at least can flow
through now and no recriminations. She is quite a remarkable person
and has handled what, especially for her, was a devastating thing, with
courage and wisdom. How wonderful when people do begin to make
themselves and one can see it happen! The best thing is that I believe
she and her husband have come to a *modus vivendi,* and that, curiously
enough, the thing with me was in the end a help toward this.

Then I had to get to work very late to finish this damned French
thing, utterly bad really, but it will have to go off tomorrow for a
deadline. I described this man fully in *The Bridge of Years* and said
what I had to say then,[1] but this kind of formal eulogy is really
poisonous—he was not a really good poet, alas, which makes it even
harder. Then a figure out of the past, former bus. manager of my
theatre co. suddenly rang up, and obviously wanted to talk, so he
came for a drink. A long incredible tale of despair, personal troubles
etc. poured out upon me, but not all negative, for he too is maturing
at last. And—like your friend who turned up after twenty years—it
is always sweet to be remembered. I then had just time to snatch a
sandwich and drive out to Medford for the only part of this day I had
foreseen. This was to see an elderly former missionary from Yen Ching
who wrote a best-selling novel about a Chinese garden two years ago,
named Grace Boynton. She is New England to the bone, the kind of
dry intelligent generous-minded reserved spinster for whom I have a
special place in my heart—I was touched to discover that she has
annotated all my poems very fully (it seemed so amazing that they
seemed that real to her) but the real point of this adventure was to
see her coloured slides of Peking gardens and especially one fabulous
garden high up in the mountains (which look so like New Mexico)—
where her new novel is to be laid. Isn't it an odd invention to write
a series of novels around Chinese gardens? I was by then tired and
rather hungry, so that it all imprinted itself on my mind with great
precision and it was really like taking a journey into a dream. As far
as I can make out, the point of a Chinese garden is a series of created

---

1. Raymond Limbosch, the model for the failed philosopher Paul in *The Bridge of Years*
(1946).

places of peace, opening into each other like boxes—the elements are
first, a great view of mountains in the far distance, then scooping out
of an irregular artificial lake; the scooped out earth is made into the
hills and islands, hills all around it, inside high walls. Of course that
is only the ground plan and afterwards, rocks and pavilions are carelessly
strewn about and trees planted. My guess is that light and seasonal
changes in trees take the place of flowers. This garden I saw was only
70 years old, which seemed unbelievable, built by "The Seventh Prince"
who retired there in a huff for political reasons.

My eye fell on a small item while Grace was getting us Chinese tea
after the slides—on the jacket of a book by Hsu something [Sarton
did not recall the full name] it said that her grandmother had objected
to mouse traps "because they would kill the grandchildren of the mice,
and also depress the cat."

I've got Nan Fairbrother's book from the lending library[2]—a beautiful
printing job by Knopf, by the way. It is the kind of book every writer
dreams of writing, but it is, as I feared, not *quite* good enough. I
think it would have been better to keep it a straight journal; instead
it is four long rambling essays about four seasons. The best parts are
about her two little boys—and some good descriptions of weather and
trees and things. The philosophical and aesthetic comments are rather
like the letters I used to write in my twenties, awfully self-conscious
and slightly smug. It doesn't begin to compare with Freya Stark. And
one kept longing for Virginia Woolf to be in her shoes.

I am happy that you will get off to Cummington,[3] in "the best
state in the Union" as Benny de Voto calls it. And so happy about
the Poore review[4]—which I long to see. Do send it and I'll send it
back pronto.

Dear heart, so much love, so many blessings   May

2. *An English Year* (New York: Knopf, 1954) is the account of Nan Fairbrother's year
in the English countryside with her two young sons while her doctor husband served during
World War II. Fairbrother wrote subsequent autobiographical treatises as well as serious
books on landscape gardening.

3. Bogan had written on 22 June 1954 that she planned a long weekend (around July
9th) in the countryside near West Cummington, Massachusetts, with her friend Paul Cun-
ningham (Cummington is the place in Richard Wilbur's recent poem, "A Wall in the
Woods: Cummington," *New Yorker,* 5 June 1989, 40).

4. In a post card dated 24 June 1954, Bogan mentions that the morning paper carried
a review of her *Collected Poems, 1923–1953* as well as a photograph. See Sarton's letter of 29
June 1954, n. 1, for an account of this review.

June 29th [1954], Tuesday eve

Dear Louise, I have just come back from tea with Daddy, such a gray day and on a gray day the house over there feels so full of absence, absence, I think he was glad I came. The marmalade cat ate little pieces of bread and butter, too, in a very satisfactory way and purred and rolled over in his rococo attitudes, utterly different from our austere animal, Tom Jones (whose attitudes are Anglo-Saxon). What a happy thing to find the Poore in the mail with good photograph of you.[1] I cannot quite agree about "shakes the mind," but that is unimportant and I trust the prize-givers are taking note and preparing their thimbles like the birds in Alice. Thank you, darling, for sending it, and here it is back again. I mean of course that "mind and heart" seem rather arbitrary definitions, but he says as much himself, and I would say that all good poetry begins in the heart and ends in the mind. But this sounds so much like Nan Fairbrother's kind of statement that I blush.[2]

I am a bit dizzy already with emerging from my cocoon and becoming all of a sudden such a social creature—people, people, all around and

---

1. In 1954, Noonday Press published Louise Bogan's *Collected Poems, 1923-1953* to enthusiastic reviews, particularly by John Ciardi *(Nation)*, Kenneth Rexroth *(New York Herald Tribune Book Review)*, Richard Eberhart *(New York Times Book Review)*, and Léonie Adams *(Poetry)*. The review that Bogan included in this letter appeared in the Thursday, 24 June 1954, issue of the *New York Times*. In this piece, Charles Poore also reviewed Léonie Adams's *Poems: A Selection* (New York: Funk and Wagnalls, 1954) and C. Day Lewis's volume, *An Italian Visit* (London: Cape, 1953) (a book Poore labeled as in the "Auden-Spender School of Nineteen Thirties"). The reviewed carried photographs of Adams and of Bogan (who is unsmiling, her expressive eyes cut sharply to the left). The specific passages that Sarton comments on appear below:

> When the time comes to give out the lit'ry laurels for 1954, the judges who wear the silks of the Bollingen, the Pulitzer and the National Book Awards are going to have the devil's own time deciding between the work of Léonie Adams and Louise Bogan.... They do not sound alike. Yet they are alike in this: that through the recent years while the frantic modernists were fruitlessly proving through feverish experiments that modern poetry could be obscure without being mysterious, doggedly deep without being truly profound, Miss Adams and Miss Bogan were writing timeless lyrics in the great tradition of poetry that rings true, yesterday, today and tomorrow.

> If there is a distinction to be made between them it is that Miss Adams shakes the heart, Miss Bogan the mind.

Léonie Adams and Louise Bogan shared the Bollingen Prize for Adams's *Poems: A Selection* and Bogan's *Collected Poems, 1923-1953*.

2. Nan Fairbrother (1913–71), writer and landscape architect. Sarton is referring to *An English Year* (1954), a book the *New Yorker* reviewer called "an agreeable diversion." See letter of 27 June 1954, n. 2.

not a drop of silence. Tonight I am going to a buffet supper, the final one for Maude Cam who sails tomorrow. I shall miss her though I saw her rarely—miss seeing her, wild and gray, hurrying through the square with an immense green bag of books over one shoulder and an immense paper bag of groceries in one arm. Her intellectual vitality dazzles and she is such a good old fashioned feminist—did I tell you that when she came to lunch at Daddy's awhile back she suddenly fixed me with her hawk eye and said, "You must write a book about friendship between women, nobody has."[3] —And there she is so full of learning (medieval law, is it?) but also a passionate reader of novels and poetry, an ardent socialist, etc.

And for lunch a darling old friend, mother of one of my schoolmates, came bringing pale pink roses and honeysuckle, a perfect bower on my desk, from her garden. She was so shy that she really ate and ran and I could not persuade her that I wanted her to stay on—but perhaps I frightened her. We used to fight about politics, but that is long ago.

Yesterday a magnificent drive down to Beverly on Route 128 where we drove along to our picnic—but there were the most romantic clouds, like a European sky, great flashes of light pouring through black rounded humps, *purple* they looked at times, and everything in the sky in motion. I had lunch with the Murdocks who have an enchanting airy-fairy little black ball of fluff to replace Toby, or not to replace him, but console a little.[4] Stacy first wet my best slacks completely down the front, then chewed up my red morocco cigarette case, and *I* missed grown-up Toby a great deal, I must say! I am very fond of the M's, but it is sad to me to see a man so much younger than my father who seems to be allowing himself to give up, not to embark on major work any longer, to dwindle into comfortable indolence—she on the other hand, works like a fury at getting a Doctor's degree in French literature, reads

---

3. The admonition to write "about friendship between women" indeed encourages what would become a major theme in Sarton's work, particularly so in *The Birth of a Grandfather* (1957), *Kinds of Love* (1970), *A Reckoning* (1981), and in her latest novel, *The Education of Harriet Hatfield* (1989).

4. Kenneth Ballard Murdock and his second wife, Eleanor Eckhart McLaughlin, were Boston residents and close friends of May Sarton. Murdock was Frances Lee Higginson Professor of English Literature as well as master of Leverett House at Harvard. In the 16 October 1954 issue of the *New Yorker,* Sarton published her poem about the Murdocks' dog—"Lament for Toby, A French Poodle."

Swedish for pleasure and is quite an expert on Swedish lit., cooks like a dream, and in fact does *not* go to seed, so it's not just money that corrupts.

That is all, except last night I had the most heavenly radiant dream about you—I woke up smiling and longing to go back into it, into that golden light of pure happiness—

I trust that Moore and Adams are off to press?[5] Tomorrow I go to Rockport, then the worst of this social time is over, except for a wedding on Saturday. I shall be quite glad to get away, friendly as it all is!

[Sarton's lively letter to Bogan on 1 July 1954 documents the pressure of creative work that must compete for time within the routine of practical obligations. The combination causes fatigue and depression, matters that Sarton later confronts effectively in her journals. Two notes (in handwriting on this typewritten letter) precede the salutation.]

July 1st 1954 Thursday

The final check from the *New Yorker* will be $1,466[1]— but all this must be *saved* this time (income tax, for one thing!) "Be meek and eke" in fact though what a glorious amount to "eke"!	I am dying to see the Marianne Moore.[2]

July 1st [1954]

Dear Louise, it is good to know that you have a supply of pineapples, cherries, and gooseberries and especially that you have a short breathing space—as well as good plans for work ahead. That is rather a good peaceful state, it seems to me. I'm sorry you have had to bother with

---

5. In the 4 September 1954 *New Yorker,* Louise Bogan wrote the lead piece for "Books," a review of Marianne Moore's translation of *The Fables of La Fontaine* (New York: Viking, 1954) and Léonie Adams's *Poems: A Selection.* Bogan said that Moore "has given us La Fontaine in a modern English idiom," but the most important aspect of the review comes when Bogan cites Moore's principles of translation: "the natural order of words, subject, predicate, object; the active voice when possible; a ban on dead words, rhymes, synonymous with gusto." These are, Bogan added, "the rules of the best modern poetic procedures."

1. Sarton published six prose pieces in the *New Yorker* during 1954 as well as two poems—"Provence" (20 June) and "Italian Garden" (1 August).

2. See letter of 29 June 1954, n. 5.

the books—and thank you. Most of all I loved the names of the stars
and constellations, though I'm sure Hoyle's book would frighten me
very much.[3] Astronomers are not generally suicidal but I should be,
were I one.

I am nearly exhausted as this seeing of people is a bit too much and
really it will be a very good thing to get away with my father and
lead a vegetable life for a while. Last night a cat woke me at 3:30 A.M.
and I didn't go to sleep again, but tossed around and finally got up
and wrote in sheer desperation (what is written at that hour by me
must always be thrown away; depression comes up like a tidal wave)—
but this morning I had very kind notes from Diarmuid [Russell], my
agent,[4] and two other people at Rinehart's to say the Mss had come,
and Diarmuid to say he has already read it through. He did not like
the first version at all and advised giving it up, so it is encouraging
that he thinks it "vastly improved" but (less encouraging) ends "I
think you've just picked an almost impossible subject here, and you've
probably done as well as anybody could." Still this is much better than
I feared from him. Ted Amussen promises to get it read this week-
end so I might hear by the 15th and then I can plan about coming
or not coming up, depending on what they say.

I went to town to look for an air-light suitcase to replace one that
is falling apart anyway, and luckily to drop in at AAA where I learned
that I am just in time to get an international driver's license as it takes
three weeks. That meant dashing to a photographer's so I only got
back here after one, a dead duck. There is the business of food for cat
and Judy over the long week-end—she may get back or may not but
one must (as Frost says so bitterly) "provide, provide!" Now someone
I did not expect is coming to tea and someone else to supper and then
I have to dash off at nine and say goodbye to someone else who leaves
tomorrow—and so these days go, much too chaotic, and exhausting.
I feel quite delirious at the moment, but I expect I will revive—and
I had a heavenly half hour on my bed after lunch reading the book of
Whitehead dialogues,[5] sheer pleasure.

---

3. Fred Hoyle, British astrophysicist, celebrated for his work on the stellar origin of
chemical elements.

4. Diarmuid Russell was the agent of many writers, including Eudora Welty.

5. Alfred North Whitehead, *Dialogues of Alfred North Whitehead* (Boston: Little, Brown,
1954).

My address after the 6th, or on the 6th until 20th will be: Ocean Vista, Chastellux Ave., Newport, R.I.

It was terribly sad seeing Miss Waterman my old friend in Rockport who has had a stroke, lives alone, in her eighties—she looked so frail suddenly, I felt quite frightened, and it felt like goodbye. Also I was dreadfully tired after the drive, and then a long lunch with Nancy Hale and her mother next door, and no break. I could not summon my real self and felt afterwards I had made the huge effort, but failed in the end just the same, which is always depressing. We talked about cats (which she adores) and about herself but somehow I could not say the healing or right thing. What a devil fatigue is, that slackening of the nerve, that emptying of the heart's spring so there is nothing to give. Old mother Hubbard and the cupboard bare (I used to think that the ysaddest poem in the world!)

Darling, forgive this. I'll do better soon.

[This letter relates Sarton's visit with Elizabeth Bowen and some of her relations in Ireland.]

Aug. 4th, 1954 "Corkagh," Clondalkin, Co. Dublin

Dear Louise, I really still feel like a ghost, transparency for clouds to wander across, so out of my own orbit that I hardly know who or what I am. It is a pity that we cannot go, you and I, for a walk across the soft green meadows towards the very gentle hills in the distance and disappear into your Ireland. Indeed, indeed I wish you were here to set the edges of everything blazing sharp for me. And then you would love this house—it is Elizabeth's aunt's house,[1] older than B[owen]'s Court, really more beautiful under its layers of dirt and crumbling wallpaper, also because of the casual dilapidated air, more homey. I always love being in a large family, the partings and meetings at every meal, the escape into this room at the top of the house where I resume work at some very imitation poems. But I have to discover who I am in this way and there is really no other way for me, even if it all gets thrown out tomorrow.

The scene from this window is all I have been dreaming of—the great silvery changing skies, moving across and darkening the long expanse of fields, punctuated by cows and the pools of shade under

---

1. Elizabeth Bowen (1899–1973), English novelist and Sarton's friend for many years.

each enormous tree, and off in the distance the gentle curve of the
hills. Every window looks out on something wonderful—down the
stairs on the landing one looks down at a formal rose garden enclosed
in high stone walls. I rather often go out and walk across the lawn
to another garden which is built along the sides of a brook, really a
magical place, quite hidden from the house with all the charm of a
secret.

We had a wild drive here on Saturday—five hours of fast driving
just avoiding the cows, pigs and dear donkeys, as E. is a rather absent-
minded driver, through rain and wind—it's quite *cold* and I am glad
of a heavy sweater most of the time. And it was so strange to land
like that out of nowhere and walk into the enormous hall, entirely
lined with stuffed deer heads and mounted horns—everything unbe-
lievably shabby and run-down with two huge untrained black retrievers
leaping and barking and what seems like hundreds of "family" to greet.
I like E.'s Aunt Edie very much, humorous, gentle, and wise *behind* a
rather vague exterior. Last evening we sat in her window (an upstairs
drawing room, the walls entirely covered with photographs and family
portraits, the curtains at the long windows in shreds) watching the
children play tennis on the court below and had a long talk about
Elizabeth. I love to see E. in this family atmosphere, where she spent
much of her childhood and where she is still "Bitha" and taken for
granted, teased and criticized. And she and I get off now and then
alone, yesterday to a very grand lunch at the Russell, all surrounded
by the Horse Show grandees and officers in uniform—and then to the
Zoo (my idea) but there I did miss you very much and the lions were
not up to Bronx standards. But we did see some very furry gibbons
happily living on an island, sitting in the willows eating oranges, like
a Japanese print.

I have a good poem in mind but have been letting off steam or
something with a short recalcitrant one which is no good, only I had
to finish it off somehow first. I was rather homesick for awhile—it
did all seem rather strange. And everything is very helter skelter so
one feels a bit lost at first like a newborn babe. This morning one
daughter and son went off on an ancient racing car with a boat attached
behind; at eleven (when we go down for mid-morning coffee), another
daughter and her husband, very elegant for the horse show, said their
goodbyes and were off for the day. Now there are only two little boys
left, and the dutiful unmarried sister who takes care of the gardens,

Elizabeth, her aunt, the old Biddy who does *all* the work, and me. Sometimes I feel the sadness of all this beauty going quietly to pieces— for it is a very beautiful house, but really awfully dirty and délabrée— and there will never be any money to set it to rights again.[2] So I think the aunt must suffer and feel she is holding up a collapsing thing. Her husband was too generous and gave a lot away, and then, times have changed. The Anglo-Irish are no longer "the ascendancy" but only poor relations who are allowed to stay on. Not even the Irish can hate them any longer. A brash up and coming middle-class is on the way, as one sees by the hideous suburbs. But I can see why Yeats mourned the passing of the aristocrat and the peasant; their values are linked. The sense of life is in them—Darling, how are you?

[Sarton's letter of 15 August 1954 describes the Limboschs' Belgian garden, tying the daily change of weather and garden with work and personal response. In the character portrait of "Aunty Lino" (Céline Limbosch), Sarton connects her parents' past and her own with the present hour and place.

Even though the letter is rich with detail, Sarton writes, "I'm afraid all this is very boring and I shall stop." In "Representing Two Cultures: Jane Austen's Letters," Deborah Kaplan argues that "news" conveyed in letters (i.e., "news" that is interesting and thus not boring) is "the creation of men acting in the public world and not of domestic women." Thus, because Jane Austen did not lead a "newsworthy" life—at least not as the male or "gentry culture discourse" judged—she frequently apologized in letters to her sister Cassandra "for having no news." What Kaplan calls "women's culture discourse" values the experience of domestic life.[1]

Sarton's apology for being dull reflects this pattern somewhat. But as

---

2. Elizabeth Bowen's ancestral home, Bowen's Court, would suffer the same fate. During the first ten days of January, 1960, Elizabeth Bowen came back to Ireland "to say good bye to Bowen's Court." Cornelius O'Keefe, a County Cork resident, had bought the dwelling—for the land and timber. Later the contents of the house were auctioned (in Cork) and the house itself soon demolished. The impressive site where Bowen and her many guests had spent brilliant days was gone. See Victoria Glendinning, *Elizabeth Bowen, A Biography* (New York: Avon, 1979), 234. In 1942, Elizabeth Bowen had published a history of her family home, *Bowen's Court* (New York: Knopf, 1942).

1. Deborah Kaplan, "Representing Two Cultures: Jane Austen's Letters," in *The Private Self: Theory and Practice of Women's Autobiographical Writings,* ed. Shari Benstock (Chapel Hill: University of North Carolina Press, 1988), 217.

Kaplan notes, "Everyday domestic occurrences are silly and trivial *and* they are enormously interesting and significant."]

Aug. 15th, 1954   18 Ave. Lequime Rhodes St. Genses

Dear Louise, I have an idea you are in a kind of purgatory of heat reading those blasted Mss. for the Academy, and collecting and arranging the prose book—it is high time you got off somewhere to the ocean, silence, salt air and a break. But of course early September might be very good too, a deep breath before what I always consider the year begins, the working year—what are your plans, I wonder—I have now about learned your card by heart and it is time for another. I am sorry about this typing but it is so very damp, the poor machine sticks all the time.

Actually a faint wan sun is trying to get through today and I have just been out to pick flowers quickly before it rains again, one huge bunch for the hall which is not a success (dahlias and hydrangeas of which I am not fond) and a lovely one in a black jar for the salon, all oranges and reds, marigolds, a few sweet peas, canterbury bells (for one spot of deep purple) etc. It has rained steadily and remorselessly for the last three days, rather gloomy, I must confess, and I feel rather dull, airless and disgruntled, also because I am still in a thicket with that poem about the Corkagh garden, which I fully intended to finish before I leave here tomorrow (for the Dubois about 12 miles away— it is with Eugénie Dubois that I go to Italy).

A greater contrast between Corkagh,[2] aristocratic and decadent, and this house can hardly be imagined, or between the two gardens for that matter. But I feel much more at home here, of course—partly [because] I spent two separate years here as a child, when I was seven and fourteen, and Aunty Lino[3] is like a family (she adored my mother and knew my father before he was married)—I have celebrated her in a novel *The Bridge of Years*. Then, some ten years ago or so, I was able perhaps to get at the essence, and now, alas, I see everything more critically and wonder which is the truth. Or perhaps the truth has two sides like a coin and one may deliberately choose to contemplate one

---

2. See letter of 4 August 1954 and Sarton's visit with Elizabeth Bowen to her aunt's home near Dublin.

3. Céline Limbosch (Aunty Lino) was the model for Mélanie, the strong business-woman/wife in *The Bridge of Years* (1946).

side only. She is a woman of great courage but frightfully dominating, and it is only by being adamant that one can escape. As a child I rather enjoyed being ordered about like a soldier (a thing my mother never did of course), but now it sets my teeth on edge when I hear that dominating tone of voice on the stairs. She has completely possessed her three girls, the eldest my age, so none has married, but all I think, really hate her, and they all are here in body but not in spirit, so it is a curiously heartless house. Yet at the same time, and as soon as I define her like this, I see that it is not the whole truth and am abashed. She is awfully kind to me and leaves me entirely free (of course, I would leave if she didn't and I expect she knows that)—and she is enormously kind and understanding with animals and children, or with quite primitive people, such as the little 14-year-old girl (!) whom she was training as a servant. She is a tremendous actress and can be very funny, but when she launches into sententious philosophy and "acts" then, it is simply embarrassing and I want to hide under the table. Dreadful disillusion is at the root of everything, and disillusion which came and comes from pride, from a sense of superiority and of being in the right which has acted like a blight on the whole family: Raymond, her husband, was a poet, never recognized, publishing his books himself, etc. You have often said how ludicrous a "successful" poet is, but here I've seen what total unsuccess can do, and it is very much like an illness. But I miss Raymond, his subtlety and tenderness, and there is this hole all the time because he is not here. Also Jean Dominique is not here[4]—and I used to see her every other day whenever I was in Belgium. Today is her birthday. She would have been seventy-six. Many people will lay flowers at her grave today, but I am somehow shy about such things and shan't go.

I do so wish you could see this garden, a creation like a poem— just below my window is a small orchard, the trunks of the trees whitened by lime as they always are here, I don't know why. Under one of the pears there is a tiny pond for the two ducks and the two geese (I am woken by their quacks at six each morning when Lino lets them out), under another tree we have tea and supper when it is fine (not this year!) and there are tables and chairs. In front of the

---

4. Marie Closset, the Belgian teacher at the Institut Belge de Culture Française, where Sarton went to school one year. Closset was well known as the poet Jean Dominique and, Sarton says in *I Knew a Phoenix,* was "one of the two or three primary influences in my life" (photograph caption, opposite 120).

house two very trim lawns lead to the gate with two glorious mixed English borders on each side, and all against the front of the house one sees nothing but flowers—window boxes at every window, an arbor covered with clematis and roses at the front door, and along the edge fuschias, roses, lilies in profusion. The whole impression is of a kind of careless grace—the oldest daughter, Claire, who is an interior decorator (very mondaine and successful) does the garden now, and she is a genius at it. Behind a screen of flowering bushes at the right is the vegetable garden, neat rows of lettuces, peas, beans, etc. absolutely weedless. Oh dear, how hard to give you any idea how charming it is—the small human scale after Corkagh's immensities—and here inside the house, everything immaculate, floors waxed every day, the Belgian sense of order and a kind of elegance in this particular house, because these people are artists. It is slightly "arty" in a William Morris way, perhaps. But very charming—and what was modern forty years ago when it was built now already has a period flavor.

Darling, I'm afraid all this is very boring and I shall stop. But deep down inside I am happy and at peace and have had wonderful days alone at my desk, thinking and working.

Tell me how you are—after this till the 26th c/o Madame Jean Dubois, 12 Longue Haie, Linkebbek, Brabant, Belgium.

I constantly use *The Galaxy* and have made some discoveries—such a good present.[5]

Sunday, August 22nd, 1954   12 Longue Haie, Linkebeek
Dear Louise, I am so happy that you went to the beneficent shore and were able to rest long nights and sit in the sun—and I was glad to have your clarifying letter and grateful for it. With some of it I am at odds, but these are not odds that more talk will solve, so for the present at least, I feel that my only answer in a life-giving sense is to do what you ask and tell you something of my life here. I would prefer that you take this as a sign of love, rather than of friendship, but it really does not matter.

The first effect of this return has been simply troubling and I am undeniably in the depression which was, perhaps, inevitable. The well is empty and just has to fill itself up. Belgium is a very earthy country,

---

5. *The English Galaxy of Shorter Poems* was, Ruth Limmer reports, Louise Bogan's favorite anthology.

deeply rooted in the rural—every inch of ground cultivated and used, for instance—and because of this one feels more than usually the need for roots oneself. I do love the rural scene; here we are surrounded by small farms and in the evening when Eugénie and I often take a walk across the fields, we see the families gathering in the potatoes, the workmen turning home with that slow tired walk, the cows standing at the gates waiting to be milked—it seems wonderfully ageless and soothing. But the weather has been really foul—today a kind of gray blight over everything. It is depressing to see the standing grain turning rusty brown, or blown down into disarray—to know that the honey-combs are empty and the bees will starve this winter, and the plums falling sour and green in the wind. The prevailing *mood* is not a gay one, as you can see. I rather like it, and like the long hours at my desk in this little room under the eaves, which trembles when the trains go past at night. It looks over an apple tree, in the foreground, then out across turnip fields and a hayfield where last night I watched the men haying, throwing the great *forkfuls* up with a slow heave onto a cart. The horizon is bounded by a magnificent line of beeches—if you walk to it, you find yourself in a fairy glade, a double line of absolutely straight beeches, rising forty or fifty feet into the air, the ground carpeted in copper leaves and a most intense velvety green moss. It is beautiful and satisfying like music.

And I have been working, of course. I finished a rough draft of the three-part Corkagh poem about the walled garden ["The Walled Garden at Clondalkin" in *A Private Mythology*], and yesterday a gloomy little one about the honeycombs *et al.*—there is nothing more cheering than to write gloom off into a poem and I felt wildy gay afterwards, drank a lot of wine and then we all went off, including the maid who is a character, to the tiny village movie-house, feeling our way down a steep cobbled street and then up again to where the village crowds on its hill. The movie house is approached through a café and was the café dance-hall. I was impressed as I always am, by the decadent beauty of the children in the audience—their very fair hair, their long old faces and *cernés;* especially the little boys are absolutely unlike any American child. I presume this is lack of sun rather than dissipation or extreme intelligence, but one is not quite sure. They all look, at least, like infant Rimbauds. It was really *horrible in* these surroundings to have to submit to a preview of the cheapest of American musical comedy, the absolutely *empty* faces, the slick meretriciousness of it—I blushed so much that I felt red all over. As it is, I spend a good deal of time arguing with Eugénie and telling her that she is provincial and ignorant to be so critical of the U.S.A. But honestly, Louise, the damage that American films do for propaganda purposes is immeasurable. Constantly and every day we give the world a deliberately false picture of ourselves— It is treason as far as I am concerned. No one imagines that a Vermont village or an Iowa farm is possible. Or, worst of all, that there are any *human* faces in the U.S.A. But you would laugh if you could hear how passionately I protest, defend and how very American I become, over here. It is partly that I am first aware of the great saving fact that life is opening in the U.S. or can open for anyone who wishes to open it in any way he desires—whereas here, life is in many ways, closing. I mind very much the class consciousness in England and Anglo-Ireland (*that* does not exist in the intellectual Belgian world where I am now, thank God).

Later

And all of this is the answer to your question, I think—I am forced to *evaluate* both what the U.S. means to me and what Europe does, and hence perhaps to realize what I might try to be—such a mixture— and if it is all rather disturbing, it is not an uncreative kind of disturbance.

And what am I reading? I haven't read the Holmes-Laski letters by the way but I remember Mark Howe's increasing disillusion re: Laski when he edited them, because of the awful liar he was.[1] Does it matter that he invented dinner parties or meetings with Churchill which never took place? He did meet so many people of equal interest, and went to so many *real* dinner parties! I don't know what I think. Laski was certainly a brilliant and also immensely kind man from what I glimpsed of him at one meeting.

I don't read a great deal because there is not time to write *and* read, to think *and* read—or very little. We are apt to launch into long discussions after supper and then I am sleepy. But usually fate lays in

---

1. Mark DeWolfe Howe, ed., *The Correspondence of Mr. Justice Holmes and Harold J. Laski, 1916–1935,* 2 vols., with a foreword by Felix Frankfurter (Cambridge, Mass: Harvard University Press, 1953). Laski taught at Harvard (1916–20) and was appointed to the U.S. Supreme Court by Franklin Delano Roosevelt.

my hands at some point on these journeys a work of major importance to my thinking—once it was Lavelle[2] (Le Mal et la Souffrance and especially the wonderful chapter on "Tous Les Êtres Séparée et Unie") and last time it was Simone Weil. I have a hunch that this time it may be a man called Bachelard[3] who has written a series of books on the imagination, relating each of the four to an element. I have two: "L'Air et les Songes: Essai sur l'imagination du mouvement" and "La Terre et les Rêveries de la Volonté"—I have so far only read the introduction to the latter, but it is fascinating. What I like at these times is this sort of thing, which must be read very slowly.

It has been pouring hard again and I went over to see the Limbosches through a long very green valley, where all was gloom and trees and a miserable group of spectators stood in a drenched field to watch a village football match. The one thing I regret is that I haven't yet seen my beloved forest with light in the leaves—but when I come back in October it will be all gold, so that is something.

We take off Wed. morning for Paris, just overnight to see a friend of mine who won't be there later—then Chartres, Fontainebleau, Vezelay, Dijon, Grenoble and down to the Mediterranean via Venice and Matisse's chapel and along the Italian Riviera to Pisa and Florence. So this is my last real letter till Sept. 3rd when we reach Florence—I'll send postcards along the way.

I forgot to thank you in my last for suggesting that I see Zabel in London[4]—I doubt if he would have any reason to see me and I'm a bit shy about it, you know. Also I do have a good many people in that very short month already—but who knows? It might just be the thing. Thank you anyway for the suggestion.

If I have time before I go I'll type Corkagh out again and make some corrections for you. It is a labored piece but as a rhymed letter might have a transient interest for you.

---

2. Louis Lavelle (1883–1951). *Le Mal et la Souffrance* was published in 1940, a work consisting of the two essays.

3. Gaston Bachelard (1884–1962) was a French philosopher, critic, educator, and author. A faculty member at the Sorbonne, he counted among his honors the French Grand Prix for literature awarded to him shortly before his death. He is generally considered one of the greatest psychoanalysts since Freud and highly regarded by critical theorists. At the time Sarton was reading Bachelard, his work and reputation had received little attention in England or in America. Thus, Sarton's interest reflects her affinity for French thought and writing.

4. Morton Dauwen Zabel (1901–64), scholar and critic, was a friend of Louise Bogan's.

I do hope you come back to cool weather and with a good feeling
of rest and life recaptured.

Address in Florence c/o Signora Muller-Licini, Via Sakulstio Bandini,
13 Firenze.

[Sarton's letter of 12 March 1955 assesses her desire to distance experience
before it becomes subject matter for poetry—to use material only after it
has been "sufficiently transposed and depersonalized." The note that Sarton
added in hand appears above the salutation; a line connects this note to the
poem title, "My Sisters, O My Sisters," in the first line of the letter.]

12 March 1955   14 Wright Street [Cambridge]

> I wanted you to read this for quite another
> reason originally—i.e. that I am *not* a
> special pleader for the homosexual, quite
> the contrary—but for *wholeness.*

Dear Louise, this is just a line because I have been mulling over (so
gratefully) what you said about the dangers of poems like "My Sisters,
O My Sisters"[1]—whenever you trouble to say such things I feel like
a squirrel with a nut, wish only to rush away and consider. There is
the possibility—unfashionable as it is—of a good poem of this sort, it
seems to me. Wordsworth's Toussaint sonnet for example.[2] What I
would say now is that two sections of my poem *are* poetry (though
not on the highest level), section one and 2, and the others are what
you said, indignant essays or essays and not poems.

There are times when I believe that for years I have misunderstood
the nature of poetry and hence have been battling to achieve something
which does not exist. I do think—and I believe you do—that everything
is material for poems, everything felt deeply, everything that springs
from experience, from the most inconsequential to the most conse-
quential. But there is a leap from the material to the poem and I think

---

1. "My Sisters, O My Sisters" (in *The Lion and the Rose,* 1948) celebrates the lives of
women, emphasizing wholeness and harmonious relation. This poem is one of three Sarton
poems included in Sandra Gilbert and Susan Gubar, eds., *Norton Anthology of Literature by
Women: The Tradition in English* (New York: Norton, 1985).

2. Wordsworth's 1803 sonnet, "To Toussaint l'Ouverture," celebrates the Haitian leader
who led the struggle for independence from France.

the great flaw in all my past work has been the belief that unadulterated "life," [in hand on left side of page:—not sufficiently transposed and *depersonalized*], that the formulating of everything that was happening to me was the material of poetry. I think now that I always stood on the threshold and never really got into the sanctuary and this is very frightening. I find it hard to put this into words, but now that I have got it in mind, I may be able to understand and use it at last. I have wished to include everything in fact—and I think I got this from Yeats originally. But when he had the most personal things to say he very often put them into the mouths of imaginary beings and hence achieved the leap. ("The Crazy Jane" sequence for instance.)

What I now so much wish to know is whether you believe I have ever successfully incorporated a certain kind of experience into a poem. For instance, "The Sacred Order," "What The Old Man Said," "Roman Head," "Unlucky Soldier" from that book[3]—or "Take Anguish for Companion" in the last one.[4] There is no hurry about this question— it can wait till we next meet, or forever. But eventually it would be helpful if you could put your finger on the intrinsic difference. If you feel that these poems never succeed, then it is a matter of simply not putting these themes into poetry, but rather into prose—yet, they, too, are deeply felt themes. I believe it is the craft that is lacking, and also that they have not been sufficiently translated, are too direct and simply *statements,* say too much, do not suggest enough. Does "Where Warriors Stood" do better, I wonder?[5]

From a technical point of view I was working toward a softer texture in the last book—the result was often diffuseness, I see now. And all of this sounds very mechanical, but I know you take it for granted (or hope you do) that we agree that any true poem is *first* given, just rises up, and *then* worked at and fashioned. (How fascinating though Coleridge's belief that working at poetry induces inspiration—I have not found it so.)

Well, I must stop. I wanted to express this so that someday you would tell me. I think of you poring over the proofs of that rich thick

---

3. These poems appear in May Sarton, *The Lion and the Rose* (New York: Rinehart, 1948).

4. "Take Anguish for Companion" appears in May Sarton, *The Land of Silence and Other Poems* (New York: Rinehart, 1953).

5. "Where Warriors Stood" appears in *The Land of Silence.*

book.[6] I wait for it with passionate eagerness and perhaps it will answer this question without a further word.

[The letter of 16 July 1955 expresses Sarton's affinity for the sea and foreshadows her life by the sea in York, Maine.]

July 16th, [1955]   14 Wright Street [Cambridge]
Dear Louise, good to find your card when I got back,—cutting our way through the thick jungle heat, which makes Cambridge rather like a tropical island in the rainy season. It is raining right now, but a *hot* rain!

How can Allen Tate read 25 novels in five days! I had 7 at Bread Loaf to do in two weeks and it seemed a Herculean task![1] But how good that they are in such fine form, that your lectures are going so well despite the heat. Daddy was charmed by Kinsey when he was out there for the big lecture series last spring, by the way, so I am fascinated to hear.[2]

I did up the Lamont things before we came back[3]—I think there may be considerable differences of opinion this time, though I fear the one person I did not wish to make first, will get it, and I had to give that book No. 1 for reasons too long and boring to go into. It is done anyway. We had tea on Mrs. Bullock's[4] porch (a rented house with not enough tea cups, but a beautiful view of the harbor and shipping)

6. Louise Bogan, *Selected Criticism: Poetry and Prose* (New York: Noonday Press, 1955).

1. Sarton was a lecturer at the Bread Loaf Writers' Conference from 1951 to 1953 and again in 1955.

2. In a letter dated 19 July 1955, Bogan reported on her lectures at Indiana University in Bloomington and on her encounter with Dr. Kinsey. "Everyone in Bloomington put themselves out to be pleasant and helpful; and we were compatible, on the whole. . . . The two-hour tour which [Dr. Kinsey] conducted through his sound-proofed quarters was fascinating; only toward the end did he show any sort of extra-scientific interest in his files and other possessions. His library of pornography, he smiling remarked (to Caroline [Gordon]'s well-concealed horror), is second only to the Vatican Library; and it *was* impressive: air-cooled, clean as wax, with all the leather backs shining" (Louise Bogan, *What the Woman Lived: Selected Letters of Louise Bogan, 1920–1970,* ed. Ruth Limmer [New York: Harcourt Brace Jovanovich, 1973], 299).

3. Lamont was a poetry competition for which Sarton and Bogan served as judges. Since Sarton mentions Mrs. Bullock in the same paragraph, the competition was probably sponsored by the Academy of American Poets.

4. Marie Bullock founded the Academy of American Poets.

and I liked her better than I expected, though her world *is* The World, and the immense social manner always makes me feel as if I had grown extra thumbs and were about to drop my cup. Daddy I think was quite taken by her blue eyes and she called him "enchanting" so it was a success! In fact the holiday was like childhood holidays, timeless and beautiful—I miss the ocean and feel claustrophobic here—and have to be cook till next Thurs. when Julia (d.v.) comes back from her holiday. I am really dying to get started now on the summer lectures and be done with them, such an interruption and *corvée* really. But maybe it will be cool in Boulder and I can breathe without wheezing which will be a help.[5]

I have been reading a horrifying too physical novel in Giono's latest manner "le Hussard sur le Toit," all about the cholera epidemic in the 1830s which ravaged the South of France. Pages and pages of descriptions of people dying and all the accompanying symptoms. Why? I simply do not understand. But Morison's *Maritime History of Mass.* is back in my hands now (Daddy snatched it from me) and that is simply wonderful, dreammaking stuff.

There is no news except that the *New Yorker* turned down the last story (I have ideas for five more if I ever get time to do them), that I think I shall never write another poem, and that the German edition of *Shower [of Summer Days]* is going through. Will you feed me a few meals when I am starving next spring? It is a sure thing that I shall be, at this rate.

Now the sun is out and we are going to an air-cooled refuge with Daddy for supper. Today I cooked salmon (to have cold tomorrow), whiting (for Daddy's cat), a huge pot of tea for iced tea, and soup. This all went on the stove at once and was rather fun. The garden is invaded by Japanese beetles, so my main task is to go out periodically with a bowl of hot soapy water and drown them by the dozen. Schweitzer would not approve, but I hate them with a passion. They eat all the tender buds of the roses, horrible black-carapaces and so *hungry*. When we brought Rufus the orange cat back from the kennel today and let him out, the birds went into an uproar—screaming and calling because he was back. He just wagged his tail and rolled over and over on his back, purring and purring—

That is all. Tell me you are safely back. And what next?

---

5. Sarton lectured at the Boulder Writers' Conference in 1955.

[This final selection illustrates Sarton's many excellent travel descriptions. Her delight in New Mexico began in the 1940s, when her first poetry-lecture tour took her to the valleys and deserts of the West.]

Aug. 7th, 1955 Santa Fe, N.M.

Dear Louise, good to have your card here and know that all was going well in Swampscott and that lovely border of annuals near by. Here it is actually cold this morning and I am wearing a sweater and a leather jacket, though we had breakfast in the portal looking over pinyon trees (no house in sight) dipping down to the valley and then through the interstices, glimpses, exactly as in the background of Renaissance paintings, of impossibly bright blue peaks and small formal white clouds. What a beautiful place! There are three dogs here, one old kind of collie, one old scottie, and one very young rambunctious puppy with soft teddy bear fur and an elfin face. Eleanor Bedell, with whom I am staying, is away all day, and the silence seems like a miracle after all those *words*. But I can't quite believe that it will all be over day after tomorrow and the continent flowing beneath a plane again, and all the effort to begin again at Bread Loaf. However, the Boulder thing was fruitful— in more ways than one. They want me to come back two years from now for five weeks (three weeks in the regular summer session and two weeks of the conf.) and this would pay $1,500 and be a boon in tiding over another year. And I think there is also a Texas lecture sometime next year in the offing. I liked the whole atmosphere 100% better than Bread Loaf and I like getting out West, too. On the last day, in fear and trembling, I read a long story which seemed to me to sum up everything I had been trying to say about what makes "literature"—this story was written by a woman about 35 from Oregon and was about Norwegian Americans (somewhat comparable to Willa Cather in the richness of suggestion and the good classic style). I was hoping that the class would feel the quality, but you can never be *sure* and oh, it was lovely and rewarding when she got the real accolade and they all "recognized" the artistic truth. So I left with the good feeling that the circle was closed and something completed and stated.

But what a relief to have a private life again and to be, for awhile with a total *non*-intellectual! Yesterday we had a dreamlike afternoon— and I saw a wholly new kind of New Mexican landscape. It is all far greener than usual, as there have been heavy rains (after about seven years of drought) and we drove through a kind of misty rain down into the Pecos valley—gentler greener mountains, rolling off into clouds, rich green pasturage and a silvery light over it all so that it looked to me like Scotland (which I've never seen). Of course, the minute it rains the arroyos boil up and great red rivers rush about as erratically as mercury, and when we turned in to the dirt road of the ranch where we were bound, it became clear that we would have to leave the car. So we took off our shoes and socks and waded happily through thick red mud, the most delicious sensation I must say, and intended to walk the two miles to the house in bare feet, but luckily we were seen and they came down in a truck and rescued us. It all seemed like magic to me from then on—such a beautiful lived-in set of low buildings, full of books and paintings, such lively *loveable* people, the grandmother (Eleanor's friend) a real character who there in that remote valley had read all my books (what an amazing thing!), her son who graduated from Harvard Law but now raises Angus cattle on the ranch and his pregnant wife, huge and radiant, and silent gnome of a son about two, and two thin shy little girls who kept appearing on the roofs, or suddenly in a doorway, and then vanished. Animals followed us about, an immense great dane who finally lay down with the tiger cat curled up between her paws, and they both slept, while we drank tea and whiskey and finally ate a wonderful stew in which everything had been allowed to simmer for hours.

Outside the silvery rain came down and we thought maybe we would have to spend the night, but the rushing river had become a trickling stream when we got back, and this time we walked over in our shoes to the car. I have hardly conveyed what a dreamy experience all this was—I wish you had been there. I was too happy even to get drunk on all the whiskey.

I cannot from here imagine the awful heat and dread being immersed in it again. Have to read poems the 15th at some Poet's Theatre series in Cambridge, and then off to Bread Loaf, ill-prepared I fear, but never mind.

What I am hoping is that soon your book will be coming—but when on earth shall I *ever* see you? I miss you.

[p.s. in hand] I haven't seen the *New Yorker* with your piece but it will be there when I get back.[1]

---

1. Sarton probably refers to Louise Bogan's poetry review in the *New Yorker* of 30 July 1955.

All in all, May Sarton has written interesting letters since her youth, letters filled with anecdotes, daily activities, reflections on work and reading, and self-criticism. While Sarton certainly took Louise Bogan's criticism seriously, these letters indicate that she relied on her own instincts, exercised her own judgment, acknowledged her success, admitted her weakness. Looking hard at one's own work, Sarton has said, is never a waste of energy. To take a long, dissatisfied look allows one to come back to life with renewed faith. That renewed faith has kept Sarton an active writer now for more than fifty years.

Letters are a private matter. When they become public, they allow the stranger privileged access into the life and thought of the writer. Letters let us move from our present vantage point to see into the past, hearing the words of daily life as well as seeing the progress of that life itself.

NOTES

1. Sarton's letter was dated 23 August 1943. Although Bogan declined, other prominent poets accepted Sarton's invitation to participate in a series of public poetry readings at the New York Public Library (William Carlos Williams, Marianne Moore, and Muriel Rukeyser were among those who read). Sarton's purpose in the undertaking was to emulate a successful program in England that, through readings by prominent poets, reminded the public of poetry, even in the midst of the war's disruption.

2. Louise Bogan, *What the Woman Lived; Selected Letters of Louise Bogan, 1920–1970,* ed. Ruth Limmer (New York: Harcourt Brace Jovanovich, 1973).

3. Elizabeth Frank, *Louise Bogan: A Portrait* (New York: Knopf, 1985).

4. See Mary K. DeShazer, *Inspiring Women: Reimagining the Muse* (New York: Pergamon Press, 1987). DeShazer discusses the friendship and literary affiliation of Louise Bogan and May Sarton and refers to several of the Bogan-Sarton letters in her excellent study of the muse and women poets. DeShazer's essay on Sarton in *Inspiring Women* is reprinted in this volume.

May Sarton's Lyric Strategy

William Drake

The genesis of a lyric poem, for May Sarton, lies in silence. "Silence / is infinitely more precious to me / than any word," she wrote in "Request," in her first volume of poems published in 1937.[1] And for the more than fifty years that have followed, in almost every one of her books, the theme is never out of sight. The titles *The Land of Silence* (1953), *Halfway to Silence* (1980), and *The Silence Now* (1988) indicate its permanence and continuity, culminating in what has finally become "immense ... deep down, not to be escaped."[2]

Silence, in Sarton's universe, is the inner region where the ego finds itself in touch with an infinite spiritual reality. Indeed, the self, as a whole, contains something of that wordless, silent depth even as it is contained by it. Transactions between the individual ego-self and the transcendent or spiritual self are at the heart of May Sarton's poetic practice.

Sarton's spirituality seems to have come to her naturally through her art, through the intense scrutiny of her own intuitive experience, and not through a study of religion or philosophy. Yet her kinship with Asian spirituality and Western mysticism is immediately evident. Sarton's "silence" seems virtually identical with the nameless, wordless Ground of Being that underlies Asian concepts of reality, the Brahma of the Hindus, the Tao of the Chinese. Although this unnameable reality appears to be a nothingness, a blankness to the eye trained only in visible, tangible things, it is actually the matrix out of which all created things are born. For May Sarton, creating a poem out of the inner region of one's own silent being, its language springing into form out of wordlessness, is the same as the creation of all life out of the Ground of Being.

May Sarton's sense of spiritual transcendence, then, does not lead her in the direction of inaction or meditation but to the act of creation. The Ground of Being appears not as a static state, but as Love, continually ushering into consciousness an awareness or epiphany that will expand or transform human experience. A poem begins to take shape from such moments of awareness when, activated by love, the deep silence begins to

cross the divide, to make the transition to words, and thus to a sharing
with others.

May Sarton has analyzed her own creative process in "The Writing
of a Poem."

> For the writing of poetry is first of all a way of life, and only secondarily
> a means of expression. It is a life discipline one might almost say, a dis-
> cipline maintained in order to perfect the instrument of experiencing—
> the poet himself—so that he may learn to keep himself perfectly open
> and transparent, so that he may meet everything that comes his way
> with an innocent eye. . . . He must learn to induce a state of awareness.
> I use the word *induce* here quite deliberately. The mystic induces a state
> of extreme awareness, the visionary state, by certain disciplines, fasting,
> prayer, and so on. The poet must create his own disciplines.[3]

Her own discipline has required solitude. She was surprised, and yet
not surprised, when staying at a Carmelite monastery in Indianapolis in
October 1986 that the nuns knew her work and recognized her as a mystic
like themselves. Nearly thirty years earlier she had written, ". . . poets must
serve it [poetry] as a good servant serves his master, must revere and woo
it as the mystic reveres and woos God through self-discipline toward joy."[4]

One of the commonplaces of the modernist era has been that the poet
is the voice of the broken time, generated out of nonpersonal language
rather than the spirit, not a voice that transcends or answers. Lives destroyed
by alcohol, inner contradiction, or psychosis, because the strain of modern
incoherence is too great to bear, are not uncommonly elevated to heroism,
accepted fatalistically as paying the price of genius. The separation of the
artist's personal identity from the work has indeed never been more insisted
on—as evident in the popular play *Amadeus,* where Sarton's beloved Mozart
is portrayed as a kind of idiot savant, irrelevant, himself, to the work that
pours through him. But it is precisely this gap between the supraliminal
and the conscious ego that Sarton will not leave to chance or bridge by
recourse to a romantic mystique of inspiration or deny by eliminating the
spirit. She recognizes that however tormented the artist's life may appear,
the work can only result from the harmony, lucidity, and intensity that
occur when the silence and the craftsmanlike consciousness meet. Furthermore, harmony between these realms of the self, like salvation, can never
be attained for keeps, but must continually be striven for: "It is a life
discipline one might almost say. . . ."

Any consent to disharmony or violence would be unthinkable in May Sarton's world. In the colors and design of walls and furnishings, of flowers, foods, one's daily schedule, the relations between human beings and animals, of houses and the land, of friends and family members, of lovely old objects hallowed by time and tradition, in the formal music of poetry itself, May Sarton has expressed her belief that harmony is the fundamental necessity of the creative life. As this list implies, the creative life is understood as embracing more than the work of the formal artist and includes all activity made wise by skill and experience that brings something new and valuable into being. Her poem "The Skilled Man" (in *The Silence Now*) makes this point explicitly.

> . . . all that it takes
> To make a knife new or a word
> Is the subtle exchange of a life.[5]

But May Sarton is not a figure in isolation, in spite of her focus on self-discipline, her semirural life, and avoidance of competitive literary society and politics. There is an echo of the New England Transcendentalists in her, for they, too, withdrew into concentration in order to speak more effectively to a broader audience. The highly personal medium of the journal also becomes, in her hands as it did in theirs, a means of bringing the inner life into communion and relationship with others. This passion for connection is the paradoxical driving power within withdrawal, the purpose of which, after all, is to perfect the human instrument.

The desire to serve a communal consciousness inherent in all of Sarton's work is revealed most clearly in her formative, early years when she had not yet settled on being a poet, but saw her future as lying in the theater, the most communal of all the arts. For several years in the early 1930s in New York, she worked first with Eva Le Gallienne and then with her own company as actor, director, and writer. Though giving up this work, she continued to conceive of poetry as dramatic and interactive, as having a public function.

That public function may be described in the briefest possible terms as the restoration of peace, equilibrium, and reconciliation. The poem is created out of tensions in the poet, and each successful poem is, in a sense, a crisis resolved. The poet confronting the silence is confronting herself, attempting to bring into harmonious conjunction the dissonant aspects of the self, the tensions between the conscious and the unconscious. This is the spiritual task the poet performs publicly: the enactment of the drama of self-conflict and resolution, so that the resulting harmony can be vicariously experienced by the reader or listener.

Sarton's poem "A Letter to James Stephens" (*Inner Landscape*, 1938) makes this point succinctly, contrasting the difference between her idea of the poet's task and that which strikes one as typically male and modern. Stephens is portrayed as chiding her for dwelling on personal love instead of the impersonal, the objective. To him, the poet is a lonely, heroic figure wresting words of doubtful comfort from his confrontation with an unheeding cosmos. While she honors him and their friendship, she gently insists on the validity of her own way: her "heart" also listens to the same sounds that his mind's ear hears and can also open to the universe, but hers is a universe of sheltering love rather than detached intellect.

> My honor (and I cherish it for it is hardly won)
> Is to be pure in this: is to believe
> That to write down these perishable songs for one,
> For one alone, and out of love, is not to grieve
> But to build on the quicksand of despair
> A house where every man may take his ease,
> May come to shelter from the outer air,
> A little house where he may find his peace.[6]

She denies that the love she writes about is only the "quick-burning fire of youth" that will go out; it is rather the immortal fire of God's burning bush, the "love that spins the universe." Thus, love between individuals is the manifestation of divine love, the small and personal opens to the infinite in a harmony of relatedness rather than separation.

The poet's public task, being at the same time so personal, therefore calls for profound humility so that it may be saved from the self-dramatizing, self-serving, self-inflating attitudes that undermine communal coherence. From the beginning, Sarton's work shows this sign of authentic spirituality, of greatness, one must say in honesty. She has monitored herself (more severely than any critic) to avoid the slightest jangle of posturing, false tone, verbal trickery, sentimentality, or emotional truth not won the hard way. This is essential if her work is to perform its service to the reader.

In a cynical time, when cynicism can be the cheapest and easiest attitude to fall into, Sarton's work naturally raises the question of whether her attempt at self-effacement in the very act of self-presentation is even possible, let alone valid. She would probably answer that the discipline of the artist demands it, whether it be always successful or not. But the measure of her success can be found in the fruits of her effort—the response of countless readers for whom her poetry has opened a door of self previously sealed, who still trust poetry to serve a vital, enlarging function in their lives, as it has traditionally done over the centuries.

This response, Sarton holds, is to the poem itself, to the words that perform their service, and not to herself as a person. The poet is, in this respect, like a performer on the stage whose role, voice, and gestures are an enactment and not an eavesdropping on an actual segment of the actor's life. Despite the effacement of the actor's own personality, all of her, or his, emotional and intellectual development is nevertheless brought to bear to illuminate the truth of the role. If a poem begins as the dramatization of a personal act of awareness, it enters the impersonal medium of poetic tradition for those who read it. The poem thus assumes an existence in the world quite apart from the poet, as do all beautiful and reassuring objects handed down over time. Only the inexperienced beginner, Sarton's character Hilary Stevens observes in *Mrs. Stevens Hears the Mermaids Singing,* confuses the writing of a poem with a confessional outcry. But that confusion is a normal beginner's mistake, and, unless development is arrested there, it contains the germ of development into true poetry.

The paradox of being intensely present in the poem while remaining apart from it, of setting up an emotionally charged encounter with the reader while objectifying it as a beautiful, enduring formal statement, has been at the center of Sarton's art from the beginning. She has used the word *transparency* to describe this presentation of herself. It appears in one of her earliest poems, one of the "Japanese Papers" in *Encounter in April* (1937).

> I walk among you,
> transparent—
> Why?
> Because I hope one will see
> who can answer.[7]

But transparency is actually an illusion, for, in spite of rigorous self-honesty, the poet discreetly never reveals many highly personal aspects of herself that are rightly no one else's business. Transparency is the poet's stance in her art. And while it is totally sincere and meticulously truthful, it is selective and limited.

Yet readers, like fans of public figures of all kinds, tend not to distinguish between the generosity of the poet as an artist and her generosity as a person offstage. Sarton's recent poem "Salt Lick" (*The Silence Now*, 1988) ruefully explores the cost this has had for her. People come to her work "like deer/To a salt lick":

> The salt, a mystery,
> The written word,
> Not me.
>
> But the deer, you see,
> Are confused.
> I, not the word, am used
> To fill their need . . .

Readers who have been inspired or moved by her work in personal ways write letters asking for advice or help. It has been hard for her to refuse them, since she is indeed as compassionate as the persona in her writings. Yet this demand on her personal resources is a severe drain on energies that are needed primarily for creative work.

> On some cold winter day
> I shall be licked away
> Through no deer's fault,
> There will be no more salt.[8]

May Sarton's devotion to the communal function of poetry explains, in part, her lifelong commitment to the lyric tradition. The lyric is accessible to a wide audience because it comes charged with pleasurable expectations. For an art to maintain a spiritual function in the community, it must necessarily accede to the ritual-based demand for familiar rhythms and repetitions, for elements that stir subconscious as well as conscious responses. This is obvious in ritualistic art observed from a distance in non-Western cultures, but less so in our own, where the emphasis on individualism tends to obscure a similar need for communal coherence through arts that, if not ritualistic in a strict sense, speak with a communal voice. Lyric poetry has had too long a history of serving that need, even in its limited and qualified way, and its presence is too deeply imbedded in popular consciousness to be easily ousted by competitive innovations. Sarton has been a highly successful public reader of her own lyrics and vividly describes the exhilarating moment of connection between performer and audience.

I love to hear the poems ring out and hear them *land* in that special
silence when a large audience is moved. For me a poem is a little like
a sheet of music; only when it is "played" can one truly hear it and
know what has been set down.[9]

The thrust of modernist poetry, however, has been deliberately against
the idea of a traditional, communal function for the arts, emphasizing instead
the dislocation of the artist from the community, ironic detachment, obscu-
rity, and avoidance of the musical elements that provide the emotional
underpinnings for the lyric. The lyric poem, of course, traces its origins to
song accompanied by the lyre and, by implication, requires an audience for
whom the melodies and rhythms evoke powerful and predictable responses.
As a solo song, the lyric presents a miniature narrative in which the listener
can experience the resonances of his or her own life, reconciling intimate
personal feeling with a common consciousness.

May Sarton believes that the banishment of verbal music from so much
contemporary poetry is a serious deprivation. Much of the appeal of poetry
should be "below the belt,"[10] she has said, rather than all in the head—in
one's unconscious bodily response to verbal movement and the play of sound.
A. E. Housman declared that he judged whether he was in the presence of
a "true" poem by its ability to raise the hairs on his face and neck if he
recited it to himself while shaving. His idea may seem facetious or over-
simplified, but it nevertheless states one of the primary functions of the
lyric poem: to appeal on paraverbal levels, like music and dance. Sarton also
believes that a poem should be easily remembered. By its musical patterning,
its tendency toward simplicity and succinctness, its relative faithfulness to
familiar syntax, the lyric is virtually designed to be memorable. No matter
how sophisticated in insight or complexity of thought or how strongly it
bears the stamp of a powerful personality, say a Neruda or a Yeats, or even
such a rarefied poet as Rilke, the lyric poem remains accessible to the broad
community and serves the communal consciousness by virtue of its drawing
on long-established conventions and emotional expectations.

The last great flowering of the lyric poem in English occurred roughly
between 1910 and 1950. This was also the time when women poets, the
generation of Edna St. Vincent Millay, Elinor Wylie, and Sara Teasdale,
came to prominence and virtually dominated American poetry, their pop-
ularity peaking in the 1920s. Sarton's work descends directly from that
brilliant period of women's achievement. She was most attracted, she has

said, to Millay, Wylie, and Amy Lowell, who are, not surprisingly, the most idiosyncratic and theatrical of the women poets.

There was a stronger sense of community among the women poets of the 1920s than they have been credited with, as they emerged from the isolation suffered by creative women in the nineteenth century; a sense that they were, collectively, in the vanguard of a new development. In making the lyric poem their special province, they found fertile ground for vigorous creative development. Because of the lyric's traditional emphasis on personal emotion, women were able to draw the veil from female experience and begin to voice their unique inner life. The impact this had on the consciousness of the public, and particularly on women readers, can scarcely be overestimated. The lyric may also be said to be androgynous in the sense that it seems as readily adaptable to female expression as to male. An advantage for women poets in the 1920s was that it permitted them to share equal professional status with men, to resist attempts to ghettoize them as a separate and lesser class of writers. After their heyday in the 1920s, women poets have never enjoyed as much prominence, broad acceptance, and serious critical recognition by their contemporaries, both women and men, as they did then. The lyric poem, by virtue of its traditional, quasi-ritualistic character, served as a medium between the personal and the public, bringing women's spiritual presence into popular consciousness, as it had traditionally served men.

Here one may apply retrospectively the recent work of Carol Gilligan, identifying women's unique focus on human relationships, love, and the finding of peaceful solutions to problems of conflict, as opposed to the male tendency toward competition, confrontation, and violence to settle differences.[11] It is beyond the scope of this essay to apply Gilligan's insights to the women poets of the 1920s in detail, but their chief theme, love in personal relationships, and their fascination with transcendent experience suggest that a uniquely female communal expression was developing in a form and a language they were making their own.

May Sarton's first book of poems, *Encounter in April* (1937), shows that her beginnings can be traced to these women poets who were her immediate predecessors. The Millay-like love sonnets, the meticulous craftsmanship, the sureness of emotion and aesthetic judgment, the themes centering on personal relationships, and the revelation of transcendent meaning in small, casual experiences try out the range she found in them. One finds in this first book, too, her lifelong sensitivity to color and design, a gift from her mother, a professional designer. But this echoes as well the artistic sensibility of such poets as Elinor Wylie and Amy Lowell, whose imagist ideas were particularly influential among women writers.

Sarton developed rapidly in her own direction, however, and she did it by energetically pressing beyond the agenda of the women she admired. While they hovered on the edge of self-doubt and few of them had developed a clear, critical sense of their roles as poets, Sarton proceeded with a vigor and strength they might well have envied, and saw the central necessity of defining for herself the nature of the poet's task. There was no basis at that time for a distinctively female theory of poetry, and besides Sarton considered the medium of poetry to be neutral as to gender. In her pronouncements on poetry, she has consistently referred to the poet as "he" (as the women of the 1920s did), not with the intent of sexist language, but rather to include herself in the mainstream. The chief influences on her own emerging ideas of poetic practice were Yeats and Valéry.

Yeats had appealed to other female lyric poets as well, perhaps because, like Keats, his sensibility seemed more feminine than most men's, but chiefly because he revised the diction of the lyric toward greater precision and austerity, loosened its boundaries for greater freedom of form and depth of subject matter. In Yeats's hands, the lyric proved flexible enough to change with the times while preserving its traditional power to speak for the community. Sarton has seen in Yeats the direction every artist must head toward in maturity: the poetic statement that is rigorously stripped down and simplified but much deepened, the product of an experienced and wise skill that has come to seem so easy as to conceal totally its effort. She has observed that her poems in *The Silence Now*, 1988, approach this Yeatsian standard.[12]

One can see a kinship as well with Japanese and Chinese aesthetics, with which Sarton has felt a degree of sympathy: the value placed on original, precise observation of nature, the minimum of means used to obtain the greatest effect, the purity of emotion, the awareness of a strict, demanding tradition within which one is perennially challenged to shape the fresh statement, and the somewhat indefinable assumption that all the arts, visual and auditory, proceed from the same spiritual center, like overlapping, alternative languages, so that paintings are full of literary allusions and poems are sensitive to color and design. *Encounter in April* contains, in fact, a set of haiku-like verses titled "Japanese Papers." Yet Sarton sees the danger for a Western poet to push such sympathies too far and attempt a facile borrowing

of Asian ways. Haiku in Western hands too easily serve as a quick fix, a way
to feel that a poem has been written without having to go through the self-
transforming struggle that one's own tradition imposes.[13]

If Yeats has provided a model for what can be done with the lyric
poem itself, Paul Valéry yields, for Sarton, vital insights into the poet's
relation to the craft. "The poet's poem interests me less than the subtleties
and enlightenment he acquires by way of his work," Valéry wrote. "And
that is why one must *work* at one's poem, that is, work at oneself."[14] One
recalls Sarton's assertion that "the writing of poetry . . . is a discipline main-
tained in order to perfect the instrument of experiencing." Valéry turned
the analytical prism on himself in order to discover and refine his poetic
practice. This is not the same, however, as trying to define what poetry
itself is, apart from the poet: "It is the labor of a lifetime to arrive at a
precise idea of poetry. I agree that the game is not worth the candle."[15]
One finds Sarton similarly saying little about poetry, but much about the
poet working. At the center of the mystery is the way poetry stands between
the poet and the public, belonging to both but in entirely different ways.
What begins as a personal statement becomes a voice for others whom the
poet does not even know and will never meet. "The writer—no, the poet,"
Valéry says—"passes through a strange crisis when what he first thought
of as himself, and more than himself—becomes the intermediary between
himself and a vague public."[16] Or further: "The 'meaning' of a poem, like
that of an object, is the reader's business."[17]

Valéry defined, with great precision, the subtle, sensitive interplay
between the poet and the poem, scrupulously observing the conditions and
states of mind necessary for creating it. Too much critical self-consciousness
would interfere with the flow of vague, undefined energy from the subconscious mind and feelings that gives the poem its truth and momentum:
"Verse must have a magical character or it does not exist."[18] The poem
emerges into being when the self-conscious apparatus of the poet's skill and
knowledge of language and form comes to terms with the amorphous,
boundless energy of what Sarton calls the silence.

One must conclude that such a poetic strategy is possible only where
there is living tradition and a community of like-minded response. Valéry,
like Sarton, preferred traditional verse forms because of the fruitful tensions
they set up: "One can . . . use regular verse because everybody uses it. One
can on the contrary use it 'in another spirit,' as if one had invented it, as
an originality. It is only then that one sees its strangeness . . . and its jus-
tification."[19] The transpersonal is evoked by a paradoxical union of individual

originality and traditionally given forms. Poetry always exists at the margin of the impossible, where paradoxes can be held in suspense: silence and speech, the security of rules and the "quicksand" of experience, the intensely private and its helpless exposure to the public, the male and the female; the list could go on. "Poetry consists of using words," Valéry wrote, "to produce in someone that which excludes the use, the possibility of using words. It wants words to be at every moment the negation of speech."[20]

Sarton, however, goes beyond a certain refined passivity in Valéry to propose a more active force working in the poet. She sees a deity presiding over the nearly impossible conjunctions that produce poetry: the muse, the female creative force that does not belong to the poet but visits her. The idea of the muse is explored in the novel *Mrs. Stevens Hears the Mermaids Singing*. Power comes to the poet, Hilary Stevens, through her involvement in a series of intense, challenging, transformational relationships in which love is the driving force. Such relationships are seldom, if ever, peaceful or stable. Their purpose is not to bring rest but, rather, new life, for opposites are not merely placed in juxtaposition, they must interact without destroying each other. Poems are born out of loving collisions. Thus, the meetings or conjunctions one sees in Sarton's personal relationship with the public, with tradition and form, reflect the archetypal encounter between love and resistance that creates the poem itself.

It is not surprising that May Sarton has found more pertinent guidance and clarification of her own practice in Yeats and Valéry than in American sources. She is a transplanted European who appears to be more a native New Englander than she really is. French poetry, with its greater attention to verbal music and to self-definition—"Poetry is a quest for its own self,"[21] Valéry wrote—has been not only influential, but came close to being Sarton's own tradition. Had her father not emigrated from Belgium when she was a child, she would have become, as she puts it, a poet writing in French in a small, culturally divided country. She finds English a richer and more flexible language, and though it lacks the French possibilities for musical effects, these can be overdone, rippling along too prettily, as in Verlaine's work, which she, like Valéry, does not admire.[22] Yeatsian austerity is a kind of antidote to French excess.

But the European roots are deep, not only in childhood memory and the furniture of her parents that Sarton still cherishes, but in her love of settled places where continuity counterbalances the destructive flow of time and change. It is as though creativity needs not only silence and solitude, but momentary escape from time as well. If Americans are rootless, spiritually hungry, driven by a never-satisfied quest for stability that defeats its own purpose, Sarton is authentically in touch with her own viable past and has succeeded in negotiating peace between the opposite-pulling forces of tradition and the new. Her much-undervalued novel *The Magnificent Spinster* shows how the figure of a revered spiritual ancestor is formed, embodying the mysteries of love and care that the young, in turn, absorb into themselves.

Although Sarton, because of her commitment to traditional poetic forms and her idealistic, humanistic outlook, has appeared to critics to be an anomaly, outside modernist development, she in fact offers, through her poetry, a trenchant commentary on the same world of experience addressed in modernist work and cannot be considered apart from it.

The modernist "revolution" has been defined almost exclusively in terms of certain male poets. One well-regarded critical history calls it "The Pound Era," subsuming the complexity of an age into the inflated personality of a single cultural hero. With the tools of gender analysis provided by recent feminist criticism, one can begin to see what should have been obvious all along: that modernism has been defined by male academics to eliminate women from the canon and to restore men to the center of poetic culture following the surge of power by the women poets of the 1920s.[23] The fall of the women poets from critical grace is one of the most remarkable turnabouts in literary history, and the litany of hostile criticism by men reveals its hidden agenda in often being based on stereotyped objections to female character. The denigration has been so effective that women poets of the earlier period are valued most whose work seems most in tune with what men were doing. May Sarton's courage in carrying forward the work of women who have suffered so much disparagement is indicative of her power of self-command and determination to chart the course of her own values. When the conscious line of descent between the creative women of today and those of the 1920s was almost broken, Sarton kept it alive. Her novel, *Mrs. Stevens Hears the Mermaids Singing,* portrays a poet of that great generation who has miraculously survived the intervening void of lack of attention and is flowering again in her later years, symbolizing the continuity between the generations of women.

But one must probe more deeply to expose the implications of Sarton's response to a male-dominated poetic culture. One turns to some of the more bizarre notions of Ezra Pound that, because of their very absurdity, reveal what is going on beneath the surface and is usually left unspoken. "It is more than possible," he wrote in an introduction to Rémy de Gourmont's *The Natural Philosophy of Love,* "that the brain itself is, in origin and development, only a sort of great clot of genital fluid held in suspense or reserve. . . . It would explain the enormous content of the brain as a maker and presenter of images."[24] It follows, then, that women can never rise to the same class with men as creators. Rather, "one offers women as the accumulators of hereditary aptitudes, better than men in the 'useful gestures,' the perfections; but to man, given what we have of history, the 'inventions,' the new gestures, the extravagance, the wild shots. . . ."[25] And again: "Woman, the conservator, the inheritor of past gestures, clever, practical . . . not inventive, always the best disciple of any inventor."[26] He characterized his own literary ambition as "driving any new idea into the great passive vulva of London, a sensation analogous to the male feeling in copulation."[27]

What Pound wishes to do is to eliminate the spiritual basis of poetic creation, the silent, transpersonal ground of being, and establish it instead in the individual physical brain. The brain's activity must then literally be linked with the physical (i.e., sexual) creative energy for the picture to be consistent. With this physically grounded, ego-centered view, the sense of community, which universally requires a spiritual base, vanishes along with a relevant and usable past, and the aggressive, competitive power of individual males becomes the key determinant; the mass of people are held in contempt, and tyrannical leaders become heroes. Instead of transcending the destructive, dislocating forces of the time, such a view expresses and embodies them. Pound is, in many respects, the authentic if unwitting voice of an era dominated by male militarism and expanding scientific technology, eclipsing the moral values that Gilligan and her associates attribute to women, to say nothing of the oppression of women themselves.

It is significant that Pound characterized tradition as female and inventiveness as male. And that Sarton has sought to heal such a split by proposing harmonious interaction between the two, finding them to be not divergent but halves of a whole. The male revolution against Western tradition inevitably left a gaping emptiness that even powerful, original individuals could not fill. So poets, painters, and composers turned to exotic cultures—African, Asian, Polynesian, medieval European—where examples of ritual art survived, and borrowed themes and motifs to use ironically in their work. But this practice has only increased self-consciousness and deepened the sense of loss and the confusion about what sustains the artistic imagination. One notes May Sarton's caveat against borrowing from traditions too far outside one's own.

If May Sarton's poetic strategy is viewed against the backdrop of her times, it is revealed as an answer, an attempt to heal and transcend. For her, a poem begins with an encounter with the muse—the force of love emerging from the transpersonal silence—and goes on to an encounter with the reader, continuing its work of making connections. It dwells in a community of responses, among those "who can answer." This community of aesthetic response to beauty, of the tension of love, of tradition hallowed by attention and care, would seem to be above all a women's community or perhaps the community women would build if free to do so.

And so May Sarton's ultimate strategy—a word she herself would perhaps not use, as sounding too unintuitive, too calculating—is to breathe life into that idea of community and perpetuate its possibility, carrying forward the work of those whose example inspired her.

NOTES

1. May Sarton, *Encounter in April* (Boston: Houghton-Mifflin, 1937), 49.

2. May Sarton, "The Silence Now," in *The Silence Now* (New York: Norton, 1988), 16.

3. May Sarton, "The Writing of a Poem," in *Writings on Writing,* rev. ed. (Orono, Maine: Puckerbrush Press, 1986), 40.

4. Sarton, "Writing of a Poem," 57.

5. Sarton, "The Skilled Man," in *The Silence Now* (New York: Norton, 1988), 74.

6. May Sarton, *Collected Poems, 1930–1973* (New York: Norton, 1973), 43.

7. Sarton, *Encounter in April,* 52.

8. Sarton, *Silence Now,* 23.

9. May Sarton, *Recovering: A Journal* (New York: Norton, 1980), 72.

10. May Sarton, interview with the author, San Francisco, April 7, 1989.

11. Carol Gilligan, *In a Different Voice: Psychological Theory and Women's Development* (Cambridge Mass.: Harvard University Press, 1982). See also Carol Gilligan, Janie Victoria Ward, and Jill McLean Taylor, eds., with Betty Bardige, *Mapping the Moral Domain: A Contribution of Women's Thinking to Psychological Theory and Education* (Cambridge Mass.: Harvard University Press, 1988).

12. Sarton, interview with author.

13. Sarton, interview with author.

14. Paul Valéry, "On Poets and Poetry," in *Collected Works of Paul Valéry,* ed. Jackson Mathews (Princeton: Princeton University Press, 1989), 1:397.

15. Valéry, *Works* 1:418.

16. Valéry, *Works* 1:400.

17. Valéry, *Works* 1:416.

18. Valéry, *Works* 1:416.

19. Valéry, *Works* 1:424.

20. Valéry, *Works* 1:424.

21. Valéry, *Works* 1:418.

22. Sarton, interview with author.

23. For a documented discussion of the gender politics of modernist poetry, see William Drake, *The First Wave: Women Poets in America, 1915–1945* (New York: Macmillan, 1987).

24. Ezra Pound, Introduction to *The Natural Philosophy of Love,* by Rémy de Gourmont (London: Spearman, 1957), vii.

25. Pound, Introduction, viii.

26. Pound, Introduction, viii.

27. Pound, Introduction, viii.

Rebirthing Genesis: May Sarton and Contemporary Feminist Fiction

Marilyn R. Mumford

Feminist scholars have been re-visioning Eve's experience in the Garden of Eden for more than a decade.[1] My own contribution to the discussion has been focused primarily, though not exclusively, on Eurocentric lesbian writers of fiction. In this essay I will locate May Sarton in a literary tradition of feminist re-visionings of the Fall, in which a lesbian or strongly woman-identified character experiences a second (usually more fortunate) fall after an original (usually heterosexual) loss of innocence.[2]

In the first decades of the twentieth century, for example, Inez Haynes Gillmore and Charlotte Perkins Gilman re-visioned the myth of the Fall with different results from those recorded in Genesis. Gillmore's *Angel Island* (1914) and Gilman's *Herland* (1915) are feminist Utopian fantasies. A half-century later, a very different kind of re-visioning of the creation myth occurs in May Sarton's realistic novel, *Mrs. Stevens Hears the Mermaids Singing* (1965). In a subtle parody of Genesis, Sarton replaces Adam and Eve with an eighteen-year-old homosexual boy and a seventy-year-old lesbian poet. These two characters talk about love and love's relationship to the act of creation in a setting ironically reminiscent of the Garden of Eden.

Both Gilman's feminist Utopian fantasy and Sarton's ironic parody of Genesis have analogues in contemporary feminist fiction. Like Gilman and Sarton, recent writers (Sally Miller Gearhart, Joan Slonczewski, Jeanette Winterson, Ellen Galford) have imagined what I call a second fall into feminist or lesbian feminist consciousness, a fall into a radically new knowledge of good and evil. This second fall, like any movement from innocence to experience, is never without pain, but the knowledge gained seems to many of the characters who experience it a desirable alternative to life in a kind of unconscious Eden or life among men seemingly intent on exercising their presumed right to power over the bodies and souls of women.

The striking fact about these literary re-visionings of the creation story is that many texts describe an actual *physical fall* in the course of the narrative—a conscious or unconscious "return" of the concept to non-metaphorical terms, as though the image of falling has first to be reinscribed at the site of physical action before its "translation" in the service of a feminist ideology can take place. In this essay I will compare Gilman's *Herland* and Sarton's *Mrs. Stevens* with more recent work in order to suggest significant changes in these feminist re-visionings of the creation myth. Gilman's novel reflects a heterosexual but strongly woman-identified point of view; Sarton's anticipates the powerful lesbian energy of much contemporary feminist fiction.

Gilman and Gillmore: The Feminist Utopia

In a feminist Utopia, the story is apt to be set in an exclusively female paradise into which "snakes," in the form of more-or-less human males, intrude. The males may be brutal and vicious or simply ignorant of peaceful ways of living. Invariably they first threaten and then attempt to take over the female paradise, usually with disastrous results.

The best American example of this type of re-visioning of the Genesis myth is Charlotte Perkins Gilman's *Herland* (1915).[3] Gilman's feminist utopia has never been surpassed in its exploration of what constitutes civilized behavior, although later feminists, particularly lesbian writers, have gone much further than Gilman in challenging stereotypes of "masculine" and "feminine" behavior. In *Herland,* three male protagonists—Van, Jeff, and Terry—discover and then land in a country the size of Holland that was separated from the rest of the world by an earthquake 2,000 years ago. Herland is an "enormous garden" (11), a *hortus conclusus* carefully cultivated to support a controlled population of 3,000,000 women and girls, in comfort and plenty, on a largely vegetarian diet.

In these first chapters, Gilman's satire of Genesis gradually develops a strong cutting edge, the comedy produced in part by Gilman's wild exaggeration of the creation story. In the first place, the women are there in paradise first—or, at least, they have been there, apart from men, for 2,000 years—living together happily and peacefully, producing (by parthenogenesis) thousands of happy and healthy baby girls, as opposed to thousands of tiny fratricidal Cains and Abels. Into this fertile garden Gilman inserts three Adams, intruders, and three resident Eves. The young men hear suppressed laughter coming from the branches of the tree above them, although they can see nothing. Van, the narrator, warns his two companions to "Look out for a poisoned arrow in your eye" (14), but Terry, aggressive and brutal,

refuses to unlearn American stereotypes of masculine and feminine behavior
that do not pertain in Herland. Underneath Gilman's retelling of the Genesis
story lies a grim recognition that, far from being seduced by Eve, Adam/
Terry is what almost destroys the paradise of Herland.

Terry sees the young women in the tree as fruit designed for his own
eating, and he is confident of his ability to trap one of the girls and then
take her. No literal snake appears in this scene, but there are at least three
metaphorical snakes: the poison in Terry's heart (his socialization as a predator
male), the snakelike "bait" he brings from his inner pocket, and Terry
himself, with his masculine good looks, his charm, and his willingness to
use force to get what he wants.

> "Have to use bait," grinned Terry. "I don't know about you fellows,
> but I came prepared." He produced from an inner pocket a little box
> of purple velvet, that opened with a snap—and out of it he drew a
> long sparkling thing, a necklace of big varicolored stones that would
> have been worth a million if real ones. He held it up, swung it,
> glittering in the sun, offered it first to one, then to another, holding
> it out as far as he could reach toward the girl nearest him. He stood
> braced in the fork, held firmly by one hand—the other, swinging his
> bright temptation, reached far out along the bough but not quite to
> his full stretch. (16)

This scene at the outset of *Herland* is built on layers of complex associations
derived from Genesis, the subtexts interlaced like vines climbing the giant
tree. Not only has Gilman turned one of the Adams into a parody of the
devil, but with great skill and good humor she has also associated the
swinging necklace, in its glittering, snakelike movements, with the phallus,
a "bright temptation" to innocent girls who have never before laid eyes on
a man.

This scene is also a parody of a modern courtship ritual in which the
male buys expensive gifts for the female in order to "prove" his love. Terry's
promiscuity back home is satirized in his offering the necklace to all three
girls. His unabashed acknowledgment that he is using bait as a fisherman
would use bait reveals the true dynamics of courtship in a capitalist system:
the woman is "caught" or "bought" to provide free labor for the man's
household. This time, however, the devil's plan fails, thanks to the careful
education by the Overmothers of the girls in Herland. Alima proves more
than a match for Terry, first feinting with her right hand, then seizing the

necklace with her left and, in the same moment, dropping beyond his reach
to the bough below. In effect, Alima castrates Terry, grabbing the source
of his power, meant to betray her, for herself and for all the women of
Herland. It is a measure of Gilman's skill that most of this ideological
business is accomplished with the lightest of comic touches. At some level,
we are aware that the tables in Genesis have been turned: women are in
charge, and men are there not to dominate and instruct, but to listen and
be educated. No wonder *Herland* has lost none of its appeal in the seventy-
five years since its publication!

Ironically, in Gilman's feminist text it is a male narrator, Van, most
sympathetic of the three adventurers, who experiences the fall into feminist
consciousness. During the abortive escape attempt, Van falls down a cliff
and narrowly escapes death.

> Terry slid down first—said he'd show us how a Christian meets his
> death. Luck was with us. We . . . made this scramble quite successfully,
> though I got a pretty heavy fall just at the end, and was only kept
> on the second ledge by main force. The next stage was down a sort
> of "chimney"—a long irregular fissure; and so with scratches many
> and painful and bruises not a few, we finally reached the stream. (37)

Intensifying the irony, Van's fall is also a birthing scene, both for him and
for his idealistic friend, Jeff. Both Jeff and Van achieve awareness of new
and mutually fulfilling relationships between men and women; the churlish
Terry is exiled for trying to rape Alima when she won't submit to him.

Herland is a brilliant achievement, but it has its limitations. As Ann
J. Lane points out in her introduction to the 1979 edition of *Herland,* Gilman
does not allow room for sexual passion in her vision of a pacifist feminist
community—a crucial omission.[4]

Much less well known than *Herland,* Inez Haynes Gillmore's *Angel
Island* (1914) puts five shipwrecked American men on an island paradise
where they are discovered by five beautiful, winged women.[5] Eventually the
men trap and imprison the beautiful creatures, savagely shearing their wings
again and again to render them fit for marriage to patriarchal males. In this
novel, the Fall, for the winged women in general, is from free flight to
earthbound imprisonment, a graphic metaphor for the disillusionment of
conventional marriage.

But for Julia, leader of the women, the one who "thinks" (259), the
last to succumb to marriage, there is, before the capture, a spectacular

individual fall that we see twice, first through Billy's eyes (144–47) and, much later, in a first-person account. Julia tells the story of her attempted suicide to her four friends, who have been "domesticated" by marriage and motherhood.

> "One day, I flew up and up. . . . I flew deliberately higher and higher until I became cold and colder and numb and frozen—until my wings stopped. And then . . . I dropped. I dropped like a stone. But—but— the instant I let myself go, something strange happened—a miracle of self-revelation. I knew that I loved Billy, that I could not live in any world where he could not come to me. And the instant that I realized that I loved him, I knew also that I could not die." (252)

Painfully, Julia describes how she fell from beauty, power, independence, free flight, into a different, for her less noble, mode of being. Julia's recognition that she loves Billy is a fall into terrible knowledge: her wings fail her for the first time in her life, and she weeps for the first time since childhood.

The profound irony of this passage, with its sexual (and possibly lesbian) subtext, is that Julia falls temporarily *out* of feminist consciousness *into* knowledge of her love for Billy, as though the two were, for Gillmore, mutually exclusive states of being. Knowing that she loves Billy, Julia believes that she "[can] not die." But as the novel proceeds, we learn that Julia and the other women do suffer a kind of death in the shearing of their wings, the loss of their freedom, their transformation into "regular" wives and mothers. Julia's fall moves Billy, who has witnessed her near death, to join with those of his companions who want to imprison the women; loving her, he wants to protect her from falling, though she claims she will never try that suicidal flight again (254). Julia's fall out of feminist consciousness and Billy's defection to the side of the cynical and opportunistic Ralph is the turning point of the women's fate.

Trapped in an endless round of trivial chores and meaningless conversation, the women of Angel Island do not rebel until they find out that the men intend to treat daughters in the same way as wives, cutting their wings when the girls reach the age of eighteen. What they can bear for themselves, the women will not allow to happen to Angela or to any other girl-child born to them (338). Under Julia's leadership, the women teach themselves to walk, an activity they have always regarded with contempt. Gaining strength, they hide themselves and their children in a cave until the men agree to their terms . . . and, in the interval, the women's wings grow back. What they are capable of after marriage and motherhood, however, can hardly be called flight; Gillmore describes it as a "grotesque performance . . . their wing-stumps [beating] in a very agony of effort" (347).

Angel Island ends with the death, in childbirth, of Julia, formerly the strongest of the winged women. She dies giving birth to a *son with wings,* a sacrifice of heroic womanhood to the crass interest of the author in a "new Adam." Despite her imaginative conception of a new way for women to be, Gillmore sells out, at the end, to what Ursula Le Guin calls her "perfectly conventional ideas" (viii) of male and female behavior: "If she didn't see through the patriarchal constructions of gender as clearly as Charlotte Perkins Gilman, at least she was trying to poke some peepholes in the wall."[6]

May Sarton: The Realistic Novel

A half-century after Gilman's *Herland,* May Sarton published *Mrs. Stevens Hears the Mermaids Singing* (1965),[7] arguably one of her best novels. In this work, the myth of a "second Fall" into lesbian consciousness is clearly articulated. As early as *The Small Room* (1961)[8] and as recently as *The Education of Harriet Hatfield* (1989),[9] however, Sarton wrestled with the issue of a lesbian observer or protagonist, often using imagery reminiscent of Genesis to suggest both the "trauma" and the "blessing" (*Mrs. Stevens,* 144) of a fall into lesbian consciousness. Sometimes this issue becomes a matter of life and death, but, in the earliest of these novels, the issues are professional disgrace and ostracism for a feminist professor who eventually sees the error of trying to force a brilliant student to ever-greater heights of achievement.

In *The Small Room,* the image of a single, strangely symbolic tree, reminiscent of the tree of knowledge, occurs at the outset of the novel: " . . . an open field with a single wine-glass elm standing alone among the goldenrod, a solitary splendor, a green fountain" (13). This resonant image is entirely appropriate to the form of a novel, a *Bildungsroman* of a young Ph.D. in her first year of teaching.[10] The protagonist's painful initiation into the knowledge of the complexities of love, both heterosexual and lesbian, is the central focus of the novel. Moreover, the frequently recurring image of the "old universal wound" (49) strongly suggests the concept of Original Sin. There are many references to gardens, to animals of all sorts, to poison, and to falling: leaves fall (89), snow falls (118), Fanny Burney falls like a shadow over the pages of Keats (114). And finally people fall: the brilliant student, Jane Seaman, and her aggressive and tyrannical professor, Caryll Cope, who observes that "Of course it does give most people real pleasure to see the mighty fall" (189). These images, however, while reminiscent of Genesis, are incidental compared to the much stronger associations with the re-visioned myth in *Mrs. Stevens Hears the Mermaids Singing*.

Mrs. Stevens is a complex *Künstlerroman* about a variety of love relationships in the remembered life of a seventy-year-old poet. In Hilary Stevens's memories, Sarton juxtaposes two relationships: a failed heterosexual relationship between a passionate older woman (Willa MacPherson) and the married man who betrays Willa, and, years later, a failed lesbian relationship between Willa and the younger Hilary Stevens. The physical consummation of Hilary's love for Willa is followed by the older woman's literal fall down a flight of stairs, ending the relationship.

Early in the novel, Sarton creates an ironic and subtle variation on the Garden of Eden as the setting for conversation on the subject of art. Hilary's paradisiacal garden is haunted by a gloomy homosexual youth called Mar. Both Mar and the lesbian (or perhaps bisexual)[11] protagonist, Hilary Stevens, are poets, the boy at the beginning of his career and the woman in her fullest maturity. A bond of love grows between these two, love so powerful they seem to change places: Hilary seems (to herself) to recover the energy of a young girl and Mar is described at one point as looking like an old man (22).

All of the other elements of a classical paradise are present in generous profusion.[12] In this garden by the sea, it is spring, there are shade trees and fruit trees (including an apple tree); narcissus and other flowers are in bloom. Some birds and animals are literally present: an oriole, the white cat Sirenica, two pet turtles, and a bee. A profusion of metaphorical animals, images of fertility and energy, crowd the pages of this important first chapter. These include the battered seabird and wild animal to which Hilary compares Mar (17 and 23), the frog to which she compares herself (25), two young men described as cawing like crows (28), the lion of the poet's desire to get away to solitude (29), "great amoral beasts" (33) of the classical myths, the need to "fight like a tiger" (35) for a moment's peace and quiet, metaphorical mice (36) and literal earthworms (35). The garden is even bordered by stone walls, like the medieval *hortus conclusus* of the unicorn tapestries.

In this enclosed setting, Hilary reflects on her experience as a wife, as a lover of women, and as a poet, at the same time trying to lead Mar away from a dangerous temptation to subside into black depression and despair. Hilary tries to get Mar to see his homosexuality not as something to be despised and feared but as part of his identity, as the source of his *power* as an artist. Before our eyes, we see Mar transformed into a vigorous young poet under the aegis of Hilary's skillful and sensitive tutoring. Often their conversation occurs with Mar (a very youthful Adam) half-hidden in a tree, presumably pruning branches, and Hilary (a wise old Eve) at the foot of the tree looking up at him (22). Comic touches are everywhere, yet the comedy is so affectionate that the black moods and violence of Mar's youth are seen in perspective as necessary to growth rather than as flaws in his character. One of the most striking characteristics of Sarton's ironic parody of Genesis in this scene is the balance she achieves between the two characters: each learns something from the other, both are initiated into the mysteries of love and art, Mar for the first, Hilary perhaps for the hundredth time.

Evocations of Genesis also occur in a sexual (as opposed to Platonic and aesthetic) context in this novel, but with almost no humor and with a far less positive outcome. Speaking with two reporters, Jenny and Peter, who have come to interview her, Hilary Stevens recalls in a flashback the year when she was twenty-nine and fell in love with Willa MacPherson, a heterosexual woman of forty-five. In this part of the novel, the emotional "second Fall," a fall into lesbian consciousness, occurs, but for one of the characters the shock is too great, and she never recovers.

In contrast to the earlier scene of brilliant springtime in an earthly paradise, the breaking of reserve between Hilary and Willa occurs on a cold November night in a London shrouded by mist and fog. The scene is the interior of Willa MacPherson's house. Sarton's evocations of Genesis here are not based on a physical landscape but on psychological and moral forces of love and sexuality, "flesh and the devil," as Willa recounts for Hilary the story of her affair with (and betrayal by) Seamus O'Connor, an Irish novelist.

"'There is nothing so frightening to an Irish Catholic as passion in a woman.' Willa laughed a hard dry laugh. 'It's all right for a man, but a woman capable of passion—that is the flesh and the devil!'" Seconds later she observes, "He loved me so much that he had to murder me!" (138). Seamus's guilty response to his own adultery, and to her passion, is to treat Willa with enormous cruelty, as something alien and other, something to be punished for her passionate commitment to love and to the needs of the body.

Feelings of guilt and shame associated in some Christian traditions with sexual pleasure in male-female love relationships are here acted out in the

aborted affair between Willa and Seamus, but when Hilary falls in love
with Willa and their love is finally expressed sexually, the possibility of
guilt is radically intensified. The morning after a passionate sexual consummation has taken place, Willa falls down a steep flight of stairs and has a
stroke or has a stroke and falls down a flight of stairs—we are not sure
which. She never fully recovers, and, although the narrator rationalizes the
end of the relationship as a transmutation of love into art, contemporary
readers are not likely to accept the "necessity" of the narrator's argument.
It seems wrongheaded, if not perverse—romantic in the worst sense of the
word.

> Whatever the psychiatrists may have told us, there are no repetitions.
> Never again would Hilary experience passion as pure light. The con-
> summation was as absolute as the initial break-through into personal
> feeling. There was, in fact, nowhere to go from there. And what had
> seemed to her, as she walked home early the next morning, the begin-
> ning of a new life, was in fact, the end of an episode. They did not
> meet again as lovers. (144)

Several ways of reading this highly problematic scene suggest themselves.
On the literal level, as K. Graehme Hall points out,[13] Willa serves as an
important muse in the development of Hilary Stevens's art; out of her
profound sexual feelings for Willa, which she cannot for many months
express, Hilary creates a book of sonnets. Willa serves not only as muse,
but also as critical audience.

> Willa listened. She accepted the poems as the true Muse does with
> detached, imaginative grace: she brought to bear her critical intelligence,
> illuminated by something like love, the inwardness, the transparency
> which had been opened in spite of herself. . . . Above all she succeeded
> in making Hilary accept that the poem itself was the reality, accept,
> at least at first, that together, for some mysterious reason, they made
> possible the act of creation. It was intimacy of a strange kind. (141)

In other words, Willa fills the same function for Hilary that her first muse,
Phillippa Munn, had served when Hilary was only fifteen. The powerful
energy of lesbian love, which, in this novel and others, Sarton seems to have
regarded as catastrophic if acted upon, can function as a beneficent demon, if
one of the lovers is an artist and the intensity of feeling is white-hot. In a

crucible of repression and renunciation, sexual love in such cases is transmuted
into art.

In addition to this reading of Willa MacPherson as Hilary's muse, a
biographical note may be of interest. Susan Swartzlander called my attention
to the fact that the character of Willa in *Mrs. Stevens Hears the Mermaids
Singing* is almost certainly based on Sarton's friend, Edith Forbes Kennedy,
one of the most powerful of the twelve "portraits and celebrations" in *A
World of Light* (1976).[14] Like Willa, Edith Kennedy, a reserved and brilliant
older woman much admired by Sarton, fell down a flight of stairs and
suffered a disastrous stroke, never regaining her brilliance and wit. When
I noticed in Sarton's chapter on Edith Kennedy the fact that Kennedy knew
Irish novelist Sean O'Faolain, I speculated that Sarton may have based the
character of Seamus O'Connor (Willa's lover) on O'Faolain. The possibility
of a biographical basis for the fictional characters and for the failed relationship
between Willa and Seamus encourages an exploration of possible autobiographical subtexts in the relationship between Willa and Hilary.

A third way of reading Willa's fall is to suggest that Sarton "punishes"
both characters. She punishes the older woman, who is apparently fatally
heterosexual, for giving in to Hilary's passionate demands. Thus, in the
case of Willa MacPherson, the fall into lesbian experience is tantamount to
death. The heterosexual woman may be blamed and subsequently punished
for betraying her own "better instincts."

> "Hilary, you force me to speak plainly. I simply am not one of those
> ambidextrous people who can love women as well as men. You'll have
> to accept me as I am." (143)

Seen in this light, Willa's fall may reflect unconscious, internalized homophobia on the part of Sarton, who was writing *Mrs. Stevens* in 1964, before
it was common for a writer to acknowledge her lesbianism, especially if
she had already lost a job because of it.[15] In this reading, Sarton can also
be seen as punishing her lesbian protagonist (Hilary) for dreaming of "the
beginning of a new life" (144) with a consciously heterosexual woman.

But it is equally likely that the stroke and subsequent remoteness of
the fictional Willa may reflect Sarton's unconscious feelings of resentment
against heterosexual women who trifle with the emotions of lesbians. In
an interview with Robin Kaplan and Shelley Neiderbach in 1982, Sarton
observed,

But I think the worst thing . . . is the fashion for lesbianism, that it's the "in" thing, and so, let's try it . . . this I think is dangerous, just because I think any sexual act boomerangs, if it doesn't come from feelings.[16]

Many women might agree with Sarton that sexuality divorced from feelings is dangerous, but the relationship between Willa and Hilary in *Mrs. Stevens* is patently not motivated by idle curiosity. Just as severely as her character Seamus O'Connor punishes Willa for expressing, and valuing, intensely passionate sexual feelings for him, Sarton punishes Willa as though her character has *done wrong* in giving way to the sexual passion of the younger woman. Many years later, in *The Education of Harriet Hatfield* (1989), as K. Graehme Hall demonstrates, Sarton's lesbian protagonist is more comfortable with her identity, although the shooting of the dog can also, in a curious way, be read as punishment. In this most recent novel, however, imagery reminiscent of Genesis (gardens, trees, animals, fruit), where it occurs, is incidental to the plot, as in *The Small Room*.

Contemporary Progeny

Thus far I have examined two kinds of feminist re-visioning of the Garden of Eden: utopian fantasies of a female paradise invaded by evil in the form of uncivilized male intruders (Gilman and Gillmore), and the realistic novel in which sexual guilt between a lesbian woman and a heterosexual woman is punished in terms of an expulsion or fall (May Sarton). Both of these genres influenced contemporary fiction by American and British feminists.

Among the best of the contemporary feminist utopias are Sally Miller Gearhart's lesbian classic, *The Wanderground* (1979)[17] and Joan Slonczewski's *A Door into Ocean* (1986).[18] Gearhart and Slonczewski envision radical departures from the patriarchal arrangements implicit in most accounts of the Garden of Eden. As in the earlier novels by Gillmore and Gilman, men in *The Wanderground* are seen as aggressive power seekers who are cruel to each other, to women, and to animals. In this powerful lesbian novel, women reclaim their right to political autonomy, and, more important, to sexual autonomy, meeting their own emotional and physical needs without recourse to men.

A more recent example of utopian (or dystopian) re-visioning of a creation myth is Joan Slonczewski's engaging novel, *A Door into Ocean* (1986), in which male and female values are so polarized they take the form of separate worlds: the "watery world of women" called Shora and the military, male world of Valedon.

Even the best of the feminist utopias, however, are rather like extended fables: imaginary universes created to illustrate the shortcomings of the real world rather than for their inherent narrative interest. The greatest danger in such works is the writer's tendency to didacticism, which bogs down even such a short novel as *Herland,* most notably in the second half of the book.

Unencumbered by didacticism (except as the target of satiric attack), realistic novels by contemporary feminist writers also play variations on biblical constructs; in the best of these, re-visionings of Genesis do not preclude the possibility of a positive, fulfilling relationship between women, whether or not they are lesbian lovers (as they often are). Two extraordinarily good novels of this type were published in Britain by feminist presses and have subsequently been reprinted in the United States. Jeanette Winterson's moving autobiographical novel, *Oranges Are Not the Only Fruit* (1985),[19] and Ellen Galford's zany satire, *The Fires of Bride* (1986),[20] make heavy use of biblical imagery to rewrite lesbian lives from an ironic or comic perspective, but the devastating fall that Sarton's characters suffer is absent, less problematic, or even a truly fortunate fall in the works of these younger writers.

Oranges Are Not the Only Fruit is a lesbian *Bildungsroman* narrated by an orphan, also named Jeanette, who, like Winterson, was adopted by a fundamentalist mother from a bleak industrial city in northern England. The structure of the novel is based on books of the Old Testament: the chapters are titled "Genesis," "Exodus," "Leviticus," "Numbers," "Deuteronomy," "Joshua", "Judges," and a chapter for the biblical character of Ruth. This explicitly biblical scheme is reinforced by pervasive allusions to Adam and Eve and paradise throughout the novel. In "Ruth," for example, an imaginary character named Winnet encounters a sorcerer.

> She recognized the clothes and would have run away had not the figure called to her . . . "I know your name." And so she stopped, afraid. If this were true she would be trapped. Naming meant power. Adam had named the animals and the animals came at his call. (142)

Recognizing the creative power of naming, Winterson also acknowledges the significance of the taboo, a promise of immortality threatened by a peculiarly postmodern image of hell as mutation. Speaking of London, she writes that "Like paradise it is bounded by rivers, and contains fabulous beasts.... If you drink from the wells ... you might live forever, but there is no guarantee you will live forever as you are. You might mutate.... They don't tell you this" (161).

Oranges Are Not the Only Fruit, an ironic title that itself implies the apple of Genesis, ends on an ambiguous note. Winterson's lesbian protagonist has been cast out of family and church for her "unnatural passions." She escapes this oppressive context for the city of London, and the two worlds are contrasted almost as Blake contrasts two states of being in *The Songs of Innocence* and *The Songs of Experience.* At the end, the protagonist returns home to make peace with her mother, an uneasy truce at best. But the last words of the novel are "Kindly Light," a name the mother has chosen for herself when she talks on the CB ... perhaps suggesting a ray of hope for the mother-daughter relationship, despite the mother's stubborn and damaging disapproval of her daughter's sexual preference.

Ellen Galford's witty and complex satire of lesbian identity, *The Fires of Bride,* is more positive than Winterson's novel and lighter in tone. Like Winterson, however, Galford blasts an unloving Christian tradition of excluding gay men and lesbians from participation in a religion supposedly based on love. Both Winterson and Galford replace the devil in their novels with sanctimonious and corrupt "ministers of God" whose chief goal in life is to condemn and destroy rather than to embrace and nurture. Both ministers are richly punished for their sins.

The Fall in *The Fires of Bride* is, for the young protagonist Maria Milleny, a gradual fall into lesbian consciousness and, at the same time, into consciousness of her strength and integrity as an artist. This gradual (and very positive) awakening to herself is foreshadowed by Maria's physical fall down a flight of stone stairs during her first days on the island of "Cailleach." Maria is being shown the site of the tenth-century Convent of St. Bride by her mentor and host, Dr. Catriona MacEochan, when she falls.

> "Damn!" Maria, distracted by a far away blue hill, framed by a gap in the chapel wall, trips over a bush growing out of the broken stone floor, and falls headlong.
>
> "Are you all right?" Catriona appears at the top of a steep staircase set close to the wall, and leading to nowhere. (50)

Maria is not hurt, and shortly after this significant fall into the precincts of St. Bride, Maria and Catriona become lovers. In this novel, the goddess Bride returns to claim her own: the remote Scottish island of Cailleach, which has been hers for centuries, and the women there, both natives and "inlanders," who love each other. Perhaps because the goddess is present, much of the novel is farcical, bawdy, and uproarious. Galford does not spare those of her characters who are selfish, excessively spiritual, or eccentric: both gay and straight, everyone who behaves foolishly comes in for more than a fair share of the satire.

As in the best comedy, however, serious issues are never far beneath the surface. In the midst of farcical send-ups of American materialism, Scottish sentimentality, lesbian seduction scenes, and ministerial hypocrisy, Galford rewrites patriarchal and biblical "history" in terms of a matriarchal society. In the chapter called "Mhairi," the story of a young novice in a scriptorium on the island at the time of the Viking invasions, Galford re-visions an entirely plausible process by means of which early Christian Fathers searched out and expropriated groves, acolytes, and rituals sacred to the Mothers. Among other things, *The Fires of Bride* is a thoroughly satisfying feminist myth of transformation in which several characters are allowed to "fall" into lesbian consciousness—and then to act out their self-fulfilling and happy destiny untrammelled by punishment from the Fathers, the Mothers, the Furies, the fates, or the narrator.

Conclusion

Authors of twentieth-century feminist myths of transformation focused on woman-identified women or on lesbian lovers re-vision Genesis in a variety of imaginative ways. In 1914 and 1915, Inez Haynes Gillmore and Charlotte Perkins Gilman created utopian visions of a women's paradise invaded by men. Alone among the writers discussed in this essay, Gilman allows a male character to experience a "second Fall" into feminist consciousness. In *Angel Island,* Gillmore created resonant images of virginal women capable of extraordinary powers of flight, but compromised her own creation by killing off the one woman capable of radical feminist consciousness.

In the 1960s, May Sarton wrote two groundbreaking novels in which lesbian characters confronted by prejudice and misunderstanding are often burdened by internalized homophobia. In *Mrs. Stevens Hears the Mermaids Singing,* comic and ironic images of Eden frame an important relationship between the lesbian protagonist and a troubled young neighbor. Sarton created a charming, enclosed garden in which young, homosexual Mar, a boyish (and gloomy) Adam hiding in an apple tree, is initiated into the mysteries of art by a wise old Eve, elderly lesbian poet Hilary Stevens. Later in the novel but earlier in the life of Hilary Stevens, Sarton juxtaposes a failed heterosexual affair and a failed lesbian relationship. Although both relationships are destroyed by feelings of guilt and shame characteristic of repressed sexuality, the lesbian relationship is punished by Willa's literal fall down a flight of stairs. Sarton's relationship to her text may have been problematized by unresolved feelings of anxiety at the time of its writing, but her most recent novel, *The Education of Harriet Hatfield* (1989), suggests a more comfortable relationship to issues of lesbian identity.

Two recent novels by British feminists re-vision Genesis to comic and ironic advantage. In Jeanette Winterson's *Oranges Are Not the Only Fruit,* books of the Old Testament structure a creation myth of a young lesbian adventurer. Winterson's protagonist is expelled from a home, school, and church that are far from paradise but at least familiar, where she receives from a variety of women, including her mother, glimmers and gleamings of love. These enable her to survive with her identity intact and her head high. In *The Fires of Bride,* Ellen Galford's witty romp across Scotland, lesbian characters receive strength and inspiration from the pagan saints of a matriarchal tradition still very much alive on a remote island in the Hebrides. The local minister, a stand-in for the devil, chokes to death on a kipper bone, and everyone with love in her heart receives her just reward.

In these recent feminist myths, demons of sexual guilt and repression are replaced by a vision of creation in which strong women or lesbian lovers locate, if not an earthly paradise, at least a world in which happiness is possible and love is more than a male-centered myth of loss of innocence and dire punishment. In the liberated, imaginative tradition envisioned by women, May Sarton must be acknowledged as having played a crucial role, bringing the subject of lesbian love relationships to a wide audience of readers, most of whom had never before encountered a sympathetic treatment of the subject. Like some of Sarton's protagonists, readers of *The Small Room* and *Mrs. Stevens Hears the Mermaids Singing* "fell" into radical new knowledge of friendship and love between women. Thanks in part to Sarton, feminist novelists in both Britain and America are creating "revised standard versions" of Genesis with revolutionary implications for Western literature.

NOTES

1. One of the best of the recent feminist commentaries on the figure is Elaine Pagels, *Adam, Eve, and the Serpent* (New York: Random House, 1988). See also the inspired re-visionings of Eve in Mary Daly, *The Church and the Second Sex* (New

York: Harper and Row, 1968); Daly, *Beyond God the Father: Toward a Philosophy of Women's Liberation* (Boston: Beacon Press, 1973); Daly, *Gyn/Ecology: The Metaethics of Radical Feminism* (Boston: Beacon Press, 1978); and Daly, *Pure Lust: Elemental Feminist Philosophy* (Boston: Beacon Press, 1984). Alicia Ostriker is currently analyzing "revisionist biblical poetry women have been writing in the postwar period, . . . especially since the sixties." In a faculty seminar at Bucknell University in May 1991, Ostriker commented that there has been " . . . an outpouring of explicit anger, indictments of God the Father for the violence inseparable from his righteousness. Poems from the point of view of the insulted and injured, the abused and abandoned women in the Bible have multiplied: Eve, Sarah, Lot's wife and daughters, Dinah, Miriam, Zipporah, Jephthah's daughter, the Levite's concubine, and so on."

2. Similar patterns may be observed in contemporary fiction by racial ethnic writers. In Toni Morrison's brilliant evocation of the loss of innocence in *Sula* (New York: Knopf, 1973), Nel and Sula lie head-to-head in a beautiful shaded grove near the river, a scene with obvious sexual (and possibly lesbian) implications. Immediately afterward, Sula urges Chicken Little to climb with her into an enormous tree from which they can look down on a foreshortened Nel. It is just after this scene that the "hand-slip" occurs, and Chicken Little "falls" (flies out of Sula's hands) and drowns (57–62). Even closer to a "second fall into feminist consciousness" are two chapters near the conclusion of *The Woman Who Owned the Shadows,* by the native American writer Paula Gunn Allen (San Francisco: Spinsters/Aunt Lute, 1983). In "A Lot Changed after She Fell" and "She Knew All about Flying," Allen's protagonist, Ephanie, suffers a brutal fall from an apple tree as the consequence of trusting her so-called friend Stephen instead of listening to the warnings of her soul's companion, Elena. Images of snakes, a paradisiacal summer day, and the end of childhood are followed in the next chapter by Ephanie's growing emotional paralysis and helplessness, which takes her years to sort out and resolve.

3. As Ann J. Lane indicates in her helpful introduction to the modern edition (New York: Pantheon Books, 1979), *Herland* had never before appeared in book form. It first appeared in a monthly magazine she wrote and published herself for seven years, between 1909 and 1916 (Lane, v–vi). For sound biographical accounts of Gilman and her family, see Mary A. Hill, *Charlotte Perkins Gilman: The Making of a Radical Feminist 1860–1896* (Philadelphia: Temple University Press, 1981); Hill, *Endure: The Diaries of Charles Walter Stetson* (Philadelphia: Temple University Press, 1985).

4. "The women of *Herland* have no way of relating to the men other than as friends. They do not understand the words 'lover' or 'home' or 'wife,'. . . . they have no sense of sexual love or passion" (Lane, Introduction to *Herland,* xv).

5. *Angel Island* was first published in 1914 by Ayer Company Publishers (Salem, N.H.). In 1988, New American Library published a paperback edition with an introduction by Ursula Le Guin, from which the quotations in the text are cited.

6. In her introduction to *Angel Island,* Le Guin notes that, except for the

climactic moment of [the women's] rebellion . . . the book and its ideas are perfectly conventional. Gillmore doesn't distinguish culturally enforced behavior from human nature, so that all the men like to work, digging and building and studying and hunting, while all the women like to laze around amidst luxury and can't resist either jewelry or mirrors. Men think, women feel; men want sex, women want babies; and so on. (xiii–ix)

Le Guin does not acknowledge that Julia is an exception to these generalizations: she is described many times as engaging in serious thought; she draws up the plans for the New Camp and other improvements on the island; she resists marriage and children until the men agree to allow Angela (daughter of Peachy and Ralph) to keep her wings.

7. First published by Norton in 1965; in 1974, Norton published a second edition with an introduction by Carolyn Heilbrun. I quote from the most recent edition (New York: Norton, 1975).

8. May Sarton, *The Small Room* (New York: Norton, 1961). Quotations are from the 1976 edition, also published by Norton.

9. References are to Sarton's most recent novel, *The Education of Harriet Hatfield* (New York: Norton, 1989).

10. For an excellent discussion of the female *Bildungsroman* in its many forms, see Elizabeth Abel, Marianne Hirsch, and Elizabeth Langland, *The Voyage In: Fictions of Female Development* (Hanover and London: University Press of New England, 1983). In this volume, Bonnie Zimmerman's essay, "Exiting from Patriarchy: The Lesbian Novel of Development," 244–57, is particularly instructive.

11. In her introduction to *Mrs. Stevens Hears the Mermaids Singing* (1975), Heilbrun observes that "Most obviously, Hilary is homosexual or, more accurately, bisexual; but for her it is the love for another woman that inspires" (xvii). Despite her marriage, Hilary seems to me unmistakably lesbian. She marries only once, very young, and the marriage obviously threatens her sense of herself as an artist. Not only are all of her muse figures women, but her sexual passion also seems reserved exclusively for women.

12. The most authoritative account of the topos of the *locus amoenus* is in Ernst Curtius, *European Literature and the Latin Middle Ages,* trans. Willard R. Trask (New York: Harper and Row, 1963), 192, 195.

13. See K. Graehme Hall, "'To Say Radical Things Gently': Art and Lesbianism in *Mrs. Stevens Hears the Mermaids Singing,*" in this volume.

14. *A World of Light* (New York: Norton, 1976), 86–101. Ethel Forbes Kennedy was mother of one of Sarton's classmates at Shady Hill School in Boston. She befriended Sarton in Paris in the winter of 1931–32, when Sarton was nineteen, and helped extricate her from an unfortunate love affair. Like the fictional character Willa MacPherson, Ethel Kennedy had "a small stroke" and fell down a flight of stairs; Sarton comments that "she was never again the person with whom I had walked through the Cambridge streets with Jean Christophe [the Briard dog] driven by extreme emotion. That current had been cut off" (99).

15. In Karla Hammond, "To Be Reborn: An Interview with May Sarton" (1978), Sarton said: "I came out long before most people did and it cost me jobs; but I was very relieved when I had done it" (236). The interview appeared first in the December 1978 issue of the *Bennington Review,* and is reprinted in *May Sarton: Woman and Poet,* ed. Constance Hunting (Orono, Me.: National Poetry Foundation and University of Maine Press, 1982), 227–38.

16. Robin Kaplan and Shelley Neiderbach, "I Live Alone in a Very Beautiful Place: An Interview with May Sarton," in *May Sarton: Woman and Poet,* ed. Constance Hunting (Orono, Me.: National Poetry Foundation and University of Maine Press, 1982), 252.

17. Sally Miller Gearhart, *The Wanderground: Stories of the Hill Women* (Watertown, Mass.: Persephone Press, 1979).

18. Joan Slonczewski, *A Door into Ocean* (Hastings-on-Hudson, N.Y.: Ultramarine Publishers, 1986). The book was reprinted by Avon in 1987.

19. *Oranges Are Not the Only Fruit* was first published in Great Britain by Pandora Press in 1985. Quotations are from the first American edition, published by Atlantic Monthly Press in 1987.

20. Quotations are from *The Fires of Bride* (London: The Women's Press, 1986). Galford's novel has subsequently been published in this country by Firebrand Books.

Art and Artist

The Artist and Her Domestic Muse: May Sarton, Miriam Schapiro, Audrey Flack

Janet Catherine Berlo

What would happen if one woman told the truth about her life? The world would split open.

—Muriel Rukeyser

Carolyn Heilbrun has characterized 1973 as a watershed year for modern women's autobiography because of the publication of May Sarton's *Journal of a Solitude,* which honestly recounts all aspects of a woman's life.[1] The first years of the 1970s were pivotal for women in the visual arts as well. In 1972, artist Miriam Schapiro asked the question "What would art look like if made in the image of domesticity by a group of women?" The answer was not only her own piece, *Dollhouse,* but the larger collaborative installation, *Womanhouse,* in which artists Miriam Schapiro, Judy Chicago, and their students took the first bold steps at exploring women's domestic iconography.[2] Schapiro planted the seed for the tremendous flowering of women's creativity in the visual arts that followed. Also in 1972, while May Sarton was writing *Journal of a Solitude,* Audrey Flack was painting *Jolie Madame,* a large, luminous painting that defied photo-realist canons of content by celebrating jewels, flowers, perfumes, and fruit.

In each of these cases, a uniquely female sensibility came of age—a sensibility combining anger, strength, sentiment, and celebration of domestic iconography. Aesthetic canons that had previously been marginalized suddenly became mainstream. May Sarton, Miriam Schapiro, and Audrey Flack empowered many of us to explore the overt dimensions of an interior female landscape. We found it at once lush and sensual, passionate and angry, tough and tender. In this essay, I explore the domestic universe that Sarton, Schapiro, and Flack celebrate in their work.

I caution the reader that I am mapping just one feature of a much more complex topography of these artists' works. May Sarton, born in Belgium in 1912, is vitally interested in multiple realms: theater, poetry, politics, old age, and the contrast between European and American sensibilities, as other essays in this volume demonstrate. The work of Audrey Flack, the American photo-realist painter born in New York in 1931, encompasses social commentary of diverse kinds. Conceived on a grand scale (usually 8' × 8'), and executed with technical precision, her work presents visual conundrums about beauty, violence, and decay. New York painter Miriam Schapiro, born in Toronto in 1923, has exhibited work that ranged from early formalist geometric grids to recent puppetlike dancing figures in collage.[3]

I use the term *domestic muse* to stress the rootedness of each of these artists in the nourishing details of daily life. Each takes the familiar, the mundane, and lifts it into the universal or the monumental. While Sarton says that individual women have been her muse, there is, nevertheless, a sense in which the domestic structure she carefully maintains (and chronicles in the journals) is often the muse of her poetry and novels. In the journals, she repeatedly documents the renewing powers of intimate friendships, animal companions, flowers, and solitude.

Canons of literary and artistic modernism have disparaged and ignored the lyrical, the feminine, the private. Through the work of Sarton, Schapiro, Flack, and other women, these traits have come to the foreground. These artists have reclaimed and transformed the structures (and the strictures) of daily life into the poetics of female domestic existence. I shall consider several facets of the domestic landscape that have meaning for Sarton, Schapiro, and Flack: aesthetic formats and the use of an iconography of the feminine, the relationship of the artist to the work, and the shaping forces of nourishment, solitude, and the past.

It is noteworthy that while Schapiro and Flack are painters, both are eloquent writers as well. Schapiro has published several reflective essays, while Flack has published two books on art.[4] Schapiro's "Notes from a Conversation on Art, Feminism, and Work" is written in the form of a memoir, while Flack's *Art and Soul* is diaristic, a commonplace book of vignettes, reflections, and conversations. Their writing as well as their visual art have much in common with May Sarton's work.

Each of these artists positions herself in a dialogue with other women, as well as with her artistic predecessors, as I shall demonstrate. So, too, in this self-reflective era of critical studies in literature and the history of art, we now recognize that the literary critic or the art historian positions herself vis-à-vis other texts, other visions, either overtly or tacitly. In this essay, I shall make my own inner dialogue overt by counterpoising quotations against my own text. These quotations are drawn from the three subjects of my essay, from others who have written about their work, and from my own life. I shall also reflect upon my own relationship to the domestic muse. I do all of this deliberately to celebrate an aesthetic format often found in women's works. This format has a number of different names and guises: in literature it appears as discontinuous or fragmented narrative, or in the piecemeal format of journal entries, commonplace books, and letters; in the visual arts, terms such as *assemblage* or *collage* are used to describe this aesthetic. Miriam Schapiro herself has given it the name of "Femmage."[5]

Femmage and the Iconography of the Feminine

On the topic of femmage, Miriam Schapiro has written that

women have always collected things and saved and recycled them because leftovers yielded nourishment in new forms. The decorative functional objects women made often spoke in a secret language, bore a covert imagery. When we read these images in needlework, in quilts, rugs, and scrapbooks, we sometimes find a cry for help, sometimes an allusion to a secret political alignment, sometimes a moving symbol about the relationships between men and women. We base our interpretations of the layered meanings in these works on what we know of our own lives—a sort of archaeological reconstruction and deciphering. . . .

Collected, saved, and combined materials represented for such women acts of pride, desperation, and necessity. Spiritual survival depended on the harboring of memories. Each cherished scrap of percale, muslin, or chintz, each bead, each letter, each photograph, was a reminder of its place in a woman's life, similar to an entry in a journal or diary.[6]

Schapiro's own work defines the visual aesthetic of femmage. *Mary Cassatt and Me,* a 1976 watercolor and fabric collage (fig. 1), uses imagery from women artists of the past in several ways. In the center, Schapiro places a reproduction of a painting by the late nineteenth-century American painter Mary Cassatt. She thereby sets up a dialogue between herself and an important artistic predecessor. The Cassatt image she chooses is significant: a young woman gazes into a mirror. The message is self-scrutiny, self-reflection.

Fig. 1. Miriam Schapiro, *Mary Cassatt and Me,* 1974, from "*Collaboration Series.*" Acrylic and fabric on paper, 30″ × 22″. Photo © 1980 by D. James Dee. Courtesy of Bernice Steinbaum Gallery, New York.

What does a woman artist see when she looks at herself and looks at the art of other women—reflections and affirmations of her own art? Framing this central image are successive borders of fabric collage, the outermost one a traditional quilt block pattern. This celebrates the work of anonymous textile artists whose work was traditionally outside the mainstream of "high" art.

Of her work in the 1970s, Miriam Schapiro says that

the new work was different from anything I had done before. I worked on canvas, using fabric. I wanted to explore and express a part of my life which I had always dismissed—my homemaking, my nesting. I wanted to validate the traditional activities of women, to connect myself to the unknown women artists who made quilts, who had done the invisible "women's work" of civilization. I wanted to acknowledge them, to honor them. The collagists who came before me were men, who lived in cities, and often roamed the streets at night scavenging, collecting material, their junk, from urban spaces. My world, my mother's and grandmother's world, was a different one. The fabrics I used would be beautiful if sewed into clothes or draped against windows, made into pillows, or slipped over chairs. My "junk," my fabrics, allude to a particular universe, which I wish to make real, to represent.[7]

Audrey Flack, too, works with the notion of femmage, although for her it is more implicit than overt. All of her works are airbrushed acrylics on canvas—not a femmagistic medium—but the subject matter and composition speaks of femmage. To make her large, ambitious still lifes, Flack assembles and arranges a large group of objects, photographing, rearranging, and rephotographing until the proper assemblage emerges.[8] Flack's photorealist paintings are painstakingly painted from projected slides of the still life set-ups. Her prop cabinet contains an array of bottles, jars, clocks, silver, and other mementos. These are combined in her still lifes with more perishable objects: lipsticks, food, flowers, and butterflies. Flack's subject matter is often drawn from the "trivial," daily world of female domestic existence: the jewelry, perfume bottles, and figurines of a woman's dressing table, as in *Jolie Madame* (fig. 2).[9] But by her sheer technical brilliance, opulent colors, and imposing scale, Flack transforms the minor icons of feminine domestic life into universal symbols. In many of her paintings, the ironic juxtaposition of emblems of sexuality and femininity with symbols of the passing of time

Fig. 2. Audrey Flack, *Jolie Madame*, 1972. Oil on canvas, 71″ × 96″. Photo by Bruce C. Jones. Courtesy of the Australian National Gallery, Canberra, and Louis K. Meisel Gallery, New York.

(a lighted candle, a clock, a calendar, fresh fruit that will spoil) speaks to us of the transience and impermanence of life as well as its beauty.

Most of Flack's photo-realist colleagues in the 1970s were men whose work glorified public male iconography: the gleaming metal of cars and airplanes, neon signs, public streets. Flack's work subverted the male order by insisting that universality was to be found in the personal domestic icons of women's lives. Of *Jolie Madame,* Flack has said that

> this still life has an angel in it which is a very favorite subject of mine; a wine glass; fruit; a brooch that I wear—a very elegant jeweled thing; a vase that I love; a ring my husband gave me; my Cooper Union ring; a watch that I wear with bracelets; two little salt shakers; a rose; and lots of reflections and glitter which is what interests me. The reason I am inventorying all these things is that they are everything I love. They are part of my world. I wouldn't paint Harnett's rabbit hanging from a barn or a gun or a hunting cap. However in the contemporary art world it has been more acceptable to paint so-called "masculine" objects like motorcycles and cars. Any objects associated with "femininity" have been derided.[10]

Miriam Schapiro says that

> in reshaping my feminism I realized that my painting itself has a political dimension. Merely to speak out, to describe the daily ways of your life, turns out to be political. To say that you make a bed, cook a meal, live with someone you love, care for a child, that you cover windows and clothe your family—to say these things is to redress the trivialization of women's experience.[11]

The diarist, too, is an artist of assemblage, for a journal is a written quilt, pieced from words, activities, and reflections selected from each day. It is deliberate and ordered, yet not pretentious. It is comforting and personal. Virginia Woolf asks,

> What sort of diary should I like mine to be? Something loose knit and yet not slovenly, so elastic that it will embrace anything, solemn, slight or beautiful that comes into my mind. I should like it to resemble some deep old desk, or capacious hold-all, in which one flings a mass of odds and ends without looking them through. I should like to come

back, after a year or two, and find that the collection had sorted itself
and refined itself and coalesced, as such deposits so mysteriously do,
into a mould, transparent enough to reflect the light of our life, and
yet steady, tranquil compounds with the aloofness of a work of art.[12]

The words of Flack, Schapiro, and Woolf are vividly evoked by other artists
as well. An elderly Texas quiltmaker says,

> ... now I have some ten big scrap bags. If someone else were to see
> them, they would seem like a pile of junk, but I've got all my pieces
> sorted according to the color. Got my cottons here and my polyesters
> there. I've been told I have a way of matching up my colors. It comes
> natural to me. I keep figuring and working with my materials, and
> thinking about my colors a long time before it feels right. I know
> how my quilt is going to look before I ever start.
>
> Different ones of my family are always appearing from one of these
> bags. Just when you thought you'd forgotten someone, well, like right
> here ... I remember that patch. That was a dress that my grandmother
> wore to church. I sat beside her singing hymns, and that dress was so
> pretty to me then. I can just remember her in that dress now.[13]

May Sarton, too, has numerous "big scrap bags," a "deep old desk"
of memory from which she fashions her memoirs and journals. Memory
animates the domestic touchstones that recur throughout her work. Particularly evocative are the discussions of the placement of her antique Belgian
furniture in *Plant Dreaming Deep,* her photos and letters from family and
friends, the arrangement of flowers in special vases that evoke her mother's
aesthetic sense.

> When the Hokusai was hung, I drew out three blue-and-white Chinese
> plates to set side by side, in Flemish fashion, at the other end of the
> mantelpiece. And under the Hiroshige I placed the deep-blue jug with
> an inset pattern of white flowers on its round sides, which my mother
> loved to use for flowers (it had come from Ghent). "There," I said as
> I planted it on the refectory table. "There."
>
> The difference these few gestures had made was simply immense.
> The house had already begun to feel inhabited by all kinds of presences
> besides my own.[14]

All of May Sarton's memoirs, but especially *Plant Dreaming Deep,* emphasize the sense of the feminine domestic sphere as a nurturing one for the artist. As Sarton assembled the bits and pieces reflective of the many facets of her rich life in her Nelson home, she created a tranquil, nurturing space in which her art could flourish. Crucial to this process was the placing of the furniture, the hanging of the Japanese prints (whose importance lay not only in their artistic significance but in Sarton's love for their giver, Jean Dominique), the positioning of a friend's lamp, a mother's embroidery, a father's Koranic inscription.

> So on that first day in this house I found the joys my parents had willed to me, and saw them take shape in concrete form on my white walls. These beautiful signs of a continuity almost erased the irony that without their early deaths I could never have invested in such a house at all, for I was able to do so only because of what I had inherited. But now I knew, in a way I had not before, that what I had inherited was life-giving and life-restoring, and would be so to the end of my life and perhaps beyond.[15]

I read May Sarton for the first time at twenty, a college junior struggling with choices: painting, creative writing, feminist theory, art history? With what bits and pieces should I construct my life as a woman, a feminist, a scholar, a creative individual? For sixteen years now I have pursued art history, through Ph.D. and professorship. I teach students, building intellectual bridges to the young. I sit in my study, solitary, surrounded by my own domestic touchstones and icons. I am tempted to write about May Sarton rather than to work on the book I have been writing for two years now, on tribal women and their arts. This is the year when I finally feel my creative powers blossom; I am thirty-six. I have written several turgid academic books on archaeological topics. The book I am writing now is informed by feminism and femmage. It celebrates women in a host of cultures. It is written for all women, not just scholarly ones. My friend Kate, reading the Tarot for me as a Christmas present, says "Are you planning some enormous changes?"

The Rhythms of Work: Structure and Sentiment

May Sarton, Miriam Schapiro, and Audrey Flack all rely on the structure and discipline of work to give shape and meaning to their lives. May Sarton has suggested that "the discipline of work provides an exercise bar so that the wild, irrational motions of the soul become formal and creative."[16] She describes the structured format of her workday in the following way.

> The form in my life is to keep my center strong and not dispersed. That's what it's all about. It's this very rigid schedule that I follow: three hours in the morning, a walk with the dog, a rest, then a different sort of mental activity or gardening in the afternoon, and early to bed.
>
> I am at my desk for three to four hours every day, and I try to keep that very much, that sacred time, because it's the time when I have energy, it's the morning time. It has to be the morning, before one's mind is all cluttered up, when the door to the subconscious is still open, when you first wake up. That's the creative time for me. Because you want, you see, that *primary intensity.* This is what my life is all about—creating a frame in which I can have that primary intensity for three hours a day. That's all I ask.[17]

Even the structure and layout of Sarton's house in Nelson, New Hampshire, served as an ordering principle for the work.

> Here again the house itself helps. From where I sit at my desk I look through the front hall, with just a glimpse of staircase and white newel post, and through the warm colors of an Oriental rug on the floor of the cosy room, to the long window at the end that frames distant trees and sky from under the porch roof where I have hung a feeder for woodpeckers and nuthatches. This sequence pleases my eye and draws it out in a kind of geometric progression to open space.[18]

In a sense, Sarton's entire domestic universe serves as a muse for the work, from the nourishment of the gardens (discussed subsequently), to the ordering of the rooms and the vistas beyond: realms of beauty and the poetics of daily life structured by a devotion to the work.

Miriam Schapiro, too, has commented upon the juxtaposition of structure and domesticity in her work. Of her painting *The Architectural Basis* (1978) (fig. 3), she has said

> I crunch the handkerchiefs on a grid in the paintings. The grid is there to indicate that this is about order, this is about form, but the hand-

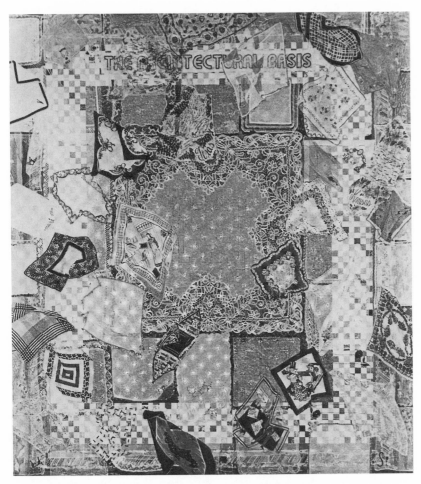

Fig. 3. Miriam Schapiro, *The Architectural Basis*, 1978. Acrylic and fabric on canvas, 72″ × 80″. Courtesy of Bernice Steinbaum Gallery, New York.

kerchiefs are there so you can cry when you remember all the tears which soaked all the handkerchiefs from time gone by. My curious esthetic sense counts on the merger of the grid and the handkerchief.[19]

What Schapiro calls "the merger of the grid and the handkerchief"— the successful blending of structure and sentiment—is key to understanding each of these artists. Each has been criticized for "sentimentality," that opprobrious term reserved for the work of women in particular. In defiance, Flack proclaims: "I approve of sentiment, nostalgia, and emotion (three heretical words for modernism)."[20] Flack's works are profusely inhabited by the objects of a woman's life. *Jolie Madame* is characteristic of the structure of Flack's paintings, exhibiting a "complex hierarchy of objects that occupy a spatial maze."[21] Order and structure coexist with lushness and profusion in Flack's works, as they do in Schapiro's collages and Sarton's prose.

Despite the beauty and sensuality of the domestic environment, none of these artists romanticizes the artistic quest that takes place there. Schapiro warns that

> when a woman decides to be a painter—a decision for which, until the past few years, there has been no precedent—she assumes the primary responsibility for her life. She becomes responsible for her perceptual, emotional, and intellectual experience. The responsibility is overwhelming. Every coffee cup she places on every table, every table on every rug, in relation to every floor, has meaning for her. Everything in her life becomes a part of her perceptual encyclopedia. She goes into a studio that is empty, bare. Here she must act on the decision she has made; here her responsibility is tested. Nothing could be more painful. However talented, however gifted she is, it is very painful.[22]

Similarly, May Sarton has endeared herself to many readers because of her uncompromising chronicling of the difficulties, storms, and griefs of the solitary artist. Sarton hopes that, through the work, "every grief or inexplicable seizure by weather, woe, or work can—if we discipline ourselves and think hard enough—be turned to account, be made to yield further insight."[23]

In her book *Art and Soul*, Audrey Flack lists "Rules for a Young Painter." The third and final rule states: "However large or small, work in a beautiful space. A studio is a haven, a place to grow, to learn and explore, a place of light and joy."[24] This rule is one that May Sarton lives by and chronicles in her many memoirs. Her description of poet Louise Bogan's apartment could as easily describe Sarton's own home.

> . . . the habitation reflected in a very special way the tone, the hidden music, as it were, of a woman, and a woman living alone, the sense of a deep loam of experience and taste expressed in the surroundings, the room a shell that reverberated with oceans and tides and waves of the owner's past, the essence of a human life as it had lived itself into certain colors, objets d'art, and especially into many books.[25]

When the work is going well, the monasticism of Sarton's daily life ("this nunnery where one woman meditates alone")[26] combines with a highly developed aesthetic sense, so that she can celebrate the "festival" of her solitary creative pursuits.

> I have a fire burning in my study, yellow roses and mimosa on my desk. There is an atmosphere of festival, of release in the house. We are one, the house and I, and I am happy to be alone—time to think, time to be.[27]

My work space, a large aerie that forms the entire third floor of my Victorian house, is light grey, white, and red. My ethnic icons are arrayed around me, mementos of a life devoted to the history of Native New World arts, women's textile arts in particular. Navajo rugs form geometric islands on the grey, wall-to-wall carpet. Maya weavings are stacked on the white bookshelves, a riot of color. On my desk, a small stone carving of a dog, by an Eskimo woman, is the tutelary canine-spirit-companion of my work. Over my desk, a lucite frame contains a postcard (changed weekly) that mirrors my mood. This week, Georgia O'Keeffe's *Spring Tree #1, 1945* wears its festive yellows and blues. This season, my work is going well. I, too, have an atmosphere of festival in my study.

Solitude and Sustenance

For each of these artists, the creative path balances the demands of solitude with the need for sustenance by others. I have already quoted Miriam Schapiro on the pain and responsibility the artist must assume for her own development. In *Journal of a Solitude,* as well as in other memoirs, May Sarton provides a continuous chronicle of the solitary creative life—its inner richness as well as its terrors and pains—for the domestic muse may, on occasion, transform to harpy.

The loving support of artistic peers (whether contemporary or long dead) goes a long way in nourishing the artist and her work. Nonetheless, Audrey Flack warns that one must banish the critical voices of others during the heat of the creative process.

> When you're in the studio painting, there are a lot of people in there with you. Your teachers, friends, painters from history, critics . . . and one by one, if you're really painting, they walk out. And if you're really painting, you walk out.[28]

Yet at other times, the solitude of the studio is animated and enlivened by the spirits of other women, other artists, permitting the artist to engage in a dialogue with her *consoeurs*. For May Sarton, this dialogue is often in the memories of youthful encounters with Virginia Woolf, and her more recent, deep friendship with Carolyn Heilbrun.[29] She also observes that "painters are enriching friends for a poet,"[30] referring to her friend, Anne Woodson. Sarton remarks that the criticism offered by a friend in the visual arts is free of the shadow of competition: "the criticism we give each other, the way we look at each other's work, is pure and full of joy, a spontaneous response."[31] She also joyfully anticipates Woodson's visits for the attentive way her painter-friend looks at the colors in the garden.[32]

For Miriam Schapiro, women met briefly during her lecture tours give her handkerchiefs, doilies, and quilt scraps that are the raw materials for her femmages. The work then forms a web of sisterhood extending across time and geography. Schapiro's work, constructed in solitude, engages in dialogue with her artistic predecessors both famous and obscure. "Mary Cassatt and Me" draws upon work by Cassatt as well as the work of anonymous quiltmakers. Audrey Flack's discovery of the seventeenth-century Spanish female sculptor, Luisa Roldan, influenced her own imagery. The opulence of the Spanish Baroque sculptor's style helped free Flack to affirm, in her own work, her love of richness, ornament, jewels, and flowers.[33]

In the solitude of my own study, I engage in inner dialogue with the women whose textiles I write about: Maya weavers from Chichicastenango, San Antonio Aguas Calientes, Almolonga; Navajo weavers from Teec Nos Pos, Chinle, Burnt Water. The names evoke music, brush fires, trips to distant canyons and mountain villages. Of course, I am also nourished by my own friends, and by a world of women writers and artists from my own culture, among them the subjects of this essay. On my desk, an old-fashioned pop-up card of a pansy bouquet from my oldest friend, Nancy Lane Fleming. Beside it, a postcard I bought at Sissinghurst, England, of Vita Sackville-West's writing desk in her medieval tower: on her desk, four bouquets of flowers from her garden, a dish of pencils, a photo of her beloved friend, Virginia Woolf. For all of us, creative solitude resonates with the whispers of other women and their work.

Nourishment

The concept of nourishment is central to the domestic muse. Sarton, Flack, and Schapiro are visually, orally, and spiritually nourished by similar things. In essence, this is what the concept of femmage is all about: the female artist taking sustenance from her domestic universe. Food, tranquil surroundings, quilts, and the memorabilia of daily life are transformed by the artistic vision.

Works by Sarton, Schapiro, and Flack honor the place of food, or food preparation, in women's lives, albeit in very different ways. In her journals, Sarton repeatedly comments on the ritual of fixing lobster salad and champagne for special guests. She often remarks on the pleasures of food.

> The best thing of the weekend was a bowl of salad—the small dark-green lettuce leaves, strewn about with brilliant orange nasturtiums and two marigolds . . . [34]

> I had it in mind not only to pick the last flowers, just in case, and that I did too, but also (madness!) to make jam from green cherry tomatoes . . . there are dozens of them, so I picked four cupfuls and have just now got them all ready under a layer of lemon, cinnamon, and ginger, mixed with two cups of sugar, and shall cook them before I go off on my expedition tomorrow. [35]

In *Wonderland* (1983) (fig. 4), Miriam Schapiro incorporates crocheted doilies, aprons, table runners, and cut-out fabric tea cups into a monumental (90″ × 144″) collage that celebrates the icons of women's domestic existence. In *Water is Taught by Thirst* (1976),[36] the artist superimposes on a patchwork background scores of embroidered names that she has torn from an old tablecloth. This is covered by a sheer organdy apron. Schapiro observes that

Fig. 4. Miriam Schapiro, *Wonderland*, 1983. Acrylic and fabric on canvas, 90" × 144". Photo by Pelka/Noble. Courtesy of Bernice Steinbaum Gallery, New York City.

you might say the transparent apron has two functions; it unites all the names by being a common sign of service to others and it also gathers the women together under the roof of domestic creativity.[37]

Audrey Flack has done a series of paintings in which fruit, cheese, and pastry are key still life elements.[38] The fruit is not only a prop, but nourishes a hungry artist after her work.

> Photographing a beautiful still life of Rome Beauty apples and pears, an homage to Melendez, the Spanish eighteenth-century still life painter—a lit candle at dusk, cherries. I shot for two days. I just disassembled the set-up, ate one of the pears, put the rest in the refrigerator, put the props back in the cabinet.[39]

The meanings of food in Flack's paintings are multiple; these are among the elements that pull her paintings into the realm of female iconography. This imagery also links Flack to the world of seventeenth-century Dutch painting with its carefully rendered details of daily life. Flack was first drawn to Dutch still lifes after viewing a 1668 painting by Maria van Oosterwyck.[40] In many works in her *Vanitas* series, Flack combines food and flower arrangements with symbols of the fleetingness of time: a watch, an hour glass, a miniature skull (fig. 5). All of these are arranged in a well-lit, carefully constructed composition that nourishes the viewer's eye while it gives her pause to meditate on the transience of moments of beauty and composure.

Sarton, too, is drawn to the world of clarity and light that the seventeenth-century Dutch painters expose. She observes that

> I suppose these paintings speak to me with such force because they represent all that I hope to do in the novels and in the poems. They compose the world without ever imposing a rigid schema upon it and make us see even the domestic scene at its most banal with a sudden sense of revelation, with poignant recognition. The painters look at reality with devotion, and what we see is life never sentimentalized, but enhanced.[41]

In their paintings and collages, Flack and Schapiro proclaim, as Sarton does in her poem "Dutch Interior,"

> The atmosphere is all domestic, human,
> Chaos subdued by the sheer power of need.
> This is a room where I have lived as woman....

Fig. 5. Audrey Flack, *Time To Save,* 1979. Oil over acrylic on canvas, 80″ × 64″. Photo by Bruce C. Jones. Courtesy of Louis K. Meisel Gallery, New York.

Sarton goes on to reveal more about this seemingly calm woman of the Dutch still life painting. Her words describe the "remaking chaos into an intimate order" that is the artistic process for Flack, Schapiro, and Sarton herself.

Bent to her sewing, she looks drenched in calm.
Raw grief is disciplined to the fine thread.
But in her heart this woman is the storm;
Alive, deep in herself, holds wind and rain,
Remaking chaos into an intimate order
Where sometimes light flows through a windowpane.[42]

May Sarton was born in 1912, the same year as my mother. I was born in 1952. I first read May Sarton at twenty; her work has been constant nourishment for me since then. At thirty-six, going back and rereading the words that helped shape me at twenty, I see the ways in which she and I are nourished by the same things: the tranquility of a writing table with fresh flowers in the foreground and a beautiful vista for the eyes' refreshment; the longing for a few good early hours at the writing desk before other demands take over; food carefully prepared, whether for oneself alone or for guests; a special dog companion; a few beloved friends.

Dear Nancy,   Dec. 1, 1988
    I love novels with recipes in them. And Miriam Schapiro says that recipes are part of femmage. But for me the problem remains: how can I incorporate recipes into my art historical writing? My friend Aldona is doing an exhibit of Northwest Coast Indian carved bowls and other ornate food vessels. She intends to have recipes in the exhibit and catalogue as well. Now that's my idea of feminist/revisionist art history!
                                                    Love, Janet

Dear Janet,   1974
Women's Stew—a recipe especially for those who want to throw out the Fem-Iron and the Geritol and keep themselves. The virtue of this stew is that it tastes good, is good for your body, has nice symbolic qualities, and can be adjusted to fit varying economic situations. Like a good woman, it improves with age.

3 T. flour	2 T. shortening
1 tsp. salt	1 can tomatoes (the fat can)
½ tsp. celery salt	3 medium onions, sliced
¼ tsp. garlic salt	⅓ c. red wine vinegar
¼ tsp. black pepper	½ c. molasses
½ tsp. ginger	6–8 carrots, cut in 1″ diagonals
3 lbs. chuck in 2″ cubes	½ c. raisins

Combine first 7 ingredients in bag and shake. Brown in hot fat in heavy kettle. Add next 4 ingredients and ½ c. water. Simmer about 2 hours. Add carrots and raisins and simmer about 30 minutes longer. Serve over rice (8–10 servings). Note: sometimes I use stew meat instead of chuck, and I cut it smaller. I made it this weekend with the following limitations:

1) I had neither garlic salt, nor celery salt, nor ginger. I used a little nutmeg.
2) I used half a can of tomato juice, ½ cup blackstrap molasses, and *circa* ⅓ c. white cider vinegar. It was great.

The secret seems to be those combined flavors, along with the onion, which I prefer chopped to sliced. (I borrowed half an onion from the guy next door.)

I think this is a great dish for the revolution. Girds the womb and flourishes on resourcefulness. Hope you like it. I do.

Love, Nancy[43]

In May Sarton's world, flowers too provide nourishment, "quite as necessary as food."[44] They nourish the artist's eye and soul, and she speaks of them as if she were a painter.

I was stopped at the threshold of my study by a ray on a Korean chrysanthemum, lighting it up like a spotlight, deep red petals and Chinese yellow center, glowing, while the lavender aster back of it was in shadow with a salmon-pink spray of peony leaves and the barberry Eleanor picked for me. Seeing it was like getting a transfusion of light right to the vein.[45]

On an excursion, she notices fringed gentians in a field: "That vivid blue standing up in the cut stubble is extravagantly exciting."[46] And the patience of a gardener mirrors the patience needed for creative work:

... everything that slows us down and forces patience, everything that
sets us back into the slow cycles of nature, is a help. Gardening is an
instrument of grace.[47]

Of patience, and the mutability of the natural world, Sarton observes that

it does not astonish or make us angry that it takes a whole year to
bring into the house three great white peonies and two pale blue iris.
It seems altogether right and appropriate that these glories are earned
with long patience and faith (how many times this late spring I have
feared the lilacs have been frost-killed, but in the end they were as
glorious as ever before), and also that it is altogether right and appropriate that they cannot last.[48]

In 1986, while I was teaching a course on Women and the Visual Arts,
Simone de Beauvoir and Georgia O'Keeffe died within six weeks of each
other. For my entire adult life I had been comforted by O'Keeffe's presence
in the desert in Abiquiu, New Mexico. I was compelled to do something
to honor her. For days I worked on a poem, entitled "Directions for a
Performance Piece Upon the Death of Georgia O'Keeffe." One section of
it reads:

Send seed packets to your artist friends, with instructions:
Dear Phyllis, plant hollyhocks in your front yard.
Dear Joanna, make ladyslipper gardens in the forest.
Dear Nancy, train sweetpeas up the cedar fence.[49]

These have always been the fixed constellations in my universe of heroic
women: Georgia O'Keeffe in the Southwest, Simone de Beauvoir in Paris,
May Sarton in New England. Though two of these are gone, all three
nourish me still.

In exhorting my friends (a painter, a performance artist, a writer) to
plant flowers, I was encouraging a gesture in celebration of O'Keeffe's
famous, sensual floral imagery. Yet I had May Sarton in mind, too. Her
literary and personal aesthetic has always encompassed the structure of work
and the splendor of the flower garden. Earlier, I quoted Sarton's words on
the legacy of her parents ("what I had inherited was life-giving and life-
restoring"). The talent, ambition, and aesthetic sensibility that May Sarton
inherited and transformed in her own life is, for the rest of us, a legacy

that is life-giving and life-restoring and will be so to the end of her life and, most assuredly, beyond.[50]

NOTES

Epigraph published in Martha Kearns, *Käthe Kollwitz: Woman and Artist* (Old Westbury, New York: Feminist Press, 1976), 227–31.

1. Carolyn G. Heilbrun, *Writing a Woman's Life* (New York: Norton, 1988), 12.

2. Miriam Schapiro, *Miriam Schapiro: Femmages 1971–1985* (St. Louis: Brentwood Gallery, 1985), unpaginated; Schapiro, "The Education of Women as Artists: Project Womanhouse," in *Feminist Collage,* ed. Judy Loeb (New York: Teacher's College Press, 1979), 247–53.

3. Audrey Flack's work is profusely illustrated with large color photographs in Audrey Flack, *Audrey Flack on Painting* (New York: Abrams, 1981). An impressive sampling of twenty-seven years' worth of Schapiro's work is illustrated in Thalia Gouma-Peterson, ed., *Miriam Schapiro: A Retrospective, 1953–80* (Wooster, Ohio: College of Wooster, 1980).

4. See Flack, *Flack on Painting;* Audrey Flack, *Art and Soul: Notes on Creating,* (New York: Dutton, 1986). For Schapiro, see especially Miriam Schapiro, "Notes from a Conversation on Art, Feminism, and Work," in *Working It Out,* ed. S. Ruddick and P. Daniels (New York: Pantheon Books, 1977), 283–305. A full bibliography of Schapiro's published writings up to 1980 can be found in Gouma-Peterson, *Miriam Schapiro,* 112.

5. Elsewhere I have suggested that this is characteristic of women artists' work in indigenous Amerindian cultures as well. See J. C. Berlo, "Beyond *Bricolage:* Women and Aesthetic Strategies in Latin American Textiles," in *Textile Traditions in Mesoamerica and the Andes,* ed. M. B. Schevill, J. C. Berlo, and E. Dwyer (New York: Garland, 1991). For an example of this aesthetic in a literary critic's work, see Rachel Blau DuPlessis, "For the Etruscans" in *The New Feminist Criticism: Essays on Women, Literature, and Theory,* ed. Elaine Showalter (New York: Pantheon Books, 1985), 271–91. For more radical examples of it in women's writings of the 1970s, see Monique Wittig, *Les Guérillères,* trans. David Le Vay (New York: Avon, 1973); Mary Daly, *Gyn/Ecology: The Metaethics of Radical Feminism* (Boston: Beacon Press, 1978).

6. Miriam Schapiro and Melissa Meyer, "Femmage," *Heresies* 4 (1978): 66–69.

7. Schapiro, "Notes," 296–97.

8. See Jeanne Hamilton, "Drawing with the Camera," in *Flack on Painting,* 96–100, in which Flack's photographic assistant discusses the painstaking process.

9. See also Flack's painting, *Chanel* (1974), illustrated in Flack, *Flack on Painting,* 59.

10. "Audrey Flack," in Cindy Nemser, *Art Talk: Conversations With Twelve Women Artists* (New York: Scribner's, 1975), 311.

11. Schapiro, "Notes," 300.

12. Journal entry dated 20 April 1919, as quoted in Mary Jane Moffat and Charlotte Painter, eds. *Revelations: Diaries of Women* (New York: Vintage, 1975), 227.

13. Patricia Cooper and Norma Bradley Buford, *The Quilters: Women and Domestic Art* (New York: Doubleday, 1978), 75.

14. May Sarton, *Plant Dreaming Deep* (New York: Norton, 1968), 45.

15. Sarton, *Plant Dreaming Deep*, 48–49.

16. May Sarton, *Journal of a Solitude* (New York: Norton, 1973), 109.

17. May Sarton, *May Sarton: A Self-Portrait*, ed. Marita Simpson and Martha Wheelock (New York: Norton, 1982), 19.

18. Sarton, *Plant Dreaming Deep*, 59; see also 57–61.

19. Gouma-Peterson, *Miriam Schapiro*, 45.

20. Flack, *Flack On Painting*, 77.

21. Lawrence Alloway, "Introduction," in *Flack on Painting*, 27.

22. Schapiro, "Notes," 304.

23. Sarton, *Journal of a Solitude*, 108.

24. Flack, *Art and Soul*, 130.

25. Sarton, *Journal of a Solitude*, 130.

26. Sarton, *Journal of a Solitude*, 73.

27. Sarton, *Journal of a Solitude*, 81.

28. Flack, *Art and Soul*, 15.

29. Sarton's book of word portraits, *A World of Light* (New York: Norton, 1976), celebrates relationships with twelve creative individuals, eight of them women.

30. Sarton, *Journal of a Solitude*, 127.

31. Sarton, *Journal of a Solitude*, 127.

32. Sarton, *Journal of a Solitude*, 157.

33. See Audrey Flack, "The Haunting Image of the Macarena Esperanza," in *Flack on Painting*, 32–43.

34. May Sarton, *The House by the Sea: A Journal* (New York: Norton, 1977), 164.

35. Sarton, *House by the Sea*, 158.

36. Illustrated in Schapiro, *Miriam Schapiro: Femmages*, n.p.

37. Schapiro, *Miriam Schapiro: Femmages*, n.p.

38. See for example, Flack, *Flack On Painting*, color plates 59, 60, 61, 67, 71, 72, 76, 82.

39. Flack, *Art and Soul*, 52.

40. Alloway, "Introduction," 27.

41. Sarton, *Journal of a Solitude*, 112.

42. May Sarton, "Dutch Interior, Pieter de Hooch (1629–1682)," in *May Sarton: A Self-Portrait*, 79.

43. Recipe from Nancy Lane Fleming, Houston, Texas, 1974.

44. Sarton, *Plant Dreaming Deep,* 57.

45. Sarton, *Journal of a Solitude,* 35.

46. Sarton, *Journal of a Solitude,* 36.

47. Sarton, *Journal of a Solitude,* 123.

48. Sarton, *Journal of a Solitude,* 169.

49. J. C. Berlo, "Directions For a Performance Piece Upon the Death of Georgia O'Keeffe," *Women Artists News* 11, no. 4 (September 1986): 33.

50. Paraphrased from Sarton, *Plant Dreaming Deep,* 16.

"The Subtle Exchange of a Life":
May Sarton's Feminist Aesthetics

Susan Swartzlander

Feminists have tended to regard May Sarton's work with suspicion. The initial enthusiasm over such works as "My Sisters, O My Sisters" and "The Muse as Medusa" has given way to the charge that Sarton is somehow not feminist enough. In her journal *At Seventy*, Sarton relates a story about a young woman who wages a campaign to enlighten her,

> sending books, referring me to Audre Lord and Adrienne Rich, as though I had never heard of them, and in general treating me like a very old party in need of help. . . . The phrase she uses about me is "a foremother," a foremother who has somehow not done what was expected of her and thus must be brought into the fold, chastised, and forgiven.

Sarton ends this account with a resounding statement: "I do not see myself in this light" (*At Seventy*, 179). The critic who surveys the poetry, novels, and prose Sarton has written over the last half-century cannot help but see her in a feminist light.

It would be difficult to find another contemporary feminist who has written as much or as explicitly about her own aesthetic philosophy and practice. Each of the five journals returns over and over again to the questions of what art is and what it means for the artist as well as for her audience. *Writings on Writing* explores in detail the act of creating art out of life, poetry and fiction out of feelings and questions. Linda Huf, in *A Portrait of the Artist as a Young Woman*, notes that "women have frequently balked at portraying themselves in literature as would-be writers—or as painters, composers, or actresses. . . . Unlike men, women have only rarely written artist novels; that is, autobiographical novels depicting their struggles to become creative artists."[1] Sharon Spencer declares that "the woman artist is a missing character in fiction."[2] Yet Sarton's first novel, *The Single Hound*

(1938) is about art, creativity. One of the main characters, a painter named Georgia, is modeled after Irish writer Elizabeth Bowen, and poet Jean Dominique appears in the guise of another character. Sarton had life-long friendships with both women. For Sarton, the woman artist is not a missing character but an inevitable one: six other novels focus on the woman artist, and she makes "cameo appearances" in several others. At least fifty of Sarton's poems, written over the last fifty-three years, are about the creative process.

As her journals, letters, essays, novels, and poetry make clear, Sarton's aesthetic philosophy emerges from a feminist ethos. Her statements about art and the artist are always couched in metaphors and images of relationship, communion, and community. Sarton differentiates between this philosophy of wholeness and a patriarchal concept of art characterized by fragmentation.

Male writers have described the artist as "priest, prophet, warrior, legislator, and emperor."[3] Sarton's artist is most often a lover. In a 1983 interview, Sarton linked "art making" with lovemaking: "I feel more alive when I'm writing than I do at any other time—except when I'm making love." She goes on to explain that the two are parallel because during both you forget time, "nothing exists except the moment."[4] There are, however, a number of other connections between love and art expressed in her work. At times she substitutes one concept for the other. For instance, we often say that love is the great healer; Sarton says the same of poetry in *Recovering* (12). She equates love and the writing process: "Tenderness is the grace of the heart, as style is the grace of the mind" (*Recovering*, 26). She links love and work when she says that through both one forges identity: "How does one find one's identity? My answer would be through work and through love, and both imply giving rather than getting" (*Recovering*, 33). She explains that she has made her style as "simple and plain as possible"; otherwise, style "makes a wall between writer and reader" (*Recovering*, 78). Thirty-seven pages later, she says that "passionate love breaks down the walls" that are barriers preventing "two isolated human beings from being joined" (*Recovering*, 115).

Not only do art and love break down barriers, but they both require that one connect fully with another person: "You learn from the person you love. You're so concentrated, really, that you almost become that person. And if you multiply this by thirty, or whatever it may be, then you have all these people you're made up of."[5] In *Journal of a Solitude*, Sarton explains how art and love operate in similar ways to expand our horizons.

At any age we grow by the enlarging of consciousness . . . that implies a new way of looking at the universe. Love is one of the great enlargers of the person because it requires us to "take in" the stranger and to understand him, and to exercise restraint and tolerance as well as imagination to make the relationship work. If love includes passion, it is more explosive and dangerous and forces us to go deeper. Great art does the same thing. (*Journal of a Solitude,* 93)

Central to both love and art is the imagination. Denise Levertov has also written that "No recognition of others is possible without the imagination. The imagination of what it is to *be* those other forms of life . . . and it is that imaginative recognition that brings compassion to birth."[6]

In the novel *Mrs. Stevens Hears the Mermaids Singing,* Sarton's protagonist, Hilary, explains that those she had loved (the women who were her muses) "were maps of the world": "Love opens the doors into everything, as far as I can see, including and perhaps most of all, the door into one's own secret, and often terrible and frightening, real self" (*Mrs. Stevens,* 25). For this reason, Sarton's artist is always portrayed as vulnerable, and she often describes in the journals her own feelings of vulnerability. In *Journal of a Solitude,* after a morning of writing, Sarton says that she "was open from the inside out" (22). In the poem "Baroque Image," written "For any Artist," a kind of warrior figure reflects the setting sun from his shield, dazzling friends and enemies, but

> They did not sense the wound
> Behind that tilted shield—For he could hardly stand
> Who dazzled the whole field!
>
> (*Private Mythology,* 107)

In discussing a love relationship, Sarton explains that "To be honest is to expose wounds, and also to wound. There is no preventing that" (*Recovering,* 115). The wound, the vulnerability, is not completely negative, however: "True power is given to the vulnerable . . . when we admit our vulnerability, we include others; if we deny it, we shut them out" (*Recovering,* 160). For Sarton, the act of creation itself is empowering.

Whatever the wounds that have to heal, the moment of creation assures that all is well, that one is still in tune with the universe, that the inner chaos can be probed and distilled into order and beauty. (*At Seventy*, 106)

Sarton sees communion as essential to her work. The poem "Innumerable Friend" includes an image of bridges from one mind to another; a novel is entitled *The Bridge of Years*. In *Recovering,* Sarton says that she has hoped to "provide the bridge between women of all ages and kinds, between mothers and daughters, between sisters, between women as friends, between the old and the young. . . ." The vision of life communicated in her work "is not limited to one segment of humanity or another. It does have to do with love, and love has many forms and is not easy or facile in any of them" (*Recovering,* 81). In a *Paris Review* interview, she says that she thinks of herself as a "maker of bridges."[7]

Sarton shares this rhetoric of connection with her feminist contemporaries. Denise Levertov has written that "to be human is to be a *conversation*—a strange and striking way of saying that communion is the very basis of human living, of living *humanly.*"[8] In an interview, Sarton quotes Elizabeth Bowen's line, "Dialogue is what people do to each other"; one of Sarton's novels uses a narrative technique linking interrelated dialogues: its title—*Crucial Conversations.*

In her letters and journals, Sarton characterizes the reader as the one who completes the circle. Home is not where the artist is, but where the reader resides: "Poems like to have a destination for their flight. They are homing pigeons."[9] She revels in the feeling when her "poems ring out" and she can "hear them *land*" (*Recovering,* 72). As William Drake suggests in an essay included in this volume, Sarton's attitudes toward her poetry and her relationship with the audience were undoubtedly shaped by her early years in theater.

At times, her images suggest love, intimacy, and even sexuality: "I experienced that marvellous stillness when I know a poem has really landed . . . because then I can 'give tongue' and make whatever meaning and music is there 'happen'" (*Journal of a Solitude,* 49). She speaks about "that intense concentration, the imaginative heave" before she writes (*Recovering,* 53), and "writing poetry is like a seizure."[10] In the film *A World of Light,* she describes the poetic moment leaving her feeling "seized and shaken." She envisions her work as making "its way, heart by heart. . . . From my isolation to the isolation of someone somewhere who will find my work there exists a true communion" (*Journal of a Solitude,* 67). In a 1929 letter to her parents, Sarton describes her own experience reading Katherine

Mansfield's journal, a work "full of arrows which I shall never be able to pluck out of my heart."[11]

The writer, according to Sarton, must be a "born friend" and have "an extraordinarily sensitive register of feeling" (*Recovering*, 58). In *Journal of a Solitude*, Sarton admits that she is "not at all discreet about anything that concerns feeling. My business is the analysis of feeling" (44). In her "Letter to James Stephens," Sarton explains to the Irish poet her commitment to a poetry of feeling. Although he has remonstrated with her to be objective, to "seek for a sterner stuff," Sarton has persisted in her belief that the personal is the "poetical": "The little world these hands have tried to fashion / Using a single theme for their material, / Always a human heart, a human passion" (*Selected Poems*, 187). Sarton describes Stephens as a "pure poet" listening to a shell, "Hunting the ocean's rumor till you hear it well," whereas she listens to another "fragile auricle," the heart, which "Holds rumor like your ocean's, is a portal / That sometimes opens to contain the miracle." Sarton believes that "If there are miracles we can record / They happen in the places that you curse" (*Selected Poems*, 187).

Most of Sarton's novels are about feeling or being afraid to feel. In an interview with Karen Saum, she explained how important this theme is to her.

> One of the themes in all I have written is the fear of feeling. It comes into the last novel where Anna asks, "Must it go on from generation to generation this fear of feeling?" I want feelings to be expressed, to be open, to be natural, not to be looked on as strange. It's not weird, I mean, if you feel deeply.[12]

In several journals and novels, Sarton recalls Yeats's line, "There's more enterprise in walking naked." In both *Journal of a Solitude* and *Recovering: A Journal*, Sarton discusses the idea in relationship to Bloomsbury. She values the Bloomsbury group's ability to discuss anything openly, "the honesty, courage, and taste with which they honored and explored personal relationships" (*Recovering*, 48). Their strength may have been "their fantastic honesty about personal life" (*Journal of a Solitude*, 76). Sarton believes that it is imperative for the artist to follow Yeats's dictum.

> If we are to understand the human condition, and if we are to accept ourselves in all the complexity, self-doubt, extravagance of feeling, guilt, joy, the slow freeing of the self to its full capacity for action and

creation, both as human being and as artist, we have to know all we can about each other, and we have to be willing to go naked. (*Journal of a Solitude*, 77)

This focus on feeling, community, and communion is inherent in the genre of autobiography. Lynn Ross-Bryant explains that by definition that genre constitutes a shared life of poet and audience.[13] In an essay included in this volume, Carol Virginia Pohli has illustrated that this is true in practice as well as in theory. Sarton's philosophy, however, is not limited to her autobiographies; it pervades all of her work, across the genres.

We see these ideas about art and life expressed in *Mrs. Stevens Hears the Mermaids Singing*, a work not typical of either men's or women's *Künstlerromane* as literary critics have defined them. The protagonist of men's artist novels is always at odds with society, like Stephen Dedalus, who longs to fly by the nets of church, nation, and family. These characters value disconnection, not communion. Linda Huf describes the artist hero as "a divided self—split between sensual longings and spiritual aspirations by which he would transcend life in art."[14]

Huf believes that the artist heroine shares with the male protagonist the desire to transcend life, but to that she adds further disharmony: "She is torn not only between life and art, but, more specifically, between her role as a woman, demanding selfless devotion to others, and her aspirations as an artist, requiring exclusive commitment to work."[15] Transcending life is antithetical to Hilary's goal; she is, however, a divided self. Although these tensions, the demands of a woman's life and an artist's life, certainly exist in Sarton's text, it seems that the predominant source of division is the balancing act of maintaining the integrity of the self, while trying to incorporate the other, balancing the inner world of self with the outer world of society (lover, reader). The female artist tries to achieve such a synthesis without being subsumed herself.

Throughout *Mrs. Stevens*, Hilary is, like Jenny, "rent in two" most of the time (77). To her interviewer, she appears as a "person advancing and retreating at the same instant, both transparent and secret . . . a person in continuous dialogue with herself" (87). Even as a young woman "she was already then two distinct beings" (102). She says that "all the time I'm myself, I'm somebody else looking on" (108). Inspired by her muse,

Hilary now felt she was two people all the time, instead of one. Her eye had been cracked open by a "you" . . . at the same time because of this huge inner reverberation, which stretched all her powers, it was as if the whole outer world also resounded in her ... landscape, literature, everything had become alive in a wholly new way. (105)

The pun on eye (I) makes it clear that her lover/muse has affected her on both personal and artistic levels. Paradoxically, the doubleness is not a negative feature as Huf characterizes it, but a pleasurable, if demanding, necessity.

In *Journal of a Solitude*, Sarton details a "female-oriented art" as "life enhancing." She believes that one cannot pick up one of Virginia Woolf's "books and read a page without feeling more alive" (*Journal of a Solitude*, 64). Sarton believes that women are centered in a unique way, "the whole and original and continual creative process is from within outwards, and it is the woman's prerogative to possess that place and power" (*Journal of a Solitude*, 139). Hilary Stevens tells her interviewer that women's work is

never to categorize, never to separate one thing from another—intellect, the senses, the imagination.... Some total gathering together where the most realistic and the most mystical can be joined in celebration of life itself. Women's work is always toward wholeness. (*Mrs. Stevens*, 172)

The men in the novel really do not understand this connection of life to art, this search for wholeness. Early in her life, Hilary was hospitalized for a nervous condition; the treatment was a rest cure. Eventually she was allowed to write poetry, but her physician insisted that she "keep the poems to objects, not people" (*Mrs. Stevens*, 119). He suggests that Hilary treat poetry like an exercise, a "game," keeping emotion out of it, "like practicing the scales" (122). She "bristles" at his suggestion. He has no idea that, in her conception, emotion is inherent in art; connection with others is not an option.

Patricia Meszaros, in an article on Irish writer Mary Lavin, notes that bird imagery is often used in *Künstlerromane* to symbolize the artist's escape from society's confinement, but in novels by and about women, birds are "broken, crippled, strangled or hung."[16] In *Mrs. Stevens*, birds are healthy, if not always happy. The bird imagery, however, reinforces notions about the woman artist. When Hilary is in the hospital, Dr. Hallowell brings crumbs to feed the sparrows on the window sill, just as he doles out a few treats (books, flowers) to help Hilary endure the punishment he has imposed on her. It is significant that the sparrows are not flying, since Hilary is not free to write, to escape these restrictions. Later in the novel, she is described as an "old hawk," an eagle (*Mrs. Stevens*, 186), and a "small, belligerent hawk," with "feathers ruffled"—all images of power rather than submission.

A significant portion of the novel is devoted to Hilary's articulation of her aesthetic philosophy to two interviewers, Peter and Jenny. Peter understands even less than Dr. Hallowell. Always categorized as "breaking in," "interrupting" the conversation, Peter does not understand integration, communion, connection, wholeness. Rather than making connections, Peter categorizes and, thus, fragments the information he receives; he always misses the mark: "The style is masculine; the content is feminine . . . am I wrong?" Hilary's response: "You frighten me, young man" (*Mrs. Stevens*, 127).

When Hilary discusses Sappho, Jane Austen, and Colette, Peter interrupts, "You have brought three fascinating females into the room, but we are here to interview *you*." He then asks about her changes in style, never realizing that the three writers are a part of her and her work, and that style cannot be divorced from that. Everything is interrelated, but he cannot begin to see it. He looks for change rather than continuity (*Mrs. Stevens*, 113). Hilary finds it difficult to answer his questions because she is incapable of thinking the way he does: "How can I ever tell them? It was like trying to extricate one straw from a tightly bound up bundle, bundle of living, bundle of writing" (131).

Hilary again tries to explain herself, pointing to poems she wrote as she was learning, "how to be there inside the poem yet outside of it" (151). Peter responds by asking her if she would "like to come back to the craft itself for a moment" (151), not realizing that what she had been describing is the very heart of her craft. Hilary, waving "aside Peter's attempt to interrupt," tells the interviewer that "art is the constant attempt to rejoin something broken off or lost, to make it whole again. It is always integrating, don't you know?" (*Mrs. Stevens*, 190). He doesn't know.

Criticism is not excluded from this aesthetics of integration, involvement, emotion. Hilary mentions a critic whom Peter dismisses as "one of those French critics for whom criticism becomes a *mystique*, who seem to be examining themselves as well as the subject" (175). Peter dislikes what he calls "this personal kind of criticism. It seems suspect" (175). Hilary asks, "You have to clothe your personal idiosyncracy in some sort of Olympian pseudo detachment?" (175) To Hilary, "criticism seems . . . always personal, however disguised in abstract lingo" (*Mrs. Stevens*, 176). This part of their discussion becomes even more ironic when one remembers that, earlier on, Peter had assured Hilary she would not have to worry about how he characterized her in his article because, "we are not critics, we are recorders" (128).

The other major male character is a young man named Mar, in whom Hilary recognizes her younger self. He is just beginning to write poetry and to learn about love. Mar, rejected by his first love, tries to obliterate emotion by having a one-night stand with a sailor who steals his wallet in the morning. When Mar confides the humiliating experience to Hilary, she explains that when she gets "stirred up, it's the whole of me that gets stirred. I can't separate soul and body" (*Mrs. Stevens*, 209). Mar insists that he wants that separation. He wants "to be sexy without all the devastating conflict and *feeling*. I want sex without love" (209). Hilary, his mentor, warns him that this is impossible for the artist: "there are no casual encounters, for you or for me. Every one is a collision, reverberates, and, because it reverberates, is costly" (216).

As Hilary Stevens tries to explain the relationship of art and passion to Mar, she talks about the quarry in front of them.

> Odd, isn't it? How these quarries, blasted open by dynamite, the scene of so much violence, so much lifting and carrying too, after they are abandoned, become magic places, deep ponds. (*Mrs. Stevens*, 211)

For Sarton, the quarry is a striking image of artistic creation. In "The School of Babylon," she writes about Katharine Sturgis's "semiabstract water color of a piece of granite being lifted out of a quarry." She bought the painting ten years after seeing it for the first time because the image "haunted" her.

> The image was evidently one of those complex ones which had something to reveal if I could explore it by making a poem out of it. . . . I sensed slowly that one of the reasons why is the fact that we dig down deep into the earth to bring up stones that will eventually soar in the cathedrals—as we dig down to the subconscious matrix to bring up images that fertilize the imagination. No height without depth. (*Writings on Writing*, 21)

When the poet "digs down deep" she finds not only images, but passions: "For poetry exists to break through to below the level of reason where the angels and monsters that the amenities keep in the cellar may come out to dance, to rove and roar, growling and singing" (*Writings on Writing*, 72).

May Sarton has been accused of not being feminist enough, yet her aesthetic philosophy, her vision of life as it is expressed for more than fifty years of writing fiction, poetry, and prose, is one that celebrates feeling, relationship, communion, and community. She recognizes that the woman artist is in a unique position to connect with others. She shares with us the values that have always united and empowered feminists. She teaches us that art, like love, requires "the subtle exchange of a life."

NOTES

1. Linda Huf, *A Portrait of the Artist as a Young Woman: The Writer as Heroine in American Literature* (New York: Frederick Ungar, 1983), 1.

2. Sharon Spencer, "'Femininity' and the Woman Writer," *Women's Studies* 1, no. 3 (1973): 247.

3. Susan Gubar, "'The Blank Page' and the Issues of Female Creativity," *Critical Inquiry* 8 (Winter 1981): 244.

4. Janet Todd, ed., *Women Writers Talking* (New York: Holmes and Meier, 1983), 4.

5. Dolores Shelley, "A Conversation with May Sarton," *Women and Literature* 7 (Spring 1979): 38.

6. Denise Levertov, *The Poet in the World* (New York: New Directions, 1973), 53.

7. Karen Saum, "The Art of Poetry XXXII: May Sarton," *Paris Review* (1983): 86.

8. Levertov, *Poet in the World*, 49.

9. Letter of 16 August 1940 from Sarton to Margaret Foote Hawley, the Berg Collection, New York Public Library. I gratefully acknowledge Susan Sherman for bringing some of Sarton's letters to my attention.

10. Todd, *Women Writers*, 11.

11. Letter of 29 December 1929 from Sarton to her parents, Berg Collection, New York Public Library.

12. Saum, "Art of Poetry," 99.

13. Lynn Ross-Bryant, "Imagination and the Re-Valorization of the Feminine," *Journal of the American Academy of Religion. Thematic Studies* 48, no. 2 (1981): 111–12.

14. Huf, *Portrait*, 5.

15. Huf, *Portrait*, 6.

16. Patricia K. Meszaros, "Woman as Artist: The Fiction of Mary Lavin," *Critique* 24 (1982): 54.

"Toward Durable Fire": The Solitary Muse of May Sarton

Mary K. DeShazer

"We have to make myths of our lives," May Sarton says in *Plant Dreaming Deep*. "It is the only way to live them without despair."[1] Of the many twentieth-century American women poets who are mythmakers, Sarton speaks most urgently and often about what it means to be a woman and a writer and about the female muse as a primary source of poetic inspiration. In the fourth "Autumn Sonnet" from *A Durable Fire,* she describes the crucial relationship between the woman poet and her muse.

> I never thought that it could be, not once,
> The Muse appearing in warm human guise,
> She the mad creature of unhappy chance
> Who looked at me with cold Medusa eyes,
> Giver of anguish and so little good.
> For how could I have dreamed that you would come
> To help me tame the wildness in my blood,
> To bring the struggling poet safely home?[2]

As "sister of the mirage and echo," Sarton's muse parallels, in some respects, the quasi-erotic, mystical inspirer invoked by Robert Graves, her "whom I desired above all things to know."[3] Furthermore, in her "warm human guise," Sarton's source of inspiration represents a female variation on contemporary poet Gary Snyder's theme of the muse as the "clearest mirror," the "human lover."[4] But for Sarton the muse is also a demonic shadow, a crucial Medusa-self against whom the poet struggles and yet through whom she ultimately transforms the "wildness in my blood" into vital creative energy. In the words of Hilary Stevens, Sarton's poet-protagonist and alter ego in *Mrs. Stevens Hears the Mermaids Singing,* "the muse destroys as well as gives life, does not nourish, pierces, forces one to discard, renew, be born again. Joy and agony are pivoted in her presence."[5]

To understand Sarton's theory of the muse, we must examine her view of female creativity, which centers on the antithesis between artist and woman. "I was broken in two / By sheer definition," she exclaims in "Birthday on the Acropolis," and though she is reacting here to the "pitiless clarity" of the stark Greek light and landscape, the statement describes as well her conflict in attempting to reconcile her femininity with her art.[6] Like writers from Emily Dickinson to Virginia Woolf to Adrienne Rich, Sarton struggles to overcome psychic fragmentation, a feeling of self versus self. For Sarton, this quest to name and claim her female creative identity is complicated by an acceptance of the patriarchal definition of woman as Other—as beloved rather than lover, object rather than subject; in short, as inherently "other than" active creator. She aligns herself with a perspective both Jungian and ahistorical in assuming an archetypal feminine principle innately separate from an active masculine principle. This assumption has enormous implications for her poetics, which posits an inevitable dichotomy between the feminine and the artistic sensibilities. "The woman who needs to create works of art," Hilary Stevens asserts, "is born with a kind of psychic tension in her which drives her unmercifully to find a way to balance, to make herself whole. Every human being has this need: in the artist it is mandatory. Unable to fulfill it, he goes mad. But when the artist is a woman, she fulfills it at the *expense* of herself as a woman."[7]

"At the *expense* of herself as a woman"—this statement recalls Robert Southey's famous pronouncement to Charlotte Brontë in 1837: "literature is not the business of a woman's life, and it cannot be."[8] For May Sarton, Southey's assertion contains a modicum of truth. "After all, admit it," Mrs. Stevens says to Jenny Hare, her youthful interviewer and a budding writer, "a woman is meant to create children, not works of art. . . . It's the natural order of things that [a man] constructs objects outside himself and his family. The woman who does so is aberrant."[9] Sarton's argument hinges on an acceptance of traditional definitions of *masculine* as active, objective, dynamic, and of *feminine* as passive, subjective, static. Any woman who writes seriously, according to this paradigm, assumes a masculine role. "I settled for being a woman," Hilary's mother-in-law tells her. "I wonder whether you can."[10] Like Aphra Behn, who spoke of "my masculine part, the poet in me," Sarton suggests that the aggressive, male side of the female self, the Jungian animus, creates literary works.[11] Yet Sarton neither claims nor desires to "write like a man"; as Peter Selversen, Hilary's other interviewer, says of her work, "the style is masculine; the content is feminine."[12] Sarton is aware of the difficulties the woman writer confronts in attempting to reconcile her gender and her creativity. How, then, does she incorporate her view of the creative enterprise as a masculine phenomenon into her definition and perception of herself as a woman writer?

For one thing, she views the woman writer's aberrance not as a liability but as an asset, a source of unique creative power. In this respect she takes issue with Sandra M. Gilbert and Susan Gubar, who suggest that, in the nineteenth century, at least, the woman who writes typically "experiences her gender as a painful obstacle or even a debilitating inadequacy."[13] According to Sarton's schema, in contrast, the woman writer's aberrance serves as a constructive rather than a destructive force, for it catapults her not toward neurosis but toward health. Anxiety is especially acute in the creative woman, Sarton acknowledges, as are frustration, fragmentation, rage; but these feelings of being "rent in two ... most of the time," as Jenny describes herself in *Mrs. Stevens,* are precisely the raw material from which female art is sculpted, the female self validated.[14] In a sense, therefore, Sarton agrees with Southey: literature is *not* a woman's business if the woman in question expects or wishes to assume traditional female roles as well as the nontraditional guise of artist. If the woman writer accepts and indeed relishes her incongruity, however, if she celebrates her aberrance as a source of artistic nourishment, literature becomes life's *only* business. "For the aberrant woman," Mrs. Stevens explains, "art is health, the only health! It is ... the constant attempt to rejoin something broken off or lost, to make whole again. It is always integrating."[15]

Once her aberrance is acknowledged as a given, the woman writer can set about the process of self-discovery that Sarton believes lies at the root of meaningful art, especially of poetry. Although she has worked for fifty years in three genres—in addition to fifteen volumes of poetry, she has published twenty novels and seven nonfiction works—Sarton focuses her theory of female creativity on poetry and the process of attaining poetic autonomy. "Poetry and novels are absolutely different," she asserts in *World of Light,* a film about her life and work. Whereas a novel represents a dialogue with others, poetry focuses on the inner world: "you write poetry for yourself and God."[16] In *Journal of a Solitude* she muses further on this subject: "Why is it that poetry always seems to me so much more of a true work of the soul than prose? I never feel elated after writing a piece of prose, though I have written good things on concentrated will. ... Perhaps it is that prose is earned and poetry given."[17] Poetry, then, is a gift; the poet an instrument. One elects to be a novelist but is "chosen" to be a poet: "you have to be willing . . . to give something terribly intimate and secret of yourself to the world—and not care."[18]

As the crucial source that inspires the poet, Sarton's muse "throws the artist back upon herself," thereby facilitating this essential psychic exchange. "When the Muse comes," Hilary explains, "the dialogue begins. . . . The Muse opens up the dialogue with oneself and goes her way."[19] "The Muse is always a question," she continues. "That's what sets up the dialogue . . . not with the Muse, but with oneself."[20] In some respects, Sarton's muse resembles the classic, passive, inspirational source of the male poet, the traditional female lover: she is mysterious, she cannot be pinned down, she "goes her way." But, as a shadow to the woman poet, she also represents a vital, active aspect of the poetic process, a potent and demonic force against whom the poet is constantly pitted. "Think of a mixture of properties in a chemical test tube," Hilary says to Jenny and Peter; "sometimes when two elements are mixed, they boil; there is tumult; heat is disengaged. So in the presence of the Muse, the sources of poetry boil; the faculty of language itself ferments."[21] Like Plato, Sarton believes that creative energy is often a product of irrationality, "frenzy," and that the primary source of this tumult is the "honeyed muse."

Whether she manifests herself as a serene visitant or a tempestuous "precipitating presence," the muse for Sarton is irrevocably and quintessentially female; there neither is nor can be, she asserts, a male muse. "What seems to me valid and interesting," Peter tells Jenny before they meet Hilary Stevens,

> "is the question posited at such huge length by Robert Graves in *The White Goddess*—who and what is the Muse? Here we have a poet who has gone on writing poems long after the Muse, at least in a personal incarnation, has become irrelevant. What sustains the intensity? Is there a White God?" he asked, and immediately felt how funny it sounded. They both laughed.
> "Of course not!"[22]

Later, when Peter toasts the muse, "whoever she or he may be," Hilary Stevens protests "'Whom I desired above all things to know. Sister of the mirage and echo!' . . . the Muse, young man, is *she*!"[23] For Sarton, this female muse is erotic, demonic, and maternal. In her guise as human lover, feminine inspiration incarnate, Sarton's muse resembles alternately Plato's

Diotima, Petrarch's Laura, and Dante's Beatrice; she evokes either passionate love—Plato's "frenzy"—or a strong sense of spiritual connectedness or both. Yet the extreme tension that Sarton considers essential to the exchange between poet and muse often suggests not a meeting of lovers but a collision of wild, animal-like forces: "I am the cage where poetry / Paces and roars."[24] These two extremes—the muse as lover and the muse as demon—merge finally in the image of the mother, Sarton's ultimate metaphor for poetic inspiration. "My mother still remains the great devouring enigma," Hilary Stevens admits, "the Muse, you see. . . ."[25]

This concept of the muse as mother suggests the complex struggle for female identity that the woman writer experiences: how to bring into her scope the Other, whether lover or demonic shadow or mother, without destroying the self. As psychologists and anthropologists from Sigmund Freud to Dorothy Dinnerstein have pointed out, human awe of and ambivalence toward the mother spring from her dual nature: as nurturer of life, she also holds the power of negation, destruction, and death. In the woman this ambivalence may be especially acute, since the biological mother is a powerful same-sex role model whom the daughter must simultaneously reject and emulate.[26] If the muse is ultimately the mother, as Sarton claims, she represents, for the woman poet, a source not only of love and nurture but also of anger and ambivalence. From the tension engendered by these conflicting emotions, Sarton concludes, springs impassioned poetry.

Although the female muse is the most crucial ingredient in the "witch's brew" that Sarton as a poet boils, a second element is also very important: solitude. "I have become enamored of solitude . . . my last great love," she admits in the film *World of Light,* and indeed silence and isolation provide her with a major source of artistic nourishment. As the condition that breeds art, solitude is especially important to the woman poet, who frequently has had little access to a "room of her own." "Solitude itself is a way of waiting for the inaudible and the invisible to make itself felt," Sarton explains. "And that is why solitude is never static and never hopeless."[27] Neither is it always easy, however. "The value of solitude—one of its values—is, of course, that there is . . . nothing to help balance at times of particular stress or depression."[28] Such attacks from within, she insists, force the woman artist to struggle with her art. For Sarton, then, female creativity is fertilized through a solitude shattered by visitations from the muse, who both intrudes upon and enhances this delicate but crucial way of living. The ideal result of such exchanges is a sense of balance, a reconciliation of selves.

Sarton's aesthetic views will be clarified and elaborated if we examine her depictions of the muse in *Mrs. Stevens Hears the Mermaids Singing,* a novel that might be considered poetic theory in the guise of fiction. The novel's protagonist, Hilary Stevens, serves as Sarton's double, mirror and mouthpiece for her creator. Like Sarton, she objects to her lack of serious critical attention, and she wishes to be considered foremost as a poet rather than a novelist. Hilary Stevens and May Sarton each live alone in a remote New England house to which each is strongly attached. Finally, both women discuss frankly their lesbianism, particularly as it affects their art.[29] As the poet's double, Hilary reveals Sarton's poetic theory, elaborates her perception of the female muse, and paints a lyrical portrait of several female incarnations of this muse.

Three distinct inspirational sources, or three aspects of a single muse, emerge in *Mrs. Stevens:* the detached lover, the demonic Other, and the all-pervading mother. Hilary Stevens must come to terms with all three forces during her interview with Peter and Jenny. The first incarnation of the muse that she recalls is the lover, distant and remote. Surfacing initially in Hilary's rememberings is her former governess, Phillippa Munn, the impetus behind the young poet's sexual and artistic awakening, her initial "instrument of revelation." Spurned by Phillippa, who views her as child and student, the youthful Hilary turns to poetry to express her "multiplicity of sensation."

> Everything could now be *said*—this was the intoxicating discovery Hilary made. She could go the limit with her feeling; she could come to terms with it by analyzing it through the written word.[30]

From this response to Phillippa, Hilary produces her first poetry, "a series of crude, passionate love poems" whose intensity shocks the governess and frightens their creator. Recalling Phillippa, the adult Hilary recognizes the value of this adolescent epiphany.

> The sign of the Muse, she thought: impossible, haunting, she who makes the whole world reverberate. Odd that I recognized her at fifteen! And she felt some remote tenderness for that quaking, passionate being whose only outlet had been poetry—, bad poetry, at that!—But who had learned then to poise the tensions, to solve the equation through art.[31]

A much later manifestation of the lover-muse, Willa MacPherson, is another force behind Hilary's ongoing efforts to "poise the tensions, to solve the equation through art." After years of intellectual exchange, Hilary becomes emotionally involved with Willa almost by accident: she brings her a recording of the Brandenburg Concerti and learns from Willa's violent response of her former liaison with a well-known musician. Hilary's awareness of Willa's unrequited passion arouses her own, and she unleashes a torrent of new poems that she presents to Willa, who accepts them with a detachment reminiscent of the attitude that medieval troubadours and Renaissance sonneteers attributed to their ladies.

> Willa listened. She accepted the poems as the true Muse does with detached, imaginative grace; she brought to bear her critical intelligence, illuminated by something like love, the inwardness, the transparency which had been opened in spite of herself. . . . Above all, she succeeded in making Hilary accept that the poem itself was the reality, accept, at least at first, that together, for some mysterious reason, they made possible the act of creation. It was intimacy of a strange kind.[32]

Despite her detachment, Willa differs from the male poet's courtly muse in her willingness to take Hilary's art seriously, to help the poet define and refine the power of the poetic word. She is distant, that is, but not disdainful. This relationship ends painfully, yet the elderly poet acknowledges Willa as a key inspirational force. "After all, the poems existed. That strange marriage of two minds, from which they had flowed, still lived there on the page."[33]

The passion that Hilary Stevens unleashes at times toward both Phillippa and Willa suggests a second manifestation of the muse as a demonic Medusa-self, violent yet essential to the tension that produces poetry at "white heat." "Women are afraid of their demon, want to control it, make it sensible like themselves," Hilary asserts; indeed, much of her artistic struggle hinges upon the recognition that one's demons must be confronted instead of denied.[34] Hilary's most incorrigible demons are "they," those "enemy" voices that accompany old age with its attendant forgetfulness, its doubts as to one's creative capacities. "Who were *they* exactly?" Mrs. Stevens asks herself. "Old fool, *they* are your own demons, . . . the never-conquered demons with whom you carry on the struggle for survival against laziness, depression, guilt, and fatigue."[35] This effort is exhausting at times, the poet admits, but it can also be energizing, particularly when "they" become "she," a demonic lover-muse against whom the poet is pitted and through whom she is mirrored and defined.

For Hilary, this muse appears forcefully in Dorothea, a sociologist with whom she lived during middle age. Unlike Willa, who accepted poems as a goddess might receive supplicants, Dorothea and Hilary interact as equal forces; hence their exchanges are charged with a "concentrated violence." Through Dorothea, Hilary is "once more in the presence of the Muse, the crucial one, the Medusa who had made her understand that if you turn Medusa's face around, it is your own face. It is yourself who must be conquered."[36] As a source of renewed vitality, Dorothea forces Hilary to confront "the enemy," herself, with a vengeance at once "a strange sort of love."

> But whatever it was, the poems began to pour out. Hilary walking down Fifth Avenue on the way to her job, would be pursued by poems, lines running through her head, lines of dialogue. Day and night, it seemed, she was struggling like a little bull against the wall, and the wall was Dorothea. Well, she thought, I have met my match.[37]

As Hilary's "match," a powerful Other who is also a part of the self, Dorothea evokes an ambivalence that emerges finally as a "devastating, destructive rage." This hostility kills any hope of dialogue between poet and muse, as the two engage in a furious battle of wills. At last, Hilary realizes that "the creative person, the person who moves from an irrational source of power, has to face the fact that this power antagonizes. Under all the superficial praise of the 'creative' is the desire to kill. It is the old war between the mystic and the nonmystic, a war to the death."[38] Mystic versus nonmystic, artist versus social scientist, Other versus self—despite their apparent differences, Hilary and Dorothea mirror each other; each sees in the other a self whom she feels driven to destroy. "I was the enemy, the anarchic, earth-shaking power,"[39] Hilary can admit years later. Broken into irrevocable halves, Hilary and Dorothea separate so that each may reconstruct herself. But Hilary learns a valuable lesson through her shadow: "It would have been better . . . to let the furies out instead of trying to contain them. I got split up, and those poems were the means of trying to knit myself together again."[40] With poets such as Louise Bogan and Muriel Rukeyser, Sarton acknowledges the importance of controlling her furies in order to keep them from controlling her. "She of the disciplined mind had had to come to terms with the anarchic Aphrodite buried so deep in herself," Hilary Stevens declares. Yet both she and Dorothea gain much from their mutual agony. "We had turned the Medusa face around and seen our *selves*. The long solitude ahead would be the richer for it."[41]

As a final act of self-discovery, Hilary Stevens confronts the muse as mother—not only the literal, biological mother but also the Great Goddess in her fierce duality: angry as well as loving, life denying and life affirming. The interaction of maternal muse and female poet, Mrs. Stevens claims, "is what is meant by fertilization."[42] Early in the novel, Hilary acknowledges both awe and ambivalence toward her mother, whom she remembers in two ways: as a tired woman sitting at a desk, "overwhelmed by what she had failed to accomplish," and as a rare intelligence who "flourished in social situations, loved good conversation with a passion, enjoyed pitting her mind and her personality against those of her peers."[43] Yet like many children sent away to boarding school or summer camp, the young Hilary feels painfully rejected by her mother, to whom she is never totally reconciled.

Despite this resentment, it is her mother with whom Hilary holds her most crucial dialogue. In recalling her mother's death, the poet recognizes in her a compelling force that the daughter seeking artistic and personal validation must confront. "Yes, let us end this dialogue with the beginning," she says to Peter and Jenny. "I have sometimes imagined that my last book might be about my mother; it is time to die when one has come to terms with everything. My mother still remains the great devouring enigma... the Muse, you see."[44] If reconciliation between mother and daughter is impossible, Sarton suggests, the poet must come to terms with the maternal principle in and through her art. In this sense, therefore, the mother functions as a muse to the poet-daughter, as "she whom I desired above all things to know."

Paralleling and complementing Sarton's theory of female creativity in *Mrs. Stevens* is her poetry itself—more than half a century's worth, written from 1930 to the present. "We are whole or have intimations of what it means to be whole when the entire being—spirit, mind, nerves, flesh, the body itself—are concentrated toward a single end. I feel it when I am writing a poem," she claims in *Journal of a Solitude*. "Art is always integrating.... I have written every poem... to find out what I think, to know where I stand."[45] The scope and nature of the poetic process, particularly that of the woman writer, provide the theme of "My Sisters, O My Sisters," an early poem in which Sarton explores the link between female writing and female power. In the first section, the poet looks back through her literary foremothers and affirms the difficulties the woman artist faces in her movement from silence to speech.

> Dorothy Wordsworth, dying, did not want to read,
> "I am too busy with my own feelings," she said.
>
> And all women who have wanted to break out
> Of the prison of consciousness to sing or shout
>
> Are strange monsters who renounce the treasure
> Of their silence for a curious devouring pleasure.
>
> Dickinson, Rossetti, Sappho—they all know it,
> Something is lost, strained, unforgiven in the poet.

Sarton argues that women writers are a breed apart, "strange monsters" who must set aside traditional female passivity to uncover the "curious devouring pleasure" of creativity. Such "sacrifices" are often problematical, the poet admits, and she offers a catalog of "aberrant" women writers to support her argument: George Sand, who "loved too much"; Madame de Stael, "too powerful for men"; Madame de Sévigné, "too sensitive." Yet only through the self-imposed renunciation of traditional roles, she suggests, have authentic female voices emerged.

The contemporary woman writer, Sarton continues, has much to learn from her forebears' attempts to break out of the prison of silence. In order to become "more simply human," she must come

> . . . to the deep place where poet becomes woman,
>
> Where nothing has to be renounced or given over
> In the pure light that shines out from the lover,
>
> In the pure light that brings forth fruit and flower
> And that great sanity, that sun, the feminine power.

Sarton links herself to women poets from Emily Dickinson to H.D. in appropriating as a metaphor for "feminine power" the traditional symbol of masculine energy and potency, the sun. As writing women, the poet suggests, she and her peers must find that "deep place" from which to celebrate the "pure light" of creativity.

Sarton defines "that great sanity . . . the feminine power" as a revaluation of those qualities typically associated with woman: fecundity, nurture, and love. These "riches," which have heretofore sustained men and children, "these great powers / Which are ours alone," must now be used by women to fertilize one another, to stimulate their own creativity. As models of the precarious balance for which women must now strive, she offers two biblical foremothers with equally valuable but very different heritages: Eve and Mary. The reconciliation of passion and wisdom that these two women represent is important to Sarton's paradigm, since she believes that women, especially artists, must be governed by both attributes. Like H.D. in *Trilogy*, Sarton rejects misogynistic notions denouncing Eve as evil incarnate and offering as the sole model Mary, a symbol of feminine wisdom yet also of feminine purity and passivity. Instead, she re-visions and celebrates both women as active female forces.

> To be Eve, the giver of knowledge, the lover;
> To be Mary, the shield, the healer and the mother.
> The balance is eternal whatever we may wish.

The woman poet's complex task, the poet concludes, is to affirm both branches of this full-bodied tree.

Yet Sarton acknowledges the difficulties inherent in such a quest. "Where rejoin the source / The fertile feminine goddess, double river?" In the final section she offers female creativity, woman's solitary art, as a means to "re-join the source" and thus attain balance and clarity of vision. Taking to task herself and other women who have "asked so little of ourselves and men / And let the Furies have their way," the poet calls upon women to claim the "holy fountain" of creative imagination, transforming it into a wellspring of feminine song. Only by appropriating the "masculine and violent joy of pure creation," the poet suggests, can women "come home to the earth," giving birth to themselves as artists. "That great sanity, that sun, the feminine power" will become a reality, Sarton concludes, when women "match men's greatness" with their own art.[46]

Other Sarton poems also describe the woman poet's efforts to "re-join the source," to assert a vital female voice. This struggle provides the underlying dialectic of "Poets and the Rain," which addresses the problem of poetic stasis and subsequent rejuvenation. In the first stanza, the poet-persona is debilitated by the rain, which reflects her own inertia and despair; she speaks not as an active creator but as a passive receptacle for the words of others. "I will lie here alone and live your griefs," she declares. "I will receive you, passive and devout." Yet, as she offers such disclaimers, the poet's creativity stirs, faint but intelligible. Plagued by "strange tides" in her head, she distinguishes three voices, each of which offers a different vision of life and art.

The first singer, an old man, "looks out and taunts the world, sick of mankind," his voice "shriller than all the rest." In an interesting reversal of a stereotype, Sarton associates shrillness not with a hysterical female voice but with a male cry of pessimism and derision. Although part of her sympathizes with this doomsday prophet, she ultimately rejects the model that he offers. She will "dream a hunting song to make the old hawk scream," but she will not adopt such a voice herself. Contrasted to this male voice are two female speakers whose visions, when combined, posit for the poet a more balanced and optimistic stance. The first woman represents the traditional female voice, that of nurturer, comforter, inspirer.

> Here is the woman, frustrate and most pure,
> Who builds a nest of blessings and there sits
> Singing the lighted tree and the dark stone
> (Many times to this woman I have come),
> Who bids us meditate and use our wits
> And we shall, with the help of love, endure—

Comforted by the love that this woman's song exudes, the poet herself is inspired to become a voice of feminine wisdom and maternal love. This choice, however, is not enough for the creative woman: the singer is "frustrate"; her purity and nest building are passive postures. Despite her connection to traditional female arts, or perhaps because of it, this woman's song is too simple and static a model for the poet.

The speaker is most moved by the "blurred" yet potent voice of a "great girl, the violent and strong,"

> Who walks accompanied by dreams and visions,
> Speaks with the blurred voice of a giant sleeping
> And wakes to hear the foreign children weeping
> And sees the crystal crack, the fierce divisions,
> Asking deep questions in her difficult song.[47]

This description recalls Denise Levertov's celebration in "In Mind" of a "turbulent moon-ridden girl . . . who knows strange songs," or Louise

Bogan's "The Dream," in which a "strong creature ... another woman" leaps and shouts until her passive counterpart is prodded into life-saving speech and action.[48] In Sarton's poem, the great girl's "deep questions" and "difficult song," her fierce commitment to her art and her beliefs, offer the questing poet her most inspirational model. Although she realizes the difficulties of such a vision, the persona determines that her voice, like the girl's, must emerge from an emotional and intellectual complex, a "labyrinth of mind."

> A sudden sweep of raindrops from the cloud,
> I stand, rapt with delight, though deaf and blind,
>
> And speak my poem now, leaves of a tree
> Whose roots are hidden deep in mystery.[49]

In rejecting stasis for dynamic song, the poet celebrates the complexity of her own imagination, its ability both to merge with nature and to transform it. Significantly, however, the speaker's celebration is not without its price, nor is her choice without ambivalence, for she is rendered deaf and blind in the wake of her song. She is able to sing, but she must acknowledge her impediments even as she asserts her newly found voice.

The special danger inherent in the woman poet's effort to "speak aloud," to re-vision as her own the "masculine and violent joy of pure creation," is also the subject of "Journey toward Poetry." The poet's structuring of her imaginative experience, Sarton suggests, is analogous to a dangerous journey across foreign yet somehow familiar terrain, a haunting interior picaresque that ultimately produces the ideal word or image or perspective for the chary traveler. For Sarton, such a psychic voyage usually begins in chaos, concentrated violence.

> First that beautiful mad exploration
> Through a multiple legend of landscape
> When all roads open and then close again
> Behind a car that rushes toward escape,
> The mind shot out across foreign borders
> To visionary and abrupt disorders.

An array of intensely surrealistic images accompanies such "mad exploration": hills winding and unwinding on a spool; rivers running away from their beds; a geranium bursting open to reveal a "huge blood-red cathedral";

"marble graveyards" falling into the sea. One is reminded of Yeats's "blood-dimmed tide": "the center cannot hold," Sarton implies, when the imagination runs unchecked.

Yet the center does hold. Once the poet's errant imagination is stayed, her inner landscapes soften, become pastoral. From disorder, to paraphrase Wallace Stevens, emerges a violent order.

> After the mad beautiful racing is done,
> To be still, to be silent, to stand by a window
> Where time not motion changes light to shadow,
> Is to be present at the birth of creation.[50]

Reconstructing her universe from a position of silence and stasis, the poet transforms mundane objects—"the field of wheat, the telephone pole"—into something altogether new. In Hilary Stevens's words, "intensity commands form."[51] "Journey toward Poetry" serves as Sarton's metaphoric depiction of the poetic process, fraught with danger for any poet but intensely so for the woman. Beginning in rage or anxiety, at "white heat," the poet's "beautiful mad racing" ultimately gives way to that fruitful ripening of image and idea that informs "the birth of creation."

Central to the creative process for Sarton is the female muse, perceived by the poet as "always a question . . . what sets up the dialogue" with oneself.[52] As the pivotal force upon which poetry centers, the muse, like the protean poet, wears multiple masks. Sarton is especially vocal about the inspirational power of the muse as lover: "You learn a lot from the person you love. I'm talking about women mostly. That's the whole thing for me. Women have been the muse, and it's the more aggressive side of me which falls in love with women. I feel more able to write and more myself than I do at any other time." During relationships with men, Sarton continues, she felt drained of creative energy. "With a woman, on the contrary, I felt very excited, wrote poems, you see. And that is the only way I can judge."[53]

In her poetry, this erotic manifestation of the muse appears sometimes as a human lover-visitant, sometimes as a goddess or mythological woman. One recurring figure is Aphrodite, the Greek goddess of love and sexuality, who also is linked to such ancient Eastern mother-goddesses as Ishtar, Isis, and Astarte.[54] Because the goddess's powers are both matriarchal and sexual, Sarton often envisions Aphrodite as a primordial figure of fecundity. Such a goddess is found in "These Images Remain," an early sonnet sequence in which the poet confronts the sexual tension at the heart of the poet-muse relationship. As the epitome of female beauty and eroticism, Aphrodite inspires the poet to become free and fertile.

> And you are here at last, and you are free
> To stand like Aphrodite on her shell,
> Wrapped in the wind, the net of nerves undone,
> So piercingly alive and beautiful,
> Her breasts are eyes. She opens in the sun
> And sees herself reflected in the sand
> When the great wave has left her naked there,
> And looks at her own feet and her own hand
> As on strange flowers and on her golden hair
> As on some treasure given by the seas
> To one who holds the earth between her knees.

Yet this "silent consummation" between poet and muse is as precarious as quicksand, Sarton suggests in the fifth sonnet; any union with Aphrodite must be transitory, fleeting. She images herself as a male sculptor whose creation grows "out of deprivation . . . / out of a self-denying rage," inspired by intense longing and frustration. "He gladly yields for the sake of those lips," Sarton says of the sculptor-poet, "That savage throat that opens the whole chest, / Tension so great between him and the stone, / It seems he carries vengeance in his wrist." The poet can never possess the muse, Sarton realizes, but the effort to possess results in the sculptor's images, "great and severe." From the encounter between poet and muse, from "difficult love," comes a lasting art.[55]

Though the poet is periodically estranged from her muse, such separation is rarely long-lived. "The Muse is never wholly absent," Hilary Stevens explains to Peter and Jenny, discussing her own rejuvenation after writer's block. "One must at least glimpse the hem of her garment, as she vanishes into her radiant air."[56] In "The Return of Aphrodite," Sarton describes a re-encounter with the muse.

> From deep she rises, poised upon her shell.
> Oh guiltless Aphrodite so long absent!
> The green waves part. There is no sound at all
> As she advances, tranquil and transparent,
> To lay on mortal flesh her sacred mantle.
>
> The wave recedes—she is drawn back again
> Into the ocean where light leaves a stain.[57]

Transparency is central to Sarton's muse as an extension of the self, the
Medusa through whom one can gaze upon oneself. Unlike the poet's
confrontation with Medusa, however, her exchange with Aphrodite is
depicted in images of silence and tranquility, pure light rather than white
heat. Sarton's imagery is also richly erotic: as the mortal poet receives
the goddess's "sacred mantle," the "green waves part," receding at once
after the sacred consummation and leaving in their wake a faint "stain"
of light.

The erotic muse appears as devouring in "A Divorce of Lovers,"
a sonnet sequence on the poet's efforts to restore her lapsed poetic powers
after a devastating love affair. In *World of Light*, Sarton explains that
these poems were written "in batches" during an extremely high fever;
and her subsequent discussion of the muse as "a woman who focuses
the world for me," whether in a pleasant or a painful way, suggests a
connection between the lover in the poems and the muse. The lovers
here are imagined as "two warring halves . . . cut in two," wounded
perhaps beyond repair. In an effort to heal her wounds, the poet invokes the "surgeon," Reason, doubting all the while that this "doctor"
has the power to rejuvenate her poetic energies: "We shall see / How
Reason operates on Poetry." As the surgeon wields the scalpel, images
of destruction dominate: "Old Fate" snapping the threads of life and
love; a flower dying, cut at full bloom. As her wounds heal, however,
the poet numbs to pain and feels, instead, the disorientation of a "blun-
dering bird," a "baffled wanderer" on a "lost journey . . . out of this
wilderness."

Eventually, the poet realizes that the loss of the lover can be endured;
it is the loss of creativity that must be challenged. To "force Fate at a
crucial pass," she invokes solitude as a healing balm: "Where these words
end, let solitude begin."[58] Like Louise Bogan, Sarton recognizes that harsh
words and cacophonous music must give way to an interim silence before
the creative voice can be restored to its full resonance.[59] In Sonnet 17 she
celebrates silence as a companion.

> As thoughts like clouds traverse my human eyes,
> Silence opens the world that I explore:
> Mozartian gaiety, the lightest presence,
> At last I welcome back my wandering soul
> Into these regions of strange transcendence,
> And find myself again, alive and whole.[60]

The re-integration of the self and the restoration of the poet's creative power are made possible, Sarton suggests, by a "turning back upon the self" that illuminates and indeed transforms both self and world.

Sarton's image of the muse as the beloved is especially prominent in the title sequence of *Letters from Maine*. The poet's "November Muse" is not the fierce, angry lover of her youth; rather, she gives "wisdom and laughter, also clarity." Even when the muse is absent, the speaker declares in the third poem, "I am floated on her presence, / Her strong reality, swung out above / Everything else that happens." But the erotic muse in these poems is also spiritual, an "Old Woman" who, according to a legend of the Nootka Indian tribe, is a "Primal Spirit, one with rock and wave."

> Old Woman I meet you deep inside myself.
> There in the rootbed of fertility,
> World without end, as the legend tells it,
> Under the words you are my silence.

The impact of this inspirational source becomes poignantly clear when the muse rejects the poet. Without inspiration, Sarton explains, "nothing can be said." Ultimately, however, the creative impulse perseveres, as the poet transforms painful experience into a lyrical and analytical assessment of the erotic muse's function.

> When the muse appears after long absence
> Everything stops except the poem. It rises
> In an unbroken wave and topples to silence.
> There is no way to make it happen by will.
> No muse appears when invoked, dire need
> Will not raise her pity.
>   She comes when she can,
> She too, no doubt, rising from the sea
> Like Aphrodite on her shell when it is time,
> When the impersonal tide bears her to the shore
> To play a difficult role she has not chosen,
> To free a prisoner she has no reason to love.
>
> What power is at work, then, what key
> Opens the door into these mysteries?[61]

The muse for Sarton also appears as a demonic force, a fury with whom the poet must come to terms in order to maintain creative energy. "Every visitation of the Muse is disturbing," Hilary Stevens declares, unsettling because it evokes such a conflicting array of responses: love and joy, guilt and rage. This ambivalence toward one's inspirational source is not new; women poets from Emily Dickinson to Emily Brontë to Louise Bogan have viewed their muse as a hostile force, sometimes male, sometimes female, frequently demonic. The poet, of course, is pitted against this muse in a fierce struggle for power. Sarton's demonic muse resembles Brontë's and Dickinson's in the tension it evokes, but, like Bogan and other modern women poets, Sarton envisions her muse as a female shadow rather than a male Other. Rebellious but potent, this muse stimulates the poet's creative energy but also arouses feelings of anger, shame, and ambivalence. "The deep collision is and has been with my unregenerate, tormenting, and tormented self," Hilary Stevens admits. "Women are afraid of their daemon," she continues, "want to . . . make it sensible like themselves."[62] Sarton realizes, however, that one's demons cannot and should not be "made sensible." Instead, they should be acknowledged and re-visioned as a source of vital energy, creative rage.

The muse as a fury out for vengeance and retribution appears frequently in poems on the demise of a relationship and the subsequent loss of creative energy. In the fourth sonnet of "A Divorce of Lovers," for example, Sarton accuses her lover of "chasing out the furies and the plagues of passion" rather than attempting to come to terms with them.

> My guess is that the weapon's name was Pride.
> It is a word the Furies understand;
> Their ghosts are gathering on every side,
> And they will raise the hair upon your hand.[63]

In awe of the monsters who plague her, the poet nonetheless needs such "ghosts" if they can be re-visioned. When angels and furies "fly so near," she explains, "they come to force Fate at a crucial pass."[64] This forcing of Fate, in turn, opens up a crucial dialogue with the self that ultimately transforms the poet's violence into creative energy. "Have done, poor beast," Sarton exhorts her fury. "I have come back into my world of no one . . . / And I am nourished here after the famine."[65]

In "The Furies," the poet explores the difficulties in reconciling herself to her demonic aspects. Here Sarton proffers a central psychological and aesthetic question: "How then to recognize / The hard unseeing eyes, /

Or woman tell from ghost?" The woman poet's furies are "almost" human, Sarton explains—"almost, and yet not quite." The danger inherent in one's furies lies in their capacity to strip the poet of her energy and wits, to "wrap you in glamor cold, / Warm you with fairy gold, / Till you grow fond and lazy, / Witty, perverse, and crazy." Only after coming to terms with the risks one takes as a creator, Sarton concludes, "can one drink [the Furies'] health . . . / And call the Furies kind."[66]

In this poem, Sarton looks ironically at the problems she faces in confronting her demons. Yet, despite her effort to distance through irony, her fear of the Furies is great. "Never look straight at one," she warns the reader, "for then your self is gone." At other times, however, she asserts the creative woman's need to confront these furious forces, admitting their power and thus claiming it as her own. Such is the theme of "A Storm of Angels."

> Anarchic anger came to beat us down,
> Until from all that battering we went numb
> Like ravaged trees after a hurricane.
> But in its wake we saw fierce angels come—
> Not gentle and not kind—who threshed the grain
> With their harsh wings, winnowed from waste.

Despite their harshness, these angels are rejuvenating rather than debilitating, for they come "as messengers of a true power denied." The angels "beat down" the poet, strip her of her pride, bring her agony, yet this energizing agony sets the poet free. It is a gift from the furies to their selected instrument: "Theirs is an act of grace, and it is given / To those in Hell who can imagine Heaven."[67]

Often Sarton replaces angels and furies with animals, demonic forces that must be re-visioned. In "Control," for example, the poet argues against any attempt to deny the tiger within. In restraining such a beast, Sarton explains, one exercises a heady power at great expense, for destroying the tiger's vitality also negates an essential part of the self.

> You may have complete control.
> There will be no roar or growl.
> But can you look into those eyes
> Where the smothered fire lies?[68]

If the tiger's "fire" is "smothered," Sarton concludes, the poet risks cooling the white heat that generates good poetry.

Yet Sarton is not always comfortable with the demonic part of the self. In "After the Tiger," her ambivalence toward the monster within surfaces as she alternately affirms and laments this psychic conflict. When "the tiger, violence, takes the human throat," the speaker first rejoices, "glad of the blood, glad of the lust," because "that tiger strength—oh it is beautiful!" Much of the tiger's demonic beauty lies in its purity of form, its awesome presence. "It is all success," she says of the tiger's strength. "It feels like a glorious creation." In subsequent stanzas, however, Sarton's ambivalence toward the tiger's brute strength surfaces, as she wonders what should be done with this passionate animal. After all, such wild release—however euphoric—is ultimately unsettling. "Who was a tiger once" becomes then "weak and small, / And terribly unfit for all he has to do." The poet wonders "who is a friend here, who an enemy," for the wounds that the "ghostly tiger" inflicts "sometimes do not heal for centuries." Peace after violence is possible, Sarton posits tentatively, but only if the "peacemaker" has the patience and courage to reconstruct bit by bit what the raging tiger has torn down.

> After the tiger we become frail and human
> The dust of ruins acrid in the throat.
> Oh brothers, take it as an absolution
> That we must work so slowly toward hope![69]

This poem makes an interesting companion to Bogan's "The Sleeping Fury," in which the "tiger" is a shrieking maenad who wreaks terror through the night. In both poems this fury, an aspect of the self, must "sleep off madness" after unleashed violence. Both furies are perceived as benevolent-malevolent forces: Sarton's tiger is "enemy" and "friend"; Bogan's fury is "my scourge, my sister." But, while Bogan finds strength and sustenance through her encounter with the fury, Sarton remains shaken: "After the violence peace does not rise / Like a forgiving sun to wash all clean." For Sarton, who claims to write from her aggressive, masculine side, the violent forces that clash in "After the Tiger" are depicted here as male: the tiger is a "god"; the poet in whom the tiger resides, "he"; the audience whom the poet addresses, "brothers." Bogan's "scourge," in contrast, is at once a "sister," a crucial same-sex figure more comprehensible to the woman poet. Sarton here is overwhelmed by the masculine fury. She is "frail and human," ambivalent toward the tiger's powers and unconvinced of her own. Bogan, on the other hand, concludes on a more confident note, having transformed her fury's destructive rage into creative energy: "Alone and strong in my peace, I look upon you in yours."[70]

When Sarton perceives her demonic counterpart as a female shadow rather than a male Other, however, she often experiences a creative impetus similar to that which Bogan wrests from her sleeping fury. In "The Godhead as Lynx," for instance, the poet gleans nourishment from the beautiful yet cold mother-lynx.

> Kyrie Eleison, O wild lynx!
> Mysterious sad eyes, and yet so bright,
> Wherein mind never grieves or thinks,
> But absolute attention is alight—
> Before that golden gaze, so deep and cold,
> My human rage dissolves, my pride is broken.

Sarton often uses face-to-face confrontation to dramatize the dialogue between poet and demonic muse; here the speaker, though but a "child," nonetheless challenges the lynx by meeting her "obsidian" eyes. Rather than fearing confrontation and dreading its aftermath, the speaker undertakes it on her own terms.

She goes on to envision the lynx as a "prehuman" maternal goddess into whose womb the poet-daughter is tempted to crawl.

> I feel a longing for the lynx's bed,
> To submerge self in that essential fur,
> And sleep close to this ancient world of grace,
> As if there could be healing next to her,
> The mother-lynx in her prehuman place.
> Yet that pure beauty does not know compassion—
> O cruel god, Kyrie Eleison!

Like ancient goddesses, the lynx is linked to both creation and destruction. Despite her "essential fur," her maternal comfort, she "does not know compassion"; and she is "cruel . . . / lightning to cut down the lamb, / A beauty that devours without qualm." Beneficent and demonic, therefore, the lynx offers the poet both a model and a means of self-possession and self-affirmation. As "a cruel god who only says 'I am,'" the lynx represents unharnessed male power in female flesh; thus, her splendor and unusual force awaken the poet's own strength. Through her encounter with the godhead as lynx, the poet becomes a "laboring self who groans and thinks."[71]

The demonic muse whom Sarton most often invokes is Medusa, the mythological monster whose hair writhed with serpents, whose glance turned men to stone. Because she could be viewed only indirectly and because of the mystery and danger associated with her powers, she suggests the woman poet's struggle *with* herself *for* herself. In "The Muse as Medusa," Sarton describes an encounter with this "fury" and her effort to re-vision the potent and dynamic relationship between poet and muse. In contrast to the speaker's ironic advice in "The Furies"—"never look straight at one, / For then your self is gone"—Sarton here meets Medusa as she has met the lynx: one on one, "straight in the cold eye, cold." Despite her "nakedness" and vulnerability, the poet transforms the legendary monster from a debilitating force to a source of creative rejuvenation.

> I came as naked as any little fish,
> Prepared to be hooked, gutted, caught;
> But I saw you, Medusa, made my wish,
> And when I left you I was clothed in thought . . .

Medusa's stony gaze does not destroy; it transfigures, "clothing" the naked speaker in the warm protective garment of perception. "Forget the image," Sarton exults, for this Medusa renews through her silent but vital presence: "Your silence is my ocean, / And even now it teems with life."

Yet Medusa herself is not responsible for this teeming life; it continues in spite of, rather than because of, her presence. Medusa, after all, "chose / To abdicate by total lack of motion," and abdicating is something the speaker refuses to do. Instead, Sarton creates a dynamic, fluid seascape of which this fury can become a part, her destructive rage used rather than denied. In re-visioning Medusa "in her own image," the poet acknowledges a vital female creativity and affirms the demonic part of herself: "I turn your face around! It is my face."[72] This final statement echoes Hilary Stevens's response to Dorothea: "she was once more in the presence of the Muse, the crucial one, the Medusa who had made her understand that if you turn Medusa's face around, it is your own face."[73] Sarton is eager to examine the causes of her pain, to heal herself, to speak out. In revising Medusa as a source of creative energy, she paradoxically affirms and challenges another of Hilary Stevens's assertions: "we are all monsters, if it comes to that, we women who have chosen to be something more and something less than women."[74]

The third aspect of the muse that Sarton explores in both *Mrs. Stevens* and her poetry is the mother as inspirational source. At times the mother appears as a potent demonic figure, as in "The Godhead as Lynx." In several poems, however, Sarton celebrates female fecundity and maternity without demonic trappings, invoking as muse a beneficent mother figure who inspires the woman poet through her greater widsom. In an early poem, "She Shall Be Called Woman," for example, the poet celebrates one of her most maligned yet potent foremothers, the biblical Eve, as a symbol of maternal fecundity and sexual and spiritual rejuvenation. Stripped of the demonic associations accorded her by patriarchal culture and religion, Sarton's Eve is re-visioned as an Ur-mother, created initially by God but recreated by herself, out of her own energy and will. Sarton's chronicle omits the Genesis 2 creation scene and instead describes Eve's first faint murmurs of self-identity, ironically coincidental with her initial sexual encounter. Although "she did not cry out / nor move. / She lay quite still," Eve, like Lilith before her, is nonetheless frightened and angered.

> She could not yet endure
> this delicate savage
> to lie upon her.
> She could not yet endure
> the blood to beat so there.
> She could not cope
> with the first ache
> of fullness.

In a radical re-vision of the Genesis myth, Sarton has Eve, "disrupted at the center / and torn," leave Eden and seek refuge in the maternal womb of the sea: "And she went into the sea / because her core ached / and there was no healing."

As with the muse as Medusa, however, so with Eve: "not in denial, her peace." Through her solitary journey into feminine consciousness, Eve learns not to deny her sexuality and creativity but to claim them as sources of power. She begins to derive pleasure and confidence from her physical self.

> She was aware
> down to extremity
> of how herself was charged,
> fiber electric,
> a hand under her breast

could hear the dynamo.

.   .   .   .

Nothing ever was
as wonderful as this.

In exploring her own body, Eve "clothes herself" with a female garment
of sexuality, fecundity, and power. "She would not ever be naked / again,"
the poet insists. As "the core of life," Eve casts off the vulnerability and
powerlessness that Genesis 2 portrays as woman's lot. Instead, she gives
birth "out of the infinite" to an autonomous entity: "'I am the beginning,
/ the never-ending, / the perfect tree.'" To depict Eve's birthing of the
female self Sarton uses menstruation as a metaphor.

There were seeds
within her
that burst at intervals
and for a little while
she would come back
to heaviness,
and then before a surging miracle
of blood,
relax,
and reidentify herself,
each time more closely
with the heart of life.[75]

As Eve the foremother reidentifies herself through her menstrual cycle, she
connects "more closely / with the heart of life." So, Sarton implies, must
Eve's daughter, the woman poet, rejuvenate herself through her resurgent
creativity.

The woman poet's need to become a mother to herself and her art can
be seen in a poem about Sarton's own mother, Mabel Elwes Sarton. "An
Observation" was, by the poet's own admission, very difficult to write.
But a persistent image of her mother, at work in her garden with "a rough
sensitivity," finally metamorphosed into a poetic tribute.

True gardeners cannot bear a glove
Between the sure touch and the tender root,
Must let their hands grow knotted as they move
With a rough sensitivity about

Under the earth, between the rock and shoot,
Never to bruise or wound the hidden fruit.
And so I watched my mother's hands grow scarred,
She who could heal the wounded plant or friend
With the same vulnerable yet rigorous love;
I minded once to see her beauty gnarled,
But now her truth is given me to live,
As I learn for myself we must be hard
To move among the tender with an open hand,
And to stay sensitive up to the end
Pay with some toughness for a gentle world.[76]

As inheritor of her mother's healing powers, Sarton received a crucial "truth": vulnerability must be accompanied by rigor, tenderness by toughness, else the plant, the delicate and valuable creation, is unlikely to grow. "You must remain vulnerable and tough," Sarton explained during a reading of this poem, "or else you'll die of it."[77] Vulnerability, growth, balance—the heritage that the mother-muse bequeaths the daughter-poet.

In one of her most provocative poems about female inspiration, "The Invocation to Kali," Sarton depicts the muse as both demon and mother, confronting what Hilary Stevens calls "the full motherhood, the full monsterhood" of those who try to be "something more and something less than woman."[78] By celebrating Kali as muse, Sarton affirms the close link that she perceives among demonic rage, maternal love, and female creativity. The poem opens with an epigraph from Joseph Campbell's *The Masks of God*, a description of "the Black Goddess Kali, the terrible one of many names, 'difficult of approach,' whose stomach is a void and so can never be filled, and whose womb is giving birth forever to all things." As this passage suggests, many of Kali's traits parallel those that numerous cultures have assigned to "evil" goddesses. She is elusive, loath to be controlled by man; she is devouring and insatiable; and she is constantly and oppressively fertile, fecund despite man's efforts to contain her. Like many matriarchal goddesses, therefore, Kali stands for both creation and destruction, life and death, but is usually associated only with the negative pole of this duality. As an aspect of the woman's creative self, Kali is thus both inspiring and threatening. Her dual powers intrigue the poet, yet an identification with Kali evokes shame, anger, and fear—that peculiar blend of self-love and self-loathing of one both trapped and freed by her art.

In section 1, Sarton sets forth this poem's central issue—how best to cope with Kali's demands.

There are times when
I think only of killing
The voracious animal
Who is my perpetual shame,

The violent one
Whose raging demands
Break down peace and shelter
Like a peacock's scream.

There are times when
I think only of how to do away
With this brute power
That cannot be tamed.

I am the cage where poetry
Paces and roars. The beast
Is the god. How murder the god?
How live with the terrible god?

Aware of the capacity for creation that accompanies Kali's power, the poet is nonetheless ambivalent toward this demonic force, for she recognizes also its potential for debilitation and entrapment. What then to do with Kali? the poet wonders. Is she to be murdered or lived with?

Section 2 suggests the futility of any effort to murder the goddess.

The kingdom of Kali is within us deep.
The built-in destroyer, the savage goddess,
Wakes in the dark and takes away our sleep.
She moves through the blood to poison gentleness.

. . . .

How then to set her free or come to terms
With the volcano itself, the fierce power
Erupting injuries, shrieking alarms?
Kali among her skulls must have her hour.[79]

Sarton's imagery of volcanic eruption recalls a comment by H.D. about her art: "A sort of *rigor mortis* drove me onward. No, my poetry was not dead but it was built on or around the crater of an extinct volcano. Not *rigor mortis*. No, No! The vines grow more abundantly on those volcanic slopes."[80] Although Sarton's "volcanic slopes" are far from extinct, she shares H.D.'s certainty that the explosive potential of poetry gives it its vital, living force. If Kali is denied, Sarton suggests, she will continue her bloody reign, and the result will be what H.D. so passionately fears: *"rigor mortis."* But if Kali is faced "open-eyed," her explosive powers will be revealed for what they are: forces necessary if creativity is to flourish. For every act of creation, Sarton insists, is preceded by some kind of destruction.

> Every creation is born out of the dark.
> Every birth is bloody. Something gets torn.
> Kali is there to do her sovereign work
> Or else the living child will be stillborn.

In the next section of "The Invocation to Kali" Sarton expands the image of Kali as a metaphor for the societal violence of the twentieth century. "The Concentration Camps" is packed with gruesome images depicting the horrifying results of humanity's efforts to deny its furies, to pretend that violence does not exist. "Have we managed to fade them out like God?" she asks of the most tragic of Hitler's victims, children. In "having turned away" from the "stench of bones," she continues, we have "tried to smother" fires that desperately need to burn, as vital reminders of what happens when violence is repressed and then unleashed. "What we have pushed aside and tried to bury, / Lives with a staggering thrust we cannot parry," the poet asserts. All of us are guilty, Sarton's indictment implies; refusing to meet our demons is both a cultural and an individual sickness.

In Sarton's view, the only solution to this widespread ailment is "to reckon with Kali for better or worse," to accept her violence as an essential purging force. Thus the poet turns finally to the goddess's sacred altar, offering an invocation to this "terrible one."

> Kali, be with us.
> Violence, destruction, receive our homage.
> Help us to bring darkness into the light,
> To lift out the pain, the anger,
> Where it can be seen for what it is—
> The balance-wheel for our vulnerable, aching love.
> Put the wild hunger where it belongs,
> Within the act of creation,
> Crude power that forges a balance
> Between hate and love.

Help us to be the always hopeful
Gardeners of the spirit
Who know that without darkness
Nothing comes to birth
As without light
Nothing flowers.

Bear the roots in mind,
You, the dark one, Kali,
Awesome power.[81]

In "The Invocation to Kali," Sarton explores the power of the demonic maternal muse, the woman poet's "great devouring enigma" and the
destructive/creative force through whom she must "forge a balance / Between hate and love." As Adrienne Rich has noted, motherhood is a highly
charged metaphor for the woman writer, "the great mesh in which all
human relations are entangled, in which lurk our most elemental assumptions
about love and power."[82] The woman writer, both Sarton and Rich would
argue, inevitably associates her poetic creativity with the female capacity for
giving bloody birth. As we have seen, images of maternal power inform
many of Sarton's tributes to the muse: the erotic Aphrodite "holds the earth
between her knees," taking it in as her lover and bearing it as her child;
the cold Medusa "clothes" her poet-daughter in the comforting wrap of
thought; even the demonic Kali fosters creation, however violent, "out of
the dark." For Sarton, the sexual, demonic, and maternal aspects of the
muse are joint attributes of a single violent yet essential force.

The final poem of *Halfway to Silence,* "Of the Muse," offers a powerful
and moving assessment of Sarton's creative philosophy as it has developed
over fifty years.

There is no poetry in lies
But in crude honesty
There is hope for poetry.
For a long time now
I have been deprived of it
Because of pride,
Would not allow myself
The impossible.
Today I have learned
That to become
A great, cracked,

Wide-open door
Into nowhere
Is wisdom.

When I was young,
I misunderstood
The Muse.
Now I am older and wiser,
I can be glad of her
As one is glad of the light.
We do not thank the light,
But rejoice in what we see
Because of it.
What I see today
Is the snow falling:
All things are made new.[83]

The transformative power of poetry, Sarton continues to claim, emerges from an intense encounter between the woman poet and her female muse, the symbolic source of poetic inspiration and sustenance.

Furthermore, this poem reveals Sarton's emphasis on the link between poetry and honesty, a concern of many contemporary feminist theorists and women poets. "We have been rewarded for lying," Adrienne Rich declares, yet "the unconscious wants truth, as the body does. The complexity and fecundity of dreams come from the complexity and fecundity of the unconscious struggling to fulfill that desire. The complexity and fecundity of poetry comes from the same struggle."[84] Rich's statement might well be Sarton's, so accurately does it describe the theory implicit in "Of the Muse." Struggling to fulfill its desire for truth, the woman poet's "fecund and complex" unconscious, Sarton suggests along with Rich, is awakened to vital insights and potent speech through her dialogue with that muse who is at once the self. Once misunderstood, the muse is now recognized by the aging poet as a force analogous to light. "We do not thank the light," Sarton explains, "but rejoice in what we see / Because of it." What we see is the "crude" but honest power of poetry, its transformative potential. Through the female muse, "all things are made new."[85]

NOTES

This essay is reprinted by permission of the publisher from Mary K. DeShazer, *Inspiring Women: Reimagining the Muse* (New York: Pergamon Press, © 1987 by Pergamon Press. All rights reserved.), pp. 111–35.

1. May Sarton, *Plant Dreaming Deep* (New York: Norton, 1973), 151.

2. May Sarton, "The Autumn Sonnets," in *Collected Poems, 1930–1973* (New York: Norton, 1974), 386.

3. Robert Graves, "In Dedication," prologue to *The White Goddess* (1948; reprint ed., New York: Farrar, Straus and Giroux, 1975), 5.

4. Gary Snyder, quoted in Adrienne Rich, "Poetry, Personality, and Wholeness: A Response to Galway Kinnell," *Field: Contemporary Poetry and Poetics* 7 (Fall 1972): 14.

5. May Sarton, *Mrs. Stevens Hears the Mermaids Singing* (New York: Norton, 1965), 186.

6. May Sarton, "Birthday on the Acropolis," in *Collected Poems*, 251–53.

7. *Mrs. Stevens*, 191.

8. Robert Southey, letter to Charlotte Brontë, March 1837, quoted in Winifred Gérin, *Charlotte Brontë: The Evolution of Genius* (Oxford: Oxford University Press, 1967), 110.

9. *Mrs. Stevens*, 190.

10. *Mrs. Stevens*, 47.

11. Aphra Behn, quoted in Sandra M. Gilbert and Susan Gubar, *The Madwoman in the Attic: The Woman Writer and the Nineteenth-century Literary Imagination* (New Haven: Yale University Press, 1979), 66.

12. *Mrs. Stevens*, 127.

13. Gilbert and Gubar, *Madwoman in the Attic*, 49–50.

14. *Mrs. Stevens*, 77.

15. *Mrs. Stevens*, 190.

16. *World of Light: A Portrait of May Sarton* (Ishtar Films, 1979). In this essay, I use the title *World of Light* to identify the film and to distinguish it from Sarton's collection of biographical sketches, *A World of Light*.

17. May Sarton, *Journal of a Solitude* (New York: Norton, 1973), 40.

18. *World of Light* (Ishtar).

19. *Mrs. Stevens*, 181.

20. *Mrs. Stevens*, 185–86.

21. *Mrs. Stevens*, 154.

22. *Mrs. Stevens*, 83.

23. *Mrs. Stevens*, 147.

24. May Sarton, "The Invocation to Kali," in *Collected Poems*, 316.

25. *Mrs. Stevens*, 193.

26. For a discussion of this mother-daughter link, see Dorothy Dinnerstein, *The Mermaid and the Minotaur: Sexual Arrangements and Human Malaise* (New York: Harper and Row, 1976); Adrienne Rich, *Of Woman Born: Motherhood as Experience and Institution* (New York: Norton, 1976).

27. *Plant Dreaming Deep*, 70.

28. *Journal of a Solitude*, 16.

29. See, for example, Dolores Shelley, "A Conversation with May Sarton," *Women and Literature* 7 (Spring 1979): 33–41.

30. *Mrs. Stevens,* 107.

31. *Mrs. Stevens,* 108.

32. *Mrs. Stevens,* 141.

33. *Mrs. Stevens,* 146.

34. *Mrs. Stevens,* 92.

35. *Mrs. Stevens,* 16.

36. *Mrs. Stevens,* 161–62.

37. *Mrs. Stevens,* 164.

38. *Mrs. Stevens,* 169.

39. *Mrs. Stevens,* 169.

40. *Mrs. Stevens,* 171.

41. *Mrs. Stevens,* 170.

42. *Mrs. Stevens,* 181.

43. *Mrs. Stevens,* 64.

44. *Mrs. Stevens,* 192–93.

45. *Journal of a Solitude,* 12, 55.

46. May Sarton, "My Sisters, O My Sisters," in *Collected Poems,* 74–77.

47. May Sarton, "Poets and the Rain," in *Collected Poems,* 110.

48. Denise Levertov, "In Mind," in *Poems, 1960–1967* (New York: New Directions, 1967), 143; Louise Bogan, "The Dream," in *The Blue Estuaries: Poems, 1923–1968* (New York: Ecco Press, 1977), 103.

49. May Sarton, "Poets and the Rain," in *Collected Poems,* 111.

50. May Sarton, "Journey Toward Poetry," in *Collected Poems,* 151.

51. *Mrs. Stevens,* 151.

52. *Mrs. Stevens,* 185.

53. Shelley, "Interview with Sarton," 38–39.

54. For a discussion of Aphrodite's link to dual-faceted Eastern goddesses, see Erich Neumann, *The Great Mother: An Analysis of the Archetype,* trans. Ralph Manheim (1955; reprint ed., Princeton: Princeton University Press, 1972), 80–81, 273–75.

55. Sarton, "These Images Remain," in *Collected Poems,* 144–47.

56. *Mrs. Stevens,* 153.

57. May Sarton, "The Return of Aphrodite," in *Collected Poems,* 367.

58. May Sarton, "A Divorce of Lovers," in *Collected Poems,* 201–5.

59. See, for example, Bogan's "Poem in Prose," "My Voice Not Being Proud," and "Sub Contra," all in *Blue Estuaries,* 72, 13, and 5, respectively.

60. Sarton, "Divorce of Lovers," 207.

61. May Sarton, *Letters from Maine* (New York: Norton, 1984), 18–27.

62. *Mrs. Stevens,* 92.

63. Sarton, "Divorce of Lovers," 202.

64. Sarton, "Divorce of Lovers," 205.

65. Sarton, "Divorce of Lovers," 207.

66. May Sarton, "Furies," in *Collected Poems*, 162.

67. May Sarton, "A Storm of Angels," in *Collected Poems*, 69.

68. May Sarton, "Control," in *Halfway to Silence* (New York: Norton, 1980), 32.

69. May Sarton, "After the Tiger," in *Collected Poems*, 321–22.

70. Louise Bogan, "The Sleeping Fury," in *Blue Estuaries*, 78–79.

71. May Sarton, "Godhead as Lynx," in *Collected Poems*, 352–53.

72. May Sarton, "The Muse as Medusa," in *Collected Poems*, 332.

73. *Mrs. Stevens*, 161.

74. *Mrs. Stevens*, 155–56.

75. May Sarton, "She Shall Be Called Woman," in *Collected Poems*, 20–26.

76. May Sarton, "An Observation," in *Collected Poems*, 271.

77. Sarton discussed this poem and her difficulties in writing it in a speech entitled "Proteus: The Joys and Hazards of Being a Poet," St. Benedict's College, St. Joseph, Minn., November 24, 1980.

78. *Mrs. Stevens*, 156.

79. May Sarton, "The Invocation to Kali," in *Collected Poems*, 316–17.

80. H.D., *End to Torment* (New York: New Directions, 1979), 35.

81. Sarton, "Invocation to Kali," 316–20.

82. Adrienne Rich, "Motherhood: The Contemporary Emergency and the Quantum Leap," in *On Lies, Secrets, and Silence: Selected Prose, 1966–1978* (New York: Norton, 1979), 260.

83. May Sarton, "Of the Muse," in *Halfway to Silence*, 62.

84. Adrienne Rich, "Women and Honor: Some Notes on Lying," in *On Lies*, 186–88.

85. Sarton, "Of the Muse," 62.

Self and Subtexts

"Seeing with Fresh Eyes": A Study of May Sarton's Journals

Jeanne Braham

At first grudgingly and then enthusiastically, May Sarton has acknowledged the importance of the first five of her journals as one continuous means of telling the story of a human life. Although she insists they are not strict "autobiographies" or "memoirs,"[1] Sarton's journals constitute a form of personal narrative at once sufficiently fragmentary and discontinuous to satisfy poststructuralist ideas about the vagaries of the "self" and sufficiently powerful to link a reader's consciousness to the author's testimony. Each of these journals was composed on the heels of personal crisis, when self-assessment was crucial for restoring emotional balance and spiritual health. *Journal of a Solitude* (1973) marks the end of a powerful love affair; *House By the Sea* (1977) is precipitated by the move from Nelson, New Hampshire, to York, Maine; *Recovering* (1980) emerges from a year of crisis involving cancer, a broken love affair, and frustration over mixed reviews of her work in fiction and poetry; *At Seventy* (1984) records the credits and debits of old age; *After the Stroke* (1988) describes the effects of a stroke suffered shortly before her seventy-fifth birthday. (*Endgame: A Journal of the Seventy-Ninth Year* [1992], was in press when this essay was written.)

Though rooted in idiosyncratic experience, Sarton's journals seek to connect with a wide readership by revealing the need to create order out of chaos, reentry out of withdrawal, health out of illness. Her efforts to define "self" and "values" within a communal context, in part supplied by readers' responses, link her journals to current theory exploring women's autobiography.

In her essay "Women's Autobiographical Selves" (1988), Susan Stanford Friedman argues that the female self is never defined in isolation though often examined in isolated crisis. The female autobiographical self, she contends, "does not oppose herself to all others, does not feel herself to exist outside of others, and still less against others, but very much *with* others in an interdependent existence that asserts its rhythms everywhere in the community."[2] Friedman contrasts these terms of self-definition with those found in the standard male autobiography. Using Georges Gusdorf's well-known essay, "Conditions and Limits of Autobiography" (1956), she says that

> women's autobiography comes alive as a literary tradition of self-creation when we approach its texts from a psycho-political perspective based in the lives of women. Historically, women as a group have never been the "gatherers of men, of lands, of power, makers of kingdoms or of empires." [Gusdorf's autobiographic requisites.] Instead, they have been the gathered, the colonized, the ruled. Seldom the "inventors of laws and of wisdom," they have been born into those inventions—all the more so if their race, religion, class, or sexual preferences also marginalized them. Nonetheless, this historical oppression has not destroyed women's consciousness of self. (55–56)

Other critics, notably Elizabeth Fox-Genovese, Jane Marcus, Nancy K. Miller, and Carolyn Heilbrun, reinforce Friedman's definitions by suggesting that the subject matter of women's life studies fails to dissociate the personal from the public or concrete reality from abstract principle. The female autobiographical self is an expression of a collective enterprise, a "grounding of identity" through linking with "another consciousness."[3]

Jane Marcus identifies that "other consciousness" as the reader's.

> If we agree that the writer resurrects herself through memory, then the reader also resurrects the writer through reading her. This *collaboration* is a reproduction of women's culture as conversation. It does not occur in the male model of individualistic autobiography, where the reader is not expected to take such an active role.[4]

If the story of one woman's life provides a script the reader enters, resignifies, and, in some collaborative sense, makes her own, then contemporary women's personal narratives chart rich new possibilities for the ways women may want to live their lives. As Carolyn Heilbrun has suggested in *Writing a Woman's Life* (1988), artists such as Sarton who speak about aging and death, about homophobia, about the narcissism of the academic and publishing worlds—who create new scripts from the raw data of life experience—free others to imagine original conditions by which they may live. Age and the authority of many books, says Heilbrun, confer a "bravery and power" on their authors, and writers like Sarton (and Heilbrun herself) can exercise that authority by continuing "to take risks, to make noise, to be courageous, to become unpopular."[5]

Striking up "crucial conversations," Sarton engages in a process of collaboration with the reader. In her journals, that process is gradual and cumulative. The initial impulses for keeping a journal were personal, and when passages explaining these motives are juxtaposed, they bear remarkable similarities.

> This journal began a year ago with depression, with much self-questioning about my dangerous and destructive angers, with the hope that self-examination would help me to change. (*Journal of a Solitude*, 206–7)

> I can't stop doing what I have always done, trying to sort out and shape experience. The journal is a good way to do this. . . . I find it wonderful to have a receptacle into which to pour vivid momentary insights, and a way of ordering day-to-day experience. . . . (*House By the Sea*, 27–28)

> I had thought not to begin a new journal until I am seventy, four years from now, but perhaps the time has come to sort myself out, and see whether I can restore a sense of meaning and continuity to my life by this familiar means. (*Recovering*, 9)

> Still, I find that keeping a journal again validates and clarifies. For the hour I manage in the morning at this task I am happy, at ease with myself and the world, even when I am complaining of pressure. (*At Seventy*, 50)

> It may prove impossible because my head feels so queer and the smallest effort, mental or physical, exhausts, but I feel so deprived of my *self* being unable to write, cut off since early January from all that I mean about my life, that I think I must try to write a few lines every day. It is a way of being self-supporting. (*After the Stroke*, 15)

A similarity of method also marks the journals, a method derived perhaps primarily from Sarton's other modes of artistic expression: fiction and poetry. Sarton casts herself as a character in her own story, recreating significant life experience, pondering its shape, discovering its outcome. Much like the novelist who discovers her characters beginning to exert wills of their own, Sarton sets her "plot" in motion, discovering its significance in the retelling. Simultaneously, she deepens "meaning" by concentrating on a few repeated images (home, animals, significant friendships) that function as poetic metaphors shimmering with collective content. Her awareness of audience widens from the reader-over-the-shoulder peepsight of *Journal of a Solitude* to full, front, direct address in *After the Stroke.*

Journal of a Solitude, spanning the year from September 1970 to September 1971, retells the story of her own artistic imprisonment, figured in the claustrophobic enclosure of Nelson. Sarton begins by describing her need to "break through into the rough, rocky depths to the matrix itself" (12). Since she declares she "can think something out only by writing it,"[6] this journal becomes an inspection, largely self-motivated, by which she hopes to understand a failed love affair, a writer's refuge that became a prison, and her subsequent serious depression. The third journal, *Recovering,* conveys a somewhat similar story—failure in love and the physical and psychological consequences of a mastectomy necessitate a "recovery," a way of "renewing acquaintance" with herself. Reader awareness is more evident here, as Sarton speaks of the "audience the journals have created" erupting in an "avalanche of mail" (*Journal of a Solitude,* 32). She also calls this "audience" via the post "a flotilla of letters" and "a welter of mail" (*At Seventy,* 174). Clearly part of what prompts her self-scrutiny is naming the fears that impede the progress of those learning to value themselves again.

House By the Sea, the second journal, and *At Seventy,* the fourth journal, are direct invitations to her audience. Moved by the physical beauty of York, Maine, and of her house at Wild Knoll, Sarton captures moments, "essences" as she calls them, that link landscape with consciousness. As Sarton explores the cycle of the seasons, the reader is invited to ponder growth and death. As Sarton records the antics of her birds, squirrels, "wild cats," and Sheltie dog, the reader examines loyalty, dependence, and what Maxine Kumin calls "the touching trust of the creatures, since they are without guile."[7] Sarton struggles with a censor who sits on the shoulder of all who write with the expectation of publication, insisting that honesty is the only path to what she calls "the bedrock of truth" (*Journal of a Solitude,* 150).

Forgiveness cannot be achieved without understanding, and understanding means painful honesty first of all, and then the ability to detach oneself and look hard, without self-pity, at the cause for violent behavior. (*At Seventy,* 196)

When Sarton reveals Judy Matlack's slow deterioration from Alzheimer's disease, the devastating nature of her personal loss not only reaches the reader, but also broadens into a parable of the loss of loved ones to disease or old age.

Consciousness of a large, responsive readership is clearest in *After the Stroke,* written "to help readers do what I could not do" (16). A large number of the entries record stages of mental and physical recovery. Others surge up "on the tide of memory" (*After the Stroke,* 15) to flood her with old griefs, scores not yet settled, intensities not yet relieved. Of these, the story of her fellow poet and friend Louise Bogan's devaluation of her poetry continues to rankle. Sarton struggles between conflicting needs to set the record straight and to exonerate herself. She seems at the mercy of replaying what Bogan actually thought, how it was reported, how it is misreported in a current biography, even though Bogan is long dead and the disputed episode in the distant past. Memory engulfs, with its old baggage, and Sarton is honest enough to record it, even angry enough to rebut it: "the wounds, I suppose, teach—force one to resolve, to surmount, to transcend" (*After the Stroke,* 231).

If Sarton's journals fashion an identity the reader can resignify by entering the landscape of a life as it is lived, so they also confer perspective on the process of value formation. Reading all five journals reveals an epistemology of growth, of authority, and of spiritual receptivity. Taken together, the journals create a reciprocal "context," for not only does each serve as a "revision" of its predecessor, it also extends and deepens the significance, creating a richer soil in which insight may grow. In *Women's Ways of Knowing* (1986), Belenky et al. call such referential building of character "constructed knowledge."

Most constructivist women actively reflect on how their judgments, attitudes, and behavior coalesce into some internal experience of moral consistency. More than any other group, they are seriously preoccupied with the moral or spiritual dimension of their lives. Further, they strive to translate their moral commitments into action, both out of the conviction that "one must act" and out of a feeling of responsibility to the larger community in which they live.[8]

As Carol Gilligan points out in *In a Different Voice: Psychological Theory and Women's Development* (1982), women solve problems and make value judgments not by arranging a hierarchy of logical principles and choosing one (as males do), but by endeavoring to reconstruct context, to see each participant's motive, need, or fear in relation to the whole. A "moral way of knowing" for women involves sorting and understanding relationships among people and ideas, crediting each affiliation with full authority; as Gilligan puts it, "theirs is a crisis of inclusion" (160). Seen in this light, Sarton's assessments of her own behavior create "context" for a "self," a self not autonomous, but enmeshed in and defined by others. Values are determined by contrapuntal assessments, each journal commenting on the next. As the journals progress, the text becomes what Rachel Blau DuPlessis calls "a form of intimacy . . . conversations with the reader."[9] As Sarton arrives at an insight worked and reworked through the fabric of a reconstructed life, so does the reader "caught and connected" by "sensitivity to situation and context."[10]

A revision of life is precisely what triggers *Journal of a Solitude*. It is written, Sarton suggests, in part to correct an earlier rendering of her Nelson experience in the memoir *Plant Dreaming Deep*. Published in 1968, *Plant Dreaming Deep* tells the story of a woman who, at forty-five, takes the risk of buying, renovating, and deciding to live alone in a house geographically and emotionally removed from friends and the artistic community of Cambridge. The tale is a triumphant one, the story of a great adventure that succeeds. Omitted are accounts of the destructive forces Sarton meets en route: a literary agent who fears the candor of her lesbian novel, a wrongheaded review of her selected poems, the grinding loneliness of geographic isolation, the first awareness of physical deterioration. *Journal of a Solitude* revises that earlier "script," retelling both the Nelson story and the story of Sarton's subsequent life with rage, isolation, and depression factored in.

When one chooses solitude as a condition of life, "there is nothing to *cushion* against attacks from within, just as there is nothing to help balance at times of particular stress or depression" (*Journal of a Solitude*, 16). Keeping a daily record allows Sarton to stitch emotional fragments into a pattern, one that reduces the emotional vulnerability of the moment. *Journal of a Solitude* also corrects the "myth of a false Paradise" (176) perpetrated in *Plant Dreaming Deep*. The house in Nelson that had begun as a refuge for the artist who wanted to withdraw from the clutter and demands of her life in Boston, becomes in "revision" a trap, a place of "anguish and unrest."[11]

Home is a metaphor in all of Sarton's writing, so her move from an inland village house in New Hampshire to a spacious, rambling house on the coast of Maine is crucial. "Wild Knoll" in York, with its magnificent grassy path to the sea, pulls the writer's focus outward. New geographical space has its parallel in new interior space. Solitude and companionship become a condition analogous to the ebbs and flows of the tides, and identity and values emerge from connection rather than withdrawal: "one does not 'find oneself' by pursuing one's self, but on the contrary by pursuing something else and learning through some discipline or routine . . . who one is and wants to be" (*House by the Sea*, 180).

In York, Sarton begins the reciprocal explorations common to her next three journals: what connections and what separations are healthy for the artist to maintain; how one preserves the "primary intensity"[12] necessary for art while meeting obligations to friends, neighbors, and the large literary and intellectual community responding to the work; how one maintains self-reliance and yet acknowledges the fears attendant on old age, physical deterioration, and flagging energy.

In *Recovering* (1980), *At Seventy* (1984), and *After the Stroke* (1988), the writer's relationship to her "home" is still at the vital center, but fear is recognized, weighed, and credited with its proportional cost. And, frequently, the ritual of writing in the journal is a tool for recovery, providing, as it does, the discipline necessary for renewed concentration and perspective. *Recovering* charts Sarton's physical and emotional battles with the effects of a mastectomy, the scars of a lost love affair, and the imbalance caused by a scathing and wrongheaded review of her novel, *A Reckoning*.

At Seventy balances the anxieties of old age (an irregular heart beat, a cancer scare, the death of "dearest love" Judy Matlack) with the celebrations of growing into age and its rewards: a huge and appreciative audience, excellent book sales, and the financial security to support worthy friends and projects she deeply believes in. In this journal, May Sarton's most vital values resonate: balance, commitment, connection. As the journal opens, she assesses seventy years of life experience.

> If someone else had lived so long and could remember things sixty years ago with great clarity, she would seem very old to me. But I do not feel old at all, not as much a survivor as a person still on her way. (*At Seventy*, 1–2)

As the account of a person in progress, the journal alternates between recollections of the past—the Julian Huxleys, the Woolfs, Bowen, Basil de Selincourt—to stories of currently valued friends like "Archie" MacLeish. Past and present connect to give Sarton affiliation with emotional peers.

Similarly, world politics and personal ethics interpenetrate: a comment on Reagan becomes an illustration of the sort of derivative personality and insincerity Sarton despises: "There never is any depth in [his] perceptions of the world. He behaves like an animated cartoon, wound up to perform futile gestures and careless witticisms" (*At Seventy*, 21).

Surely much of what Sarton knows about attachment comes from her relationship with Judy Matlack, always a presence in earlier journals but fully fashioned in *At Seventy*. Judy first appears in a wheelchair, the victim of Alzheimer's disease, reduced to a baby "for whom food is the only real pleasure" (*At Seventy*, 147). Although Sarton visits her in a nursing home in Concord and bravely arranges short trips for her to York, most visits carry a high price.

Only after her death, when Judy begins to live again, can Sarton remember.

—Judy was the precious only love with whom I lived for years . . . only Judy gave me a home and made me know what home can be. She was the dear companion for fifteen years, years when I was struggling as a writer. We were poor then. . . . But strangely enough I look back on those years as the happiest ones. And that is because there was a "we." (*At Seventy*, 213)

Although Judy is the primary example of a "we," Sarton's inventory of her life is packed with "connections." Friends of her youth, visiting artists, Mr. Webster (who fixes the pipes), Eleanor Perkins (who cleans the house), Nancy (who makes order out of the chaos of the files), and Sister Lucy (who plows and builds at the commune H.O.M.E. in rural Orland, Maine) crowd the pages. In *At Seventy*, Sarton clearly acknowledges the growing community of readers who buy and read her work, queue up for book signings, send her pounds of mail monthly, and turn out in staggering numbers at her readings. This community of response leads her to write, "the answer is not detachment as I used to believe but rather to be more deeply involved—to be attached" (*At Seventy*, 12). The "self" in *At Seventy* is defined by connection to others, and values become luminous in "the company of others attended by love."[13]

After the Stroke, a darker record than *At Seventy*, records not only the effects of a stroke Sarton suffered shortly before her seventy-fifth birthday but also the more incapacitating side effects of a fibrillating heart and diverticulitis, conditions that complicate and delay recovery time. The journal chronicles nine months of excruciating pain, of the anxiety that builds when one cannot depend on ever feeling wholly well, of the grief that wells up when Tamas—the Sheltie she brought to York fifteen years earlier—dies, and Bramble—the "last of the wild cats tamed at Nelson"—must be put to sleep. It is as if the sustaining metaphors of home and family have deserted her and the most vital ingredient, the concentration that solitude provides, has been replaced by grinding loneliness.

Difficult as these entries are to read, they form a convincing case study for those struggling with life-threatening illness. She documents the particular terror of memory loss, memory she acknowledges as so vital to the writer, and the special fear of losing the ability to make connections and critical judgments—a deterioration Sarton saw at close range in Judy's long bout with senility. She also records the more universal fears of the old or the infirm, prisoners in their own deteriorating bodies, at the mercy of their own thoughts and feelings.

> . . . I lie around most of the afternoon, am in bed by eight, and there in my bed alone the past rises like a tide, over and over, to swamp me with memories I cannot handle. (*After the Stroke,* 13)

The strange displacement of seeming a visitor in one's own home—watching others do the gardening, care for pets, bring in or prepare food—also plagues Sarton: "I look and admire but am not *connected*" (*After the Stroke,* 80). Speaking for herself and for those who have experienced this unwelcome dependence, Sarton says that she must "curl up deep down inside" herself and wait for things to change (74).

Visitors come, other doctors are consulted, a new cat is given to her by her friend, Carolyn Heilbrun, a new dog is promised if recovery permits, but Sarton finds her own responses merely polite or ritualistic. "I feel so cut off from what once was a self. . . . Everyone I know must be as sick and tired of this illness as I am" (97).

Change occurs as the consequence of two heart shocks. One is quite literal: an anticipated electrocardiac shock treatment to adjust and regulate her heart beat. Her heart is also required to "adjust" metaphorically from the primary role of giver to one who must accommodate to her role of receiver. This is the more difficult adjustment, and her visit with the

Carmelites at their monastery in Indianapolis, nine months after the stroke, marks the real turning point in receptivity.

> It is all so silent and at first the corridors and many closed doors so mysterious and bewildering that I would have been lost without Jean Alice to show me the way down to the first floor where the large dining room is. There I was introduced to ten of the sixteen Carmelites and we sat round a big square table with a votive candle at each place. After grace had been said the conversation began and continued at a lively pace during the whole of supper. I was inundated with questions about my work and realized that some of the sisters had read a lot of Sarton. They were of all ages, each a strong individual. . . . The atmosphere created by these remarkable women is both innocent and of great depth. How rarely am I asked such cogent questions! How rarely feel so at home . . .
>
> While I lay down looking out onto trees, I thought about what I had been experiencing here, and felt the powerful magnet a conventual life holds. But people like me who are given a taste of it cannot realize what such life costs. . . . I came to see that what looks so peaceful, so full of order, has to be won and rewon every day by hard work. I, as a guest, could feel the charisma because sixteen remarkable women had given it to me as an unearned gift. (*After the Stroke,* 166–69)

Accepting an "unearned gift" becomes the key to renewed energy and her leitmotif of the final entries in *After the Stroke.* As Sarton concludes, she reminds herself and her readers that "one of the things old age has brought me is being able to receive gladly and with joy, whereas, young, I only wanted to give . . ." (279). Although she learns to rejoice in the "life recaptured," as readers of *After the Stroke,* we are never far from the consciousness of death and the precious, fragile gift of health. It is the precariousness that lingers. If Sarton knows now that she makes a myth of her life, it is not a hoax of the perfect artistic retreat the Nelson memoir invented. Instead, it is a consciously chosen, uniquely inscribed metaphor, in Heilbrun's phrase, a new script that has been consciously and unconsciously appropriated by many as a model.

The "new script" empowers on a variety of fronts, for not only does it speak to those who wish to take control of their lives, to tend their talent even when it means risking hostility or isolation or self-doubt, but it also targets issues central to women's creativity: the courage to love other women, the celebration of female friendship in both the private and public spheres, the identification of the creative "Muse" as female.

In *Writing a Woman's Life*, Heilbrun documents how few of the women of Sarton's generation acknowledged their debts to other women. She includes in this debt not only literary apprenticeships but the forgotten or unacknowledged support of female friendship. She describes one startling exception to this historical silence by retelling the story of Vera Brittain's and Winifred Holtby's life-long and life-giving friendship after World War I. Holtby seems to anticipate much of what gender theorists now document, and, in her book *Women and a Changing Civilization* (1934), she ranges over issues everywhere apparent in Sarton's narratives.

> I think that the real object behind our demand is not to reduce all men and women to the same dull pattern. It is rather to release their richness of variety. We are still greatly ignorant of our own natures. We do not know how much of what we usually describe as "feminine characteristics" are really "masculine" and how much "masculinity" is common to both sexes. Our hazards are often wildly off the mark. We do not even know—though we theorize and penalise with ferocious confidence—whether the "normal" sexual relationship is homo- or bi- or heterosexual. We are content to make vast generalizations which quite often fit the facts enough to be tolerable, but which—also quite often—inflict indescribable because indefinable suffering on those individuals who cannot without pain conform to our rough-and-ready attempt to make all men [and women] good and happy.[14]

Sarton's script speaks to those who, as Holtby phrases it, "walk more delicately" among definitions, who celebrate "their richness of variety" and who may find in Sarton's texts liberating validation.

To read Sarton's five journals sequentially is analogous to experiencing the series of remarkable self-portraits Goya painted in his later years. The portraits move from self-enclosure, the artist locked in the self-contemplation of a window pane, mirror, or canvas to a figure in three-quarter turn, looking outward toward the audience as if to check *in their response* the authentic outline. Sarton's journals emphasize the costs and rewards of a life devoted to art, the strengths and risks of female bonding, the advantages of "growing *into* age." Sarton is increasingly conscious of moving from solitary experience into dialogue with a reader, making her experience available "as a lens of empathy."[15]

In *At Seventy,* Sarton admires a journal by Anne Truitt that Pantheon has sent her to review in proof. She emphasizes a passage in Truitt describing a Rembrandt self-portrait looking steadily, "straight out" as the testimony to being "human beyond reprieve"; as Truitt says, "he looks out from this position, without self-pity and without flourish, and lends me strength" (*At Seventy,* 50). In Anne Truitt's words, Sarton locates an objective for herself. "It is that kind of honesty that I have been after in the journals, but I envy the painter who does not have to use elusive, sometimes damaged, often ambivalent *words*" (50).

By insisting on rethinking old scripts in light of new experience, Sarton practices what Adrienne Rich means by "re-vision": "the act of looking back, of seeing with fresh eyes, of entering an old text from a new critical direction [that] is for women more than a chapter in cultural history: it is an act of survival."[16] And by deliberately inviting the reader in, Sarton engages in crucial conversations with an increasingly responsive readership.

NOTES

1. Sarton defines the memoir as a reconstruction of experience "through the shaping power of memory." While the journal is certainly "selective in recording experience," it is more spontaneous, committed to fluid chronology, written "on the spur of the moment." In the fall of 1982, when interviewed by Karen Saum for the *Paris Review* series "Writers at Work," Sarton was irritated with reviewers who cited the journals as her best work; by the time I interviewed her in July 1987, she was comfortable with the journals' "contribution to the whole work" and "the audience it has brought me."

2. Susan Stanford Friedman, "Women's Autobiographical Selves," in *The Private Self: Theory and Practice of Women's Autobiographical Writings,* ed. Shari Benstock (Chapel Hill: University of North Carolina Press, 1988), 55–56.

3. Mary G. Mason, "The Other Voice: Autobiographies of Women Writers," in *Life/Lines: Theorizing Women's Autobiography,* ed. Bella Brodzki and Celeste Schenck (Ithaca, N.Y.: Cornell University Press, 1988), 22.

4. Jane Marcus, "Invincible Mediocrity: The Private Selves of Public Women," in *The Private Self: Theory and Practice of Women's Autobiographical Writings,* ed. Shari Benstock (Chapel Hill: University of North Carolina Press, 1988), 137.

5. Carolyn G. Heilbrun, *Writing a Woman's Life* (New York: Norton, 1988), 131.

6. Sarton used this phrase during our July 1987 interview (see n. 1). In *House by the Sea,* she says, "The journal is a good way . . . to sort out and shape experience" (27). In *Journal of a Solitude,* she says, "I have written every poem, every novel, for the same purpose—to find out what I think, to know where I stand" (12).

7. Maxine Kumin, *In Deep: Country Essays* (New York: Viking, 1987), 166.

8. Mary Field Belenky, Blythe McVicker Clinchy, Nancy Rule Goldberger, and Jill Mattuck Tarule, *Women's Ways of Knowing: The Development of Self, Voice, and Mind* (New York: Basic Books, 1986), 150.

9. Rachel Blau Duplessis, *Writing Beyond the Ending: Narrative Strategies of Twentieth-Century Women Writers* (Bloomington: Indiana University Press, 1985), 17.

10. Belenky et al., *Ways of Knowing*, 149.

11. This is also a phrase from our interview. The phrase she uses at the beginning of *House by the Sea* is that Nelson was a place "contaminated by pain" (8).

12. Sarton used this phrase in the Wheelock video, "A World of Light," and she repeated it in Carol Ascher, Louise DeSalvo, and Sara Ruddick, eds., *Between Women* (Boston: Beacon Press, 1984), 423.

13. This phrase is from Saul Bellow's *Dangling Man* (New York: Vanguard Press, 1944), 92. The full passage reads: "Goodness is not achieved in a vacuum, but in the company of others attended by love."

14. Heilbrun, *Writing a Woman's Life*, 106.

15. Mary Catherine Bateson, *Composing a Life* (New York: Atlantic Monthly Press, 1989), 5.

16. Adrienne Rich, *On Lies, Secrets, and Silence: Selected Prose, 1966–1978* (New York: Norton, 1979), 35.

"To Say Radical Things Gently": Art and Lesbianism in *Mrs. Stevens Hears the Mermaids Singing*

K. Graehme Hall

May Sarton published *Mrs. Stevens Hears the Mermaids Singing* in 1965. The novel was, in many ways, ahead of its time. Lesbian protagonists were rare and provided a risk to their creator's career. The sexual revolution, the most recent wave of feminism, and the lesbian/gay rights movement were still quietly evolving. By virtue of publishing this novel, Sarton declared herself to be a lesbian feminist. Because she was firm, but quiet, in her positions, and because she preferred a life of solitude to visibility as a public figure, her contributions to the lesbian feminist movement have often been overlooked. It seems that we are finally beginning to rectify that error and include her in the lesbian feminist movement, where she belongs.

Margaret Cruikshank has written that, if "a lesbian writer is more broadly defined as a woman whose creative work sheds light on lesbian lives past and present, then Sarton is easily included. If the critic insists on seeing citizenship papers before admitting writers to Lesbian Nation, she may miss not only women of Sarton's generation, but also others whose independence keeps them from political alignments."[1] In reality, by dealing with homosexuality openly in her 1965 novel, Sarton was making a political statement. Because that statement is not so radical by comparison as statements made since, we tend to forget the original force of the word in 1965. Just as many feminist classics now seem quite tame, so lesbian feminist literature and theory have been rapidly evolving in recent years. Sarton stated, in a 1983 interview in the *Paris Review*, "The militant lesbians want me to be a militant and I'm just not."[2] Sarton's militancy was in publishing a novel cast primarily with "homosexual" characters before many of today's militant lesbians were even born.

One of my initial concerns in approaching *Mrs. Stevens* was recognizing that this novel is often taught in "women's literature" courses as "*the* lesbian novel." Just as no one work can represent a whole group of people or the body of theory about a group, *Mrs. Stevens* is appropriate as part of the lesbian canon of literature, if we can begin to think in those terms, and not as *the* representative piece. *Mrs. Stevens* must be placed within the context of its time of publication, the psychological theory of development of sexual and female-male roles used as its base—primarily Freudian, and the time span of its characters' lives. This novel is the story of a woman who had a childhood crush on her governess in approximately 1911, at the age of fifteen, and whose love relationships with women lasted from the mid-1920s through the early 1940s. It is the story of a lesbian of the past, not the present; it would be dangerous and wrong to treat the character as our contemporary. *Mrs. Stevens* is, however, a strong portrayal of some of the struggles faced by women writers and, specifically, lesbians, and of the interweaving of lesbianism and art in the life of the character of Hilary Stevens during this time period.

Hilary's character is placed into a time when love between women was newly suspect in the United States. As Lillian Faderman has explained, same-sex love between women was entirely acceptable in the early part of this century. However,

> In America it took the phenomenal growth of female autonomy during and after World War I, and the American popularization of the most influential of the European sexologists, Sigmund Freud, to cast the widespread suspicions on love between women that had already been prevalent in Europe.[3]

Increased heterosexualism, in response to the increasing visibility of women and their power in American society, was quickly felt. Buffy Dunker has written the following about this time period.

> For those of us who felt "different," the messages we received from our mothers as we were growing up in the nineteen-twenties and thirties were conflicting for us. . . . Sex was seldom talked of, if at all, and we knew very little about expressing our sexuality except through marriage . . . only a few of my 1926 college classmates chose not to get married, and in my narrow experience of close relationships between women at that time, I never heard any of the women referred to as lesbian or homosexual. Besides, many of us didn't understand either the meaning or the derivation of the word *lesbian,* if we had even heard

it. Because our strong attraction to women wasn't considered "normal," it wasn't unusual for some of us to develop bad feelings about ourselves. It seemed clear that we had to keep our true feelings secret.[4]

Mrs. Stevens was published in the middle of a decade when writing by women was often assumed to be "confessional" in nature. With this book, May Sarton was considered to be revealing, to her readers, the depths of her own relationships with women, although clearly the book is fictitious and not a disguised autobiography. Sarton has called *Mrs. Stevens Hears the Mermaids Singing* "an original book, ahead of its time, written when I was fifty-five. Because of it, I have become a sort of hero. I have lost jobs because of that book, but I have never been exposed to contempt; my neighbors have never made life difficult."[5]

Sarton's presentation of lesbianism was different—actually more positive—than many of the literary and media images of lesbians during this time. Publishing *Mrs. Stevens* drew attention to a subject most members of the public would have preferred to keep closeted. Sarton decided to approach them quietly.

I have been trying to say radical things gently so that they may penetrate without shock. The fear of homosexuality is so great that it took courage to write *Mrs. Stevens,* to write a novel about a woman homosexual who is not a sex maniac, a drunkard, a drugtaker or in any way repulsive; to portray a homosexual who is neither pitiable nor disgusting, without sentimentality; and to face the truth that such a life [as writer and lesbian] is rarely happy, a life where art must become the primary motivation, for love is never going to fulfill in the usual sense.[6]

May Sarton undertook an immense challenge with the writing of this book, and publishing it was an act of courage. One must sift through the layers she has interwoven; the neat surface—the structure—is deceiving. She deals with what it meant to be a woman in the earlier decades of this century—a woman alone, self-actualizing; with what it means to be a writer, and to be a woman writer. She writes of the complexities of art and of love, of American society's fear of feeling and subsequent escape through sex, of relationships between women and men, women and women. She reflects the subtleties of human life through landscape—indoors and out, and demonstrates the human connection with nature, of which we often forget our part. We see encounters with unseen forces (such as the presence of Anne); the struggle of coming to terms with one's parents and childhood and self; the coming together of past and present for an older woman, with aging presented in the positive context it deserves. *Mrs. Stevens Hears the Mermaids Singing* is the story of F. Hilary Stevens, more than seventy years old, as she struggles to gain an understanding of herself: it is her coming to terms with herself, her life, and her art as poet, woman, lesbian, and human being. To accomplish this task, she looks back through her life, piecing it together; the interview lends structure as she recalls her various books and the people and life circumstances that helped to birth the books.

Hilary's "talent," giving rise to art, coexists in Hilary with lesbianism. The two elements are in a complementary relationship, a coexistence. For Hilary to be a writer, she had to renounce at least some of the traditional expectations for a woman in her day. She had to step outside the norm. Her husband, Adrian, as would have been typical of men at that time, wanted her to assume a stereotypical feminine role, at least publicly.

> She married Adrian in a total revulsion from one part of herself, yet whether she ever published a word again or not she could not stop being the person she was. There was the rub! She was young, witty, on the defensive, and more than once at a dinner party, she had let herself go, had talked from her own center, honestly, had enjoyed feeling her powers in action, until she had caught Adrian's look across the table, a troubled look, a slightly hostile look.[7]

This reaction from Adrian, while expected, is also enlightening, since Hilary had already published her first book, *Bull's Eye,* an outrageous—for the times—outspoken book, before they met. Adrian knew what he was getting into.

Hilary felt caged in that relationship, "caged by being in love with, and married to, a man whose life pattern seemed to her both trivial and confining" (42). But as a woman in the 1920s, she was supposed to find happiness through life with her husband. Instead, she felt "caged also by the demands of housekeeping, by the late hours they kept, so she never woke up really fresh with the extra psychic energy at her command necessary for writing a single sentence" (42–43). Hilary wanted to be "her self," not her "married self" (45). Her mother-in-law, Margaret, questions her: "I settled for being a woman. I wonder whether you can" (47).

To step outside the perimeters of a "woman's world" to be herself,

Hilary found she could also be a woman capable of loving women, as well as men, and that women did not have the role expectations of her that men did. With the introduction in the novel of Hilary's crush, at age fifteen, on Phillippa Munn, her governess, and the development of writing poems as a way of saying to Phillippa what it was not otherwise permissible to say, the question is raised: is writing, for Hilary, partly a survival method for dealing with her own love for women in a misogynistic, heterosexist culture? Or is lesbianism simply an added conflict for her, already struggling to be a "self" outside the bounds society has set for women? Probably both.

Poets are often perceived as people of feeling, of passion, of "primary intensity" (26). That romantic image of the poet—as present today as thirty years ago—is especially true for F. Hilary Stevens, who lives "so near the surface" (161). A poet who is a lesbian will undoubtedly find at least part of the passion in her life through relationships with other women. Her muse will be female. In that sense, an involvement for her with other women is essential to her art, essential for what she, as a writer, needs in order to birth her works. The passion and inspiration in Hilary's life come from other women: from her governess, from friends and lovers. When Hilary first falls in love with Phillippa, she feels that God has "chosen to make me love you," since it seems to Hilary as true revelation: "Something far greater and more mysterious than Hilary seemed involved. She felt enlarged by goodness, not an emotion she was used to feeling at all . . ." (101). Hilary feels as if she has "emerged from her cocoon, as if she were some awkward luna moth, painfully extricating itself for a first flight into the soft darkness of a spring dusk" (102). Through Phillippa, the muse makes its first appearance: "impossible, haunting, she who makes the whole world reverberate" (108). Hilary describes that encounter in much the same way many lesbians describe their first experience of love with another woman: it feels as if one is "coming home" within one's self. Hilary's first book, *Bull's Eye,* published in 1919 when Hilary was twenty-three, was a response to that experience, transforming her feelings for Phillippa "into the very young man and his love affair" (109), and was also "about things like women falling in love with each other, took this for granted, set it in its place" (94).

Vivienne Cass's six-stage model of identity formation, as applicable to lesbians, recognizes that homosexuals acquire identity through a developmental process.[8] She offers what she describes as a "broad outline" of how identity as a "homosexual" can be "fully integrated within the individual's overall concept of self," with the assumption that a person begins the process while perceiving herself as heterosexual.[9] The six stages, to summarize briefly, are: (1) Identity Confusion ("Who am I? My behavior may be called lesbian; am I a lesbian?"); (2) Identity Comparison ("I'm different . . . I may be a lesbian"); (3) Identity Tolerance (Moving from "I probably am a lesbian" to "I am a lesbian"); (4) Identity Acceptance ("I am a lesbian; and I'm comfortable in the lesbian culture"); (5) Identity Pride ("I am proud to be a lesbian and society should accept me as a lesbian"); and (6) Identity Synthesis ("I am a woman and a lesbian and a . . . "; identity as a lesbian is integrated with other aspects of self). Cass notes that identity foreclosure is possible at any of these stages; completion is not prerequisite in the development of lesbian identity. According to this model, Hilary's attraction to Phillippa moved her into stage 1. In *Bull's Eye,* written five years after that summer in Wales with Phillippa, "the imagination had . . . crystallized, perhaps just because nothing there had been 'lived out' at all" (109). The novel was, for Hilary, a "false start," because, in it, she "simply transposed" herself (109). She left "fiction" and returned to the medium of poetry for her next book. Her first collection of poems, *From a Hospital Bed,* was published in 1925. Hilary said, "I write for one person, but the person changes" (125). This book of poems was about "objects described for the keen ear and eye of Dr. Hallowell," who had "nourished her" in the hospital, who had "understood the fundamental being in her," something her mother was never able to do (123). The person in the hospital who had "lit her up," however, was Nurse Gillespie, "with her austere closed face and clear blue eyes" (119). Dr. Hallowell, recognizing the attachment, moved Nurse Gillespie off the floor. "Keep the poems to objects, not people," he admonished Hilary (119).

Grief over the death of Hilary's husband was undoubtedly complicated by memories of her early feelings for Phillippa. Already uncomfortable with the constraints of a heterosexual female role and no longer dependent on a husband for economic survival, Hilary now had more options from which to choose. Despite her emotional relationship with Dr. Hallowell, she was attracted to Nurse Gillespie, who captured her imagination, and Hilary was not shy or apologetic about her feelings. To some degree, Hilary had already accepted her feelings for women and was beginning to feel comfortable with them. But, on other levels, she was just starting, exploring "deep mysterious waters" (121). Hilary's grief was compounded by these feelings. When Adrian died, Hilary cried "perhaps not so much out of grief, as out of some indefinable sense of being now cut off from everything, and most of all from herself" (49). Hilary was cut off from the part of herself that had internalized the hopes of her parents and of society for a young woman. Betty Berzon notes that the idea of relinquishing a heterosexual identity can arouse troubling questions: "If marriage and family are not in one's future, what is? What will there be to give form and structure to one's life?"[10] "With the letting go of a perception of self that is clearly heterosexual," Berzon writes, "one can experience a profound feeling of loss . . . grieving the loss of that heterosexual blueprint for life is an inescapable part of what is going on."[11] Writing was the one constant for Hilary, giving her self and her life both form and structure.

Hilary's second book of poems, a collection of love sonnets written to Willa MacPherson at age twenty-nine, asked "to be taken into the flood, to be part of it" (141). This relationship taught Hilary about shaping emotion with poetry to a new depth.

> Inspiration? It felt more like being harnessed to wild horses whom she must learn to control or be herself flung down and broken. The sonnet form with its implacable demand to clarify, to condense, to bring to fulfillment, became the means to control. Now for the first time she understood about form, what it was *for*, how it could teach one to discover what was really happening, and how to come to terms with the impossible, how it was not a discipline imposed from outside by the intellect, but grappled with from inner necessity as a means of probing and dealing with powerful emotion. (140–41)

Form, like content, emerges as part of the poem and as part of the struggle of creation. The creation of self—in all its aspects—was a vital part of that struggle for Hilary. In this book, there was "the emergence of a definite 'I': the change of style is organic, has to do with the emerging person" (126).

With Willa, Hilary felt passion, "passion as pure light. The consummation was as absolute as the initial break-through into personal feeling. There was, in fact, nowhere to go from there" (144). "Within those passionate kisses," Hilary remembers, "sexuality hardly existed, or was totally diffused in a fire of tenderness" (144). The episode brought both blessing, with its "poignance and . . . power" (144), and trauma, as Hilary recalls it, as she "became an actor only through being a witness of something beyond [her] understanding" (134). One could speculate that Hilary moved to stage 2 with the writing of these poems, as she more fully accepted her feelings for Willa.

Hilary's third book of poems, *Themes and Variations,* written at age forty, was about self-conquest: "how to transpose, how to be there inside the poem yet outside of it" (151). These were "musically inspired" poems, with the singer Madeleine HiRose as inspiration. Madeleine was "an impossible person, but when she sang she became a different animal. She had an impeccable sense of the exact weight of the smallest word and tone. She could sing a whisper. She could place a shade of meaning on a phrase which made shivers of realization run down one's back" (156–57). In this book, Hilary was seeking "a poetic equivalent to certain musical phrases, so the villanelle, for instance, with its echos [sic] and variations, or the sestina, or even the ode with its long ebbing lines, became appropriate" (157). Her involvement with Madeleine—literally the woman next door—inspired her to try to write poems dealing with sex. To Hilary's frustration, she found that "the language of sex is masculine. Women would have to invent a new language..." (157). Moving further into stage 2, Hilary was more accepting of the sexual component of their relationship and perhaps used writing about it as a means to gain understanding of it. While Hilary later destroyed these poems, their purpose was undoubtedly served.

The poems Hilary saved for her third book, so "sensuously rich," were in sharp contrast to the collection of poems, *Dialogues,* written five years later, at age forty-five. "Everyone of the poems in that book had to be fought through out of violence, rage. I was sick with it" (160). With the sociologist, Dorothea, ten years her elder, Hilary found herself face to face with forces that represented opposition to her—and with someone who was undoubtedly farther along in her identity formation as a lesbian. Dorothea was disciplined, logical, analytical, an "anti-mystic by nature and by profession" (162). She brought Hilary's struggle with herself to a climax: the battle between the "boy" (166), who represented what she labeled the "masculine" part of herself, with its objectivity and rationality, and the woman writer, "the creative person... who moves from an irrational source of power" (169). Hilary saw herself as

> ... a sacred animal, a kind of totem who must be destroyed for the world Dorothea represented to survive. I was the enemy, the anarchic, earth-shaking power. Oh, we threatened each other at the very source of our being! And very nearly killed each other. (169–70)

The relationship was complicated by the contrasting critical reception their most recent works received. When Dorothea's "study of a mining town in Pennsylvania" was "a great success," and Hilary's collection of Vermont poems went "almost entirely unnoticed," Hilary found her sense of self-worth, still largely dependent on her success as a writer, challenged (166). Dorothea represented the critics, who came from her sphere. Hilary felt on the brink of self-annihilation, and responded violently, as a threatened, "wounded bear" (167). Perhaps these sensations were heightened because she had also assumed a more traditionally feminine role in her relationship with Dorothea: "she was content to stay close to home," to arrange flowers, to make curtains, to swim in the shallow waters, while Dorothea would "advance into the harsh waves, dive into them, go flashing off with her strong crawl out into the deep waters where only her red cap could be seen" (166). Hilary felt "the boy in herself backing away" and "the woman buried so long, taking possession" (165–66). But Hilary was woman and writer and found herself engaged in the same struggle she had endured with Adrian: to be fully herself. She was struggling to form her identity as a participant in a lesbian domestic relationship; this was Hilary's first lesbian relationship to incorporate perceived "normal" couple standards, while she and Dorothea lived together in a house for the summer. Hilary's last experience of living with a relationship partner had been as a wife, with her husband. So the traditional teachings of appropriate "masculine" and "feminine" behavior, feeling, and attitude came again into conflict with the being whom Hilary felt herself to be and, perhaps unrealistically, if understandably, also wanted approval to be. Still operating with the desperate need for approval so often instilled in women, Hilary found herself face to face with her own Medusa: "if you turn Medusa's face around, it is your own face. It is yourself who must be conquered" (161–62). In *Dialogues,* Hilary tried to self-monitor feeling, to contain the furies: "I was trying to use my mind, a big mistake... perhaps it would have been better to run wailing down the streets of New York" (171).

Hilary moved even more deeply into stage 2 with her struggle in this relationship. She turned her "self-image further away from 'heterosexual' and more toward 'homosexual,'" which signals the end of stage 2.[12] In the intimacy and struggle she faced with Dorothea, Hilary encountered new aspects of herself that had to be faced, new issues of control, dependence, and autonomy. Although she appears to have lacked a social support system of other lesbians, it may also be imagined that, given her location and the time of this relationship, lesbian circles were limited in visibility and accessibility.[13] In need of respite from the intensity of poetry and the intensity of her struggle with herself, Hilary turned to write a second novel about the Depression years in New York. It temporarily "caused a considerable stir," then left her "feeling lost, high and dry" (169). Hilary went to France for "nursing," "when I was, so late in life, casting off my boy's clothes, emerging from a long adolescence, emerging too from a crucial and devastating encounter with the Muse. All part of the same thing . . ." (173). It is interesting to note that a common strategy in stage 2 is "moving to another city or country" as a way of reducing "the fear of negative reaction from others."[14] When Hilary was challenged by a potential lesbian identity, she moved away—from others and, perhaps symbolically, from herself— and lived a life that is reported in the novel as without sexual partners; asexuality is also a common stage 2 behavior.[15] In France, Luc Bernstein helped her to confront herself again, to "confront the essential problems" (176). The presence of Anne, the previous owner of the village house Hilary inhabited in the Touraine, filled the house with a sense of her singing: "I had all the time the sense that in that house music was just on the threshold, until I came to see that the silence itself was the music" (181). ". . . [T]ogether Luc and Anne's presence showed up my own chequered life in a pitiless light. . . . I was surrounded in every way by simplifying and unifying powers" (183). With Anne as muse, *Country Spells,* Hilary's next book of poems, was born.

The move from music (Madeleine HiRose) to spoken voice (Dorothea) to expectant silence (the nonembodied Anne) is indicative of Hilary's next move, further away from lesbian relationships and back into solitude, still trying to reconcile her past involvements. After that summer, Hilary realized it was time she "stopped borrowing other people's houses, other people's lives, and made my peace with myself in a house of my creation" (186). Her mother died about the same time, just before Hilary came to her present home. *The Silences* is "the book of this house, the intoxication of solitude," but it was her mother who haunted the book, who kept it from becoming better (192). Her mother "remains the great devouring enigma," "*the* antagonist" (193). Hilary speculates during the interview that her last book may be about her mother: "it is time to die when one has come to terms with everything . . . the Muse, you see . . ." (192–93). In the Robert Graves lines quoted in this novel, the Muse is: "Whom I desired above all things to know. Sister of the mirage and echo!" (147). But "the other side of the coin," Hilary tells us, "is the longing to *be known,* to be accepted as one is" (195). According to Hilary, her mother "understood nothing, or pretended not to understand . . . she would never, never find me acceptable as I am" (195).

Beverly Burch has written that the mother-daughter relationship, as the first female-to-female relationship experienced, brings special issues to lesbian relationships. The process of separation-individuation, which lasts throughout the lives of both women and men, "is never so complete . . . as to preclude re-engulfment in the original mother-child unity and subsequent loss of self."[16] While the development of male gender identity, and the differences of mother-son relationships, create defenses to ensure separateness, there is a strong sense of sameness between mothers and daughters. Heterosexual women have obvious barriers placed between these issues and their male partners, but lesbians lack these boundaries to intimacy in relationships: "In fact, the boundaries are doubly permeable," Burch writes, "more fluid on both sides, and the threat of loss of self may feel greater."[17]

Hilary's mother saw her daughter as being the very woman and artist that she, herself, had wanted to be: a woman who created works of art from her emotions and experience. In the ethos in Boston society where Hilary grew up, "feeling was always the threat" (193). "People who cannot feel punish those who do" (139). Hilary became herself, doing what she chose to do with her life: her *own* life. Hilary's mother "was the woman meant to be an artist who tried to do the right thing!" (193). She was a powerful woman who was "totally allergic to the chaotic suffering, the elements in life itself which make the poetry" (194). Hilary comments that "before I was eight it had devastated me, or marked me for a poet . . . what I heard in my mother's voice of longing and starvation" (193–94). Hilary felt she "had to fight my parents every inch of the way, from the beginning" (194). And, toward the end of her life, Hilary finds herself transposing her mother, living in one of the "mansions" of the Muse by the sea.

The Muse, for Hilary, is the women in her life who invoke emotional passion. The Muse has many faces. One at a time they have appeared: Phillippa Munn, Miss Gillespie, Willa MacPherson, Madeleine HiRose, Dorothea, Anne, Hilary's mother. With most of the women, the passion became romantic, in Hilary's mind if not acted out; with Hilary's mother, it was the extreme of emotion that exists between mother and daughter, particularly in a relationship where feeling is frustrated, the potential far from realized: "'Whom I desired above all things to know. Sister of the mirage and echo!'" The phrase is "prescient" (147) because it speaks of a relationship "desired," but in the past tense, because it was not achieved. It was as elusive as "the mirage and echo." Hilary's muse is always a woman, because "Women have moved and shaken me" (180). The "disturbing" visitation of the muse (184) always sets up a question, opens up dialogue: "One begins to talk *to* someone, *about* oneself. Each time one's whole life seems to be in play" (181). Once the dialogue with the muse is set up, whether the physical instrument of the muse—person or presence— is still there, "lines begin to run through one's head, without the slightest volition on one's own part" (183). The muse also demands of Hilary: "The Muse destroys as well as gives life, does not nourish, pierces, forces one to discard, renew, be born again. Joy and agony are pivoted in her presence" (186).

Hilary tells Mar, "it is the talent for poetry, this talent for love, and no true poetry without it . . . it's the talent for going naked" (218). Sarton has commented that, "Poetry is one person's immediate feelings . . . [it] does not answer to command."[18] "The deepest experiences in my life have had to do with other people I love," Sarton says. "Love, not sex, is the 'way out' of feeling."[19] Love, not sex, is the key to poetry for Hilary: "Bound to be [a] dry [quarry], if you separate sex and feeling" (212). Hilary tells Mar that

> . . . I do know something of the excitement of discovering the . . . unknown person, to break down barriers, to understand, to be enlarged, to discover, the tremendous excitement of that kind of conquest. Of course sex is mixed up with it. That's sure. But if it were only sex, it wouldn't be worth the candle. When I get stirred up, it's the whole of me that gets stirred. I can't separate soul and body. (209)

Hilary found love in her life primarily with other women, and expressed it primarily through poetry. The two are integral. Poetry was, for Hilary, a way "to poise the tensions, to solve the equation," bringing the balance to her life that was necessary to survive (108). Jane Rule wrote that Hilary

> . . . could have become only a woman, a choice she would make only if she could choose as well to have no talent. It isn't really a choice at all. She is a woman, a gifted woman, who has faced the Medusa squarely enough to know that the meeting with the Muse is really a meeting with the self, an opening of intense speculation which is the discipline and wonder of art, even when the Muse takes no interest at all. (*Lesbian Images,* 175)

The Education of Harriet Hatfield, published in 1989, also has an older lesbian as protagonist, and the novel lends insight to Sarton's presentation of women and lesbianism, and of the relationship between art and lesbianism. The structure of the book is more traditional than that of *Mrs. Stevens*, with divisions of thirty chapters, the story told in chronological fashion. The novel is written in first person, whereas *Mrs. Stevens* is written in third, so the reader immediately begins with a stronger, more personal and powerful sense of this woman, Harriet Hatfield. Harriet is sixty years old and at a turning point in her life. Her lover and life partner of thirty years, Victoria Chilton, has just died: "We had a truly happy life together for thirty years."[20] They were, as Harriet notes, engaged in what Henry James called a Boston Marriage. Vicky was "a fountain of energy and conviction . . . the editor and owner of a small publishing house" (*HH*, 9). While Vicky worked at her publishing company all day, Harriet worked at home, tending to their house and gardens. She assumed a role similar to that of many women of her time. When Vicky died, she left Harriet "comfortably off," (10) giving Harriet the opportunity to develop herself, and her life, in a new direction. Harriet opens a women's bookstore in Somerville, a working-class Boston suburb.

Much of the novel revolves around Harriet's "coming out" to family, friends, and strangers, her "coming out" more fully to herself, and the "coming out" of the bookstore in the community. The book, in essence, shows Harriet's process of "self-actualization" during this time, where she is "being stretched as a human being every day" (*HH*, 309). She is no longer in a protected relationship with Victoria Chilton, in a house with huge walls that cut her off from the rest of the world; she is a part of it. As Harriet notes in the closing line of the book: "It's the real world and I am fully alive in it" (*HH*, 320).

There are many similarities between *The Education of Harriet Hatfield* and *Mrs. Stevens Hears the Mermaids Singing*—and many differences. Both Hilary and Harriet find the primary love in their lives with women, although they are "nourished" by men and enjoy their companionship and support as well. Harriet Hatfield, like Hilary Stevens, is an older woman in search of self. Hilary lives with Sirenica, a white cat, and two turtles; Harriet has Patapouf, a Labrador retriever, for companionship. While Hilary lives by the ocean, on Cape Ann, Harriet has moved to Somerville, a "'working' community" outside of Boston (*HH*, 15). In many ways, their locations are as telling as any personal details: Hilary says that "Women do not thrive in cities" (175), but Harriet certainly does. While Hilary is isolated in her home on Cape Ann, Harriet has broken through the insulation of nature,

moving from her home and gardens to the city where she has extensive
interaction with other people. Both women are older, in good health, still
actively living their lives. Both women believe that age provides the security
and wisdom to encourage truth. Harriet is, in many ways, an evolved
Hilary. While Hilary creates art with her life, Harriet's creation of life is
her art.

The meaning of "lesbianism" used in this essay is derived from both
novels, since Sarton makes the meaning of a primary relationship between
women clearer in her more contemporary book, and the use of the term
lesbian is consistent with that found in *Mrs. Stevens* regarding female homosexuality. In *Mrs. Stevens,* Hilary tells Mar, "I loved my husband, but . . .
others touched the poet as he did not" (27). "Others," while perhaps
inclusive of the male physician and male critic who nourished her, also
indicates the women with whom Hilary fell in love, and the women who
served as her muses. The double entendre of "touch" is suggestive both of
the physical/sexual relationship usually associated with lesbianism, and, more
important, of being touched emotionally, at the heart of self. In *Harriet
Hatfield,* Harriet questions whether her friends have ever loved other women,
focusing on love and the emotional aspect of the relationship. She does not
ask if they have ever been sexually attracted to other women. It is, then,
important to broaden the common definition of lesbianism when working
with Sarton's novels, and to derive a fuller and more accurate understanding
than suggested by the terms *sexual preference* or *sexual orientation.*

As Carla Golden has commented, "Psychologists and feminists alike
tend to assume that most persons can be neatly categorized according to
membership in one of four groups: heterosexual, homosexual, bisexual, or
asexual (celibate)."[21] Both a person's sexual behavior and sexual identity are
expected to fit into the same category. The major lack of agreement comes
in defining those four categories. The label "lesbian," in particular, remains
the cause of considerable discussion. Even Alfred Kinsey, however, noted
that his homosexual-heterosexual scale is representative of the full spectrum
of sexual behaviors and experiences; the terms *masturbatory, heterosexual,* or
homosexual in his research "are of value only because they describe the source
of the sexual stimulation, and they should not be taken as descriptions of
the individuals who respond to the various stimuli."[22] "Only the human
mind," Kinsey notes, "invents categories and tries to force facts into separated
pigeon-holes. The living world is a continuum in each and every one of its
aspects."[23]

Adrienne Rich prefers the terms *lesbian existence* and *lesbian continuum*

to the use of *lesbian,* which "has been held to limiting, clinical associations
in its patriarchal definition."[24] Rich uses "lesbian existence" to refer to "the
fact of the historical presence of lesbians and our continuing creation of the
meaning of that existence."[25] The phrase "lesbian continuum" is meant "to
include a range—through each woman's life and throughout history—of
woman-identified experience; not simply the fact that a woman has had or
consciously desired genital sexual experience with another woman."[26] Rich
believes that women, in general, move in and out of the lesbian continuum
throughout our lives, with or without lesbian self-identification.[27] Ann
Ferguson disagrees, believing that self-identification is vital, and that definitions of lesbianism should recognize the importance of sexual feelings and
behavior. She offers, instead, a definition of lesbian as "a woman who has
sexual and erotic-emotional ties primarily with women or who sees herself
as centrally involved with a community of self-identified lesbians whose
sexual and erotic-emotional ties are primarily with women and who is herself
a self-identified lesbian."[28] After conducting research among college women
about their relationships with women, Carla Golden has suggested that, "To
the extent that lesbianism is very narrowly defined, the categories will restrict,
rather than give full expression to, the diversity among women who subjec-
tively define themselves as lesbian."[29] In her study, she discovered great differences in the definitions of "lesbian" given by women students at her college
who self-identified as lesbian, and major variances between those definitions
and common societal definitions of "lesbian." Sarah Hoagland has also
suggested there is a problem with defining "lesbian": "to define 'lesbian'
is, in my opinion, to succumb to a context of heterosexualism. No one
ever feels compelled to explain or define what they perceive as the norm.
If we define 'lesbianism,' we invoke a context in which it is not the norm."[30]

There is no definition of lesbianism or female homosexuality given in
Mrs. Stevens or *Harriet Hatfield.* When Harriet and Vicky were making their
lives together, they never considered themselves "lesbian"—they had no need
to label themselves. It is only when Harriet emerges into the world at large
after Vicky's death that she finds society defining their relationship as "lesbian." Similarly, in *Mrs. Stevens,* Hilary never labels her relationships with
women as "lesbian" relationships or as "homosexual," the word used instead
in that book and perhaps more commonly in the early 1960s. The heart of
the relationships between all of these women, as presented in the novels,
was beyond society and labels and based on love. The emotional aspect of
the relationships in these novels seems to outweigh the sexual or political.
In *Harriet Hatfield,* Harriet never mentions missing the sexual aspect of her

relationship with Vicky, to which an allusion is made when Harriet notes that her brothers never thought of her as a sexual being; that omitted dimension of the relationship may also be explained as the result of Sarton's belief, or her character's, that discussion of sexual activity should be treated discreetly. The reader sees Harriet grieving over the loss of the person Vicky in her life—the woman as a whole, the relationship as a whole. So the concept of lesbianism used here must be inclusive of both affectional and sexual partner preference.

Another struggle with labels in *Mrs. Stevens* is Hilary's attempt to define the parts of herself she sees as "feminine," by society's standards, and their conflict with the parts of herself included in "masculine" stereotyping. As Jane Rule has written, Sarton's insight often draws on "a cultural inheritance from Freud which makes her call a great many needs and strengths which are simply human either masculine or feminine instead."[31] This male-female polarization can be confusing and misleading, but represents part of the "rules" by which the character Hilary lives. The young Hilary did not play the masculine-feminine game as well as many of her peers, in terms of assuming specific "feminine" roles and behaviors; her peers may have done it for survival, but to her, survival came to mean not playing. Writing, for Hilary, was not just what made her different; it was a tool to help her survive outside the traditional female role.

In many ways, the actual presentation of the struggle in the novel is Hilary attempting to place what she considers the "masculine," analytical perspective on her female self. It is worth noting that the primary, experienced interviewer is a man; the person to whom Hilary most strongly relates, however, in finding "sameness" is the woman interviewer. Hilary repeatedly tries to understand and categorize herself, doing the very thing she—and Harriet—became frustrated with in society. Through discussion with Mar, Hilary finally achieves the "feminine" truth at the end of the novel: she is whole as she is. It is possible for Mar—who is picking up where she is leaving off, at the beginning stages of his life while she is moving toward the concluding stages of hers—to have "life and a talent," just as it may be possible for Jenny (22). "That every ending is a beginning" is a beginning for them all (220).

The task Hilary undertakes through this interview is common for older women who are trying to understand the circle of their lives. When reminiscing, Hilary sometimes offers dates and ages that do not coincide: her recollection is memory—her facts of experience as they now exist in her mind. Hilary has many qualities common to women in her age group: she also has characteristics that may be specific to older lesbians. Buffy Dunker contrasts "the situation of the conventional married old woman and the autonomous old lesbian."

> The lesbian has had to be self-supporting, and the conventional woman has not. The lesbian, especially the lesbian of color, has had to deal with the hazards of oppression, exclusion, and prejudice. The wife has held an honored although secondary position in society with many heterosexual privileges. The lesbian has had to seek her own friends, lovers, and communities. The wife took her place in the well-established society of couples. The lesbian has been in charge of her own life, making choices of work, recreation, and companions as she wished. The wife has had to please others in most areas; even the kinds of meals she prepared and the way she brought up the children had to conform to her husband's wishes.[32]

Even apart from her relationships with women, Hilary's dedication to the muse, and her placement of the creation of art as the priority in her life, was in direct opposition to the expectations of a woman in the early to mid-1900s. The dialogue between Jenny Hare and Hilary Stevens about the challenges facing a woman writer is particularly enlightening in this sense. Hilary, essentially, chose not to be "superwoman"; she elected not to try to have it all. The sense of regret she shares at the end of the book with Mar is because her path was difficult, and she relinquished many facets ascribed to traditional female "identity" to follow it. She did not have children. She preferred the passion of short-term relationships to the security of long-term ones. She found the muse with women instead of with men. For Hilary, art came first. If she married, her husband would be the priority; if she were a mother, her children would take precedence. Hilary responds to Jenny's question, "Why shouldn't being a writer make one more human than less so?"

> "My dear child, one is nourishing a talent, [an] expensive, demanding baby! Human? What does human mean? Having time and the wish to care intensely about someone else? This is what women will do, willy-nilly, and what then?"
>
> "But, but . . . ," Jenny persisted out of her own misery, "you seem to be saying yourself that you can't write without love!"
>
> "Love as the waker of the dead, love as conflict, love as the mirage. Not love as peace or fulfillment, or lasting, faithful giving. . . . No,

that fidelity, that giving is what the art demands, the art itself, at the expense of every human being." (156)

Mrs. Stevens Hears the Mermaids Singing was published two years after Sylvia Plath killed herself, with two young children to care for alone after separating from her husband. Less than a decade later, Anne Sexton killed herself. Hilary was saying that, in her experience, a woman can't have it all; a woman who wants to be an artist must make choices. While we may choose today to agree or disagree with that view—certainly there are more options now than thirty years ago—it was what Hilary felt was right for her in her own time, and this fictional character narrates this novel toward the end of a very full life. Hilary tells Peter and Jenny that

> the woman who needs to create works of art is born with a kind of psychic tension in her which drives her unmercifully to find a way to balance, to make herself whole. Every human being has this need: in the artist it is mandatory. Unable to fulfill it, he goes mad. But when the artist is a woman, she fulfills it at the *expense* of herself as a woman. (191)

With the writer's constant search for the muse, and the placement of the creation of art at the forefront of her life, Hilary never gives love an opportunity to fulfill in the "usual sense," through traditional long-term interpersonal relationships, through motherhood. Hilary follows love on a different path. As Hilary notes, "all poems are love poems . . . the motor power, the electric current is love of one kind or another" (125). "Love opens the doors into everything . . . including and perhaps most of all, the door into one's own secret, and often terrible and frightening real self" (25).

Willa MacPherson reflects that, from society's perspective, "a woman capable of passion—that is the flesh and the devil!" (138). One of Sarton's challenges to her readers, as voiced through Willa and Hilary, is to note that "we live in a curious age, in an age where passion is suspect. We are lepers. We are treated like lepers" (138). One of the echoes of this book resounds through the line, ". . . it is the privilege of those who fear love to murder those who do not fear it!" (138). We see this message again through the presentation of homophobia in *The Education of Harriet Hatfield*.

In looking at *Mrs. Stevens Hears the Mermaids Singing* today, we see a woman, Hilary Stevens, who represents the struggles that women writers, lesbians, and lesbian writers were facing in the early part of this century.

While Hilary evolves to stage 2 of Cass's model of development, Identity Comparison, Harriet Hatfield evolves to the sixth and final stage, Identity Synthesis. These characters are, perhaps, reflective of the progress of the social, psychological, and literary development of lesbianism between 1965 and 1989. Although stage 6 has not been reached yet, there has been substantial growth.

Hilary says that "woman's work" is "never to categorize, never to separate one thing from another—intellect, the senses, the imagination, . . . some total gathering together where the most realistic and the most mystical can be joined in a celebration of life itself. Woman's work is always toward wholeness" (172). You can't separate the woman from her work. Lesbianism and art were interwoven in Hilary's life and in her writing, as they are interwoven in Sarton's: interwoven parts of wholeness.

NOTES

1. Margaret Cruikshank, "A Note On May Sarton," *Journal of Homosexuality,* 12, nos. 3–4 (1986): 154.

2. Karen Saum, "The Art of Poetry XXXII: May Sarton," *Paris Review* 89 (Fall 1983): 86.

3. Lillian Faderman, *Surpassing the Love of Men: Romantic Friendship and Love between Women from the Renaissance to the Present* (New York: William Morrow, 1981), 298.

4. Buffy Dunker, "Aging Lesbians: Observations and Speculations," in *Lesbian Psychologies: Explorations and Challenges,* ed. Boston Lesbian Psychologies Collective (Urbana: University of Illinois Press, 1987), 74.

5. Caroline Drewes, "A Radical Feminist with a Quiet Voice," *San Francisco Examiner* 29 November 1976.

6. Drewes, "Radical Feminist."

7. May Sarton, *Mrs. Stevens Hears the Mermaids Singing* (New York: Norton, 1965), 41. Subsequent references to this book will be made in the text.

8. Vivienne Cass, "Homosexual Identity Formation: A Theoretical Model," *Journal of Homosexuality* 4, no. 3 (Spring 1979): 219–35.

9. Cass, "Homosexual Identity Formation," 220.

10. Betty Berzon, *Permanent Partners: Building Gay and Lesbian Relationships That Last* (New York: Dutton, 1988), 48. Berzon uses the Cass model in her discussion of gay/lesbian identity, particularly in chap. 3, "Feeling Good About Being Gay" (44–60). My thanks to Juli Burnell for bringing the Cass and Berzon publications to my attention.

11. Berzon, *Permanent Partners,* 48–49.

12. Cass, "Homosexual Identity Formation," 229.

13. Hilary may also have had access to a social network; there certainly were networks in existence during this time. It was either not an important memory for Hilary or it was a very private one, for she does not provide the reader with much information on this point.

14. Berzon, *Permanent Partners,* 51.

15. Cass, "Homosexual Identity Formation," 228.

16. Beverly Burch, "Barriers to Intimacy: Conflicts over Power, Dependency, and Nurturing in Lesbian Relationships," in *Lesbian Psychologies: Explorations and Challenges,* ed. Boston Lesbian Psychologies Collective (Urbana: University of Illinois Press, 1987), 133.

17. Burch, "Barriers to Intimacy," 134.

18. May Sarton, quoted in Barbara Bannon, "May Sarton," *Publishers Weekly* 205 (24 June 1974): 17.

19. Drewes, "Radical Feminist."

20. May Sarton, *The Education of Harriet Hatfield* (New York: Norton, 1989), 9–10. Subsequent references will be noted in the text as *HH.*

21. Carla Golden, "Diversity and Variability in Women's Sexual Identities," in *Lesbian Psychologies: Explorations and Challenges,* ed. Boston Lesbian Psychologies Collective (Urbana: University of Illinois Press, 1987), 19.

22. Alfred Kinsey, W. B. Pomeroy, C. E. Martin, and P. H. Gebhard, *Sexual Behavior in the Human Female* (Philadelphia: Saunders, 1953), 446–47. For discussion of the frequent misuse of Alfred Kinsey's research on sexual behaviors, particularly as applied to homosexuality, see William H. DuBay, *Gay Identity: The Self under Ban* (Jefferson, N.C.: McFarland, 1987), chap. 1.

23. Alfred Kinsey, W. B. Pomeroy, and C. E. Martin, *Sexual Behavior in the Human Male* (Philadelphia: Saunders, 1948), 639.

24. Adrienne Rich, "Compulsory Heterosexuality and Lesbian Existence," in *Women-Identified Women,* ed. Trudy E. Darty and Sandra J. Potter (Palo Alto, Calif.: Mayfield Publishing, 1984), 135.

25. Rich, "Compulsory Heterosexuality," 134.

26. Rich, "Compulsory Heterosexuality," 134.

27. Rich, "Compulsory Heterosexuality," 136.

28. Ann Ferguson, "Compulsory Heterosexuality and Lesbian Existence: Defining the Issues," *Signs* 7 (Autumn 1981): 166.

29. Golden, "Diversity," 29.

30. Sarah Lucia Hoagland, *Lesbian Ethics: Toward a New Value* (Palo Alto, Calif.: Institute of Lesbian Studies, 1988), 8.

31. Jane Rule, "May Sarton," in *Lesbian Images* (New York: Doubleday, 1975), 173.

32. Dunker, "Aging Lesbians," 77.

Double Discourse: Gilman, Sarton, and the Subversive Text

Barbara Bair

Now the image is fire
blackening the vague lines
into defiance across the city.
The image is fire
sun warming us in a cold country
barren of symbols for love . . .

The image is fire . . .
I smell it in the charred breezes blowing
over
your body
close
hard
essential
under its cloak of lies.

—Audre Lorde, "Summer Oracle"

I can tell you that solitude
Is not all exaltation, inner space
Where the soul breathes and work can be done.
Solitude exposes the nerve
. . . No one comes to this house
Who is not changed.

—May Sarton, "Gestalt at Sixty"

It is a matter of historical serendipity that Charlotte Perkins Gilman's classic feminist treatise, "The Yellow Wallpaper" (1892), reemerged into print in the same year that May Sarton's *As We Are Now* was first published (1973).[1] The two texts are mirrors of one another, double images across time. In style, structure, plot, and even, to some extent, critical reception, Sarton's account of an elderly nonconformist confined in the abusive environment of a nursing home reflects Gilman's story of a young Victorian wife sequestered under medical orders in a nursery. The two tales are also significantly paradigmatic of the basic tenets of theory predominant in feminist literary criticism of the 1970s, theory that stressed the oppression of women and the association of women's secondary status with pathology, deviance, or disease.[2]

Based primarily on nineteenth-century materials, literary and historical paradigms of oppression and subversion begin from a dualistic model of culture in which women/men are associated with private/public, submissive/ authoritative, confined/agentic, static/moving dichotomies.[3] Against this bifurcated framework, which largely denies the existence of a viable female culture to counteract patriarchal definitions, rebellious women are isolated; they are assumed to be masculinized in their instrumentalism and become lonely deviants and saboteurs, ultimately ineffectual in their reactions against gendered institutions that confine them. The female patient's or the literary heroine's "male" instrumentalism thus becomes a double phenomenon, simultaneously (positive) feminist rebellion and (negative) sickness. She—or a designated double who acts out for her—rejects normative submissive and restrictive roles that underlie the construction of female "health" and thereby is labeled as ill. Her own experience of these states of being is, however, reversed—it is in conformity that she feels ill and in subversion that she finds healing and empowerment.

The Yellow Wallpaper is styled as a series of diary entries written by an unnamed female narrator.[4] The woman patient/author is the author's double, an autobiographical characterization based on Gilman's own debilitating experience of a rest cure prescribed by the eminent Victorian physician, S. Weir Mitchell.[5] In her nameless state, she is also a signified, generic everywoman, suffering not as an individuated person, but as a representative of a category or caste of humanity—the domesticated middle-class woman— denied agency and profession and, with these, the powers of self-realization. The structure of the story is twofold and duplicitous, as, indeed, is the design of its controlling trope, the yellow wallpaper itself. Greeted by turn-of-the-century reviewers as a tale of gothic horror that charted the progressive insanity of its protagonist, its second, subversive plot, which offers a critical analysis of the normative assumptions behind the heroine's treatment, is recognized as the dominant one by modern, feminist readers.

Like Gilman's short story, Sarton's novella, *As We Are Now,* is presented as a supposed series of short and irregular copybook entries made by its female protagonist, the patient-writer Caro Spencer. Spencer is endowed by the author with many of her own personality traits, concerns, and preferences. Just as Gilman explains her authorial intention of writing *The Yellow Wallpaper* as a social tract that would awaken potential patients and current practitioners to the evils of standard psychological medical practice, so Sarton's alter ego explains her purpose in creating her copybooks as "a kind of testament" to be published in hopes of changing the ways health care practitioners "deal with people like me" (106).[6] The stories of destructive subversion thus have constructive alibis. Like Gilman's protagonist, Sarton's creates a duplicitous text alternating between her efforts at outer conformity and her interior rebellion. Instead of wallpaper (whose pattern, like a psychically distorted mirror, reflects the walls and bars that literally shape Gilman's entrapped woman's room and, ultimately, her twofold self as well), actual walls with their apertures (translucent windows, doors that can either offer sanctuary if closed or surveillance if opened) comprise the architectural embodiment of Sarton's protagonist's twoness. These walls form the boundaries of the interior of the nursing home she inhabits (and against which her own interior rebels) and of the landscape outdoors she views either as a longing spectator or as a loving participant (and where her outer demeanor is temporarily freed from its defensive falsehood). Recognized upon publication as a damning critique of American health care policy toward the aged, the feminist meanings underlying the overt purpose of Sarton's text were less commented upon.[7] While these parallels between the two stories are striking, there are also departures. Sarton's character's process of self-examination, unlike that of Gilman's persona, includes contact with outsiders who are not her keepers. These dynamics of relationship add feminist dimensions to the text that augment and reshape its subversive meanings in ways absent from Gilman's story.

Gilman's woman is incarcerated for her rest cure by her husband-physician, John, and attended by his sister, Jennie. (In *As We Are Now*, the unmarried Miss Spencer—a name close to spinster—is institutionalized by her brother, John, and his wife, Ginny). Her diary entries begin with decidedly gothic descriptions of the building John has brought her to. It seems altogether to her to be like a "haunted house," a "queer," untenanted place whose undefined past is made more questionable by its abandonment (Gilman, 9). The estate is remote from the nearby village, hedged in, walled in, with "gates that lock"; even houses for the few staff members are separated from the main mansion (11). The woman's quarters, in an attic-like space at the top of the building, is in turn cut off from the main house by a gate at the top of the stairs. The attic, with its barred windows, lockable door, and "rings and things in the walls," is at once nursery, playpen or crib, cage, prison cell, or madhouse (12). Supposedly the scene of rest and recuperation, it is instead the physical manifestation of the psychic constructions that hem the heroine in and gradually reduce her. It is the architectural embodiment of the processes of infantilization, regression, brutalization, deviance, and insanity. In it, husband-physician John patronizes his wife-patient. Referring to her with endearments usually reserved for a recalcitrant but charming child, he gathers her in his arms and carries her to bed as if she were a naughty youngster foolishly attempting to avoid the wisdom of his benevolent guidance (14–15, 21).[8] The heroine, confined and negated, eventually crawls—acting out a standard metaphor of subservience, lowered to all fours like an animal or like a child who has yet to develop the skill of walking upright. Like a prisoner or an institutionalized patient, her privacy is limited, her time is structured for her, and her behavior monitored. She receives hourly doses of medication and has "a scheduled prescription for each hour in the day," her attentive husband hardly letting her "stir without special direction" (12).[9]

The path of her diminishment is charted by two texts, the diary she writes that is perused by us, her readers, and the wallpaper, the text of which she slowly interprets for us.[10] The two come to match one another in their doubleness. In the first, the text of the physician-husband's prescriptive constructions of the heroine's needs and behaviors is subverted by the heroine's secret assertion, in her forbidden diary, of her own counter-vailing views. In the second, the putrid, "sickly," sulphuric paper, with its obnoxious, outrageous, contradictory, and revolting pattern, becomes gradually deciphered.

Initially viewed as a baffling and aggravating one-dimensional text, the wallpaper becomes personified and slowly splits into two separate texts. It seemingly begins to move and shake; the narrator attributes to it a consciousness ("as if it *knew* what a vicious influence it had"); she sees in it bulbous eyes that stare out at her from atop broken necks (16). Already torturous, the offensively patterned paper becomes violently abusive ("It slaps you in the face, knocks you down, and tramples upon you" [25]). It slowly sorts itself into two texts, an inner and outer pattern. A third person, a woman, comprises the inner subtext, crawling and shaking, struggling behind the confining boundaries of the outer text-design. She is legion, one and many. The narrator recognizes the bulbous eyes and broken necks protruding into the outer design as those of the wallpaper woman / women, their battered condition the symptoms of their efforts, like her own, to penetrate the boundary that constrains them and escape through its bars (30). With time, she identifies herself as the double of the woman she perceives in the subtext of the wallpaper. In a kind of osmosis between the two sides of the papered wall, the woman confined behind the paper emerges into the attic room, while the heroine becomes the wallpaper woman.

Her penetration of the outer pattern of the paper and her embodiment of its subtext is described in the alternate double text of the story—her diary. In her writing, the heroine shifts from the third to first person in describing the woman in the wallpaper. As the moonlight "creeps" over the gory outer pattern of the wallpaper, she reports that "I felt creepy" (23); she sees the creeping woman / women behind the overt pattern struggling to be released and she begins creeping herself, rubbing off the yellow of the wallpaper onto her own body and staining her clothes with it as she crawls, carrying the smell of the sulphurous paper with her like a putrid aura wherever she goes, creeping, about her domestic confines. She knowingly confides to her diary that "I always lock the door when I creep by daylight" (31).

The direct identification with (and subsequent embodiment of) the heroine with the wallpaper woman / women marks a turning point in the discourse of the written diary. From its beginning, the diary is an exercise in outlining basic constructions of reality from the husband-physician's viewpoint coupled with the wife-patient's deconstruction. The deconstructive voice is, at first, quite assertive ("Personally," the narrator confides, "I disagree with their ideas" [10]). The estate is *not* a restful retreat, the room chosen by her husband is *not* the one she desires, her isolation from friends is *not* improving her condition, nor is forbidding her to work—write— doing her good. Yet, she attempts to identify with her husband's diagnosis, with his power to label her condition, and to conform to the remedies he prescribes to alter it. This process of social construction and treatment provides the overt structure of her journal. Simultaneously, by secretly "working," documenting the structure imposed upon her and privately giving voice to her countervailing perceptions of that structure, she creates a subtext that exists underneath her compliance with outer definitions and restraints. The content of the private subtext shifts in its meanings, becoming progressively more subversive. It changes from a chronicle of interiority in which the writer seeks "relief to my mind" (10) through self-expression— and thus resists her confinement and limitations—to an obsessive identification with the literal interior that entraps her. The subversive aspects of the two double texts—wallpaper and diary—collapse in on one another and merge in the figure of the crawling woman.

The bars the narrator perceives in the outer pattern of the wallpaper become associated with John and his prescriptions, which make up the overt structure of the diary ("As if I couldn't see through him!" she crows [32]). Meanwhile, the covert pattern of the paper is directly associated with herself and her secret actions. Her "work"—a reference earlier in the story to her writing—becomes instead her stripping of the wallpaper (34). The inner and outer layers of the wallpaper are punctured and pulled inside out as the heroine peels the paper away, figuratively releasing the wallpaper woman/ women from her imprisonment behind the outer pattern. The covert text of the diary also becomes its dominant discourse, as the writer records her own creeping, and reports that she sees the creeping women everywhere, the yard outside the confines of the attic full of these escapees, and wonders "if they all came out of that wall-paper as I did?" (35).

The denouement of Gilman's story thus reverses the relative status of the overt and covert texts (just as John, the patriarchal authority, lies prostrate in a dead faint as his maddened wife crawls over his passive body). The subversive texts of the wallpaper/diary are brought into the open. The creeping wallpaper women metaphorically emerge to move throughout the landscape outside the barred attic windows; the creeping, mad heroine sheds her outer conformity to prescriptive behavior/"health" and openly reveals herself to others as she has covertly described herself in her journal passages for some time.

Like the Victorian wife who begins her diary soon after being brought to the remote and queer estate in *The Yellow Wallpaper,* Sarton's Caro Spencer in *As We Are Now* begins to write soon after being deposited by her brother at the Twin Elms nursing home. Announcing in the first paragraph of her journal that she has been placed in a "concentration camp for the old" (Sarton, 3), where merely obtaining the tools for writing—notebook and pen—becomes a challenge, Spencer proceeds, as Gilman's woman diarist did, to describe the new situation she finds herself in. Like the ancestral mansion that was the scene of the young wife's confinement, the rest home Spencer has been relegated to is described in gothic terms reminiscent of the House of Usher. A sense of isolation, apocalypse, or disaster and a suppressed desire for escape are expressed in her description of the remoteness of the building from any town and of the ravages of weather. She arrives in a heavy downpour that would "make almost anyone consider building an ark!" (5). The deluge obscures the route and makes it seem as if the house has been reached by a wrong turn. The building is "enclosed in darkness" without and within and seems to be sinking into a grave of its own making, its foundations covered and its front door blocked by a "sea of mud" (5).

The home is variously described as prison, purgatory, hell; "a place of punishment" (4) where it is difficult to tell the difference between deliberate indignities and "delusions of persecution" (5). From the beginning, Spencer doubts the veracity of her own perceptions. Her journal, like that of Gilman's alter ego, is her effort at resistance and self-definition, a hold on sanity through the careful labeling and exploration of reality. It makes her countervailing perceptions seem objective and concrete.

> Because it *is* written down and can be reread, it is far more substantive than my idle thoughts, or even my most intense thoughts for that matter. It is *outside* me and because I can see it and read it *outside* my mind, I know that I exist and am still sane. (40)

Literally going outside into the yard or meadow is associated with the objective "outsideness" of writing and with being herself. The only female inmate, she has a room of her own with a view of fields and gentle hills. Indoors, her behavior is checked. She is subject to surveillance and a random and unceremonious denial of her privacy. In extremes, following rare outbursts of emotion or rebellion, she is locked in a silent, dark room deprived of sensation, the promise of a return to docile conformity the price of her release. In contrast to this denial of agency and self-worth, the outside world offers warmth, beauty, and the possibility of renewal and candor. "I did get out and it was wonderful" (41) she reports with relief to her copybook, in an image of escape not unlike that of the figurative wallpaper woman pushing through the bars of the paper and of the attic window out into the yard.[11]

The outside of the institutional structure is associated not only with her own objectivity and expression, but with outsiders who confirm those powers in her. Being outdoors frees her to create the written word; it also offers her the space for uncensored verbal expression with visitors. Indoors, she hides her journals under her pillow and speaks in whispers to avoid being overheard by her keepers; outdoors, she speaks aloud (57 and 93). Indoors, communication is warped and difficult, not only because of the threat of retaliation against honest expression but because of physical barriers. Standish Flint, the one other inmate with whom she forms a bond, is deaf.

He cannot read because the women who run the home have misplaced his glasses. She must communicate with him by shouting, which bars her from truthfulness. They conspire instead by exchanged glances and the press of hands. She also communicates with Jack, a mentally disabled young man, whose "speech is a sort of gurgle" (15) that she gradually learns to "decipher" (71). The alienation induced by this disrupted discourse brings Spencer to describe old age itself as like a "foreign country with an unknown language" (17).

The word—read, written, or remembered—is her "touchstone for sanity" (88). Words are the foundation of the journal she writes, which is a kind of internal dialogue, and of the newspaper she reads, which links her to the world at large she has been removed from. Words codify the meaning of the poems she recites; of the Lord's Prayer she repeats like a rune; of the *Oxford Book of English Verse* she sets on her dresser. Words are her medium of memory and, thus, of identity. She recalls the letters she wrote to her long-ago lover and, eventually, to the lover's wife; she composes new letters in her copybook and sometimes succeeds in mailing them out to those she cares for and who know her only as the independent person she once was.[12] Rev. Richard Thornhill (his name redolent of Calvary, of suffering and redemptive sacrifice) and his daughter, Lisa, two of Spencer's outside visitors, are both linked with the outdoors and the word. Spencer has true conversations with them; they in turn mail her letters and supply her with novels and blank copybooks. Spencer's positive assessment of Thornhill when she first meets him equates him with integrity of expression; "his copybook," she metaphorically reports to her own, literal, copybook, "was surprisingly clean"(50).

Richard Thornhill is associated not only with open discourse but with the second purpose of her subversive text. While the journal serves as a means for clarifying and maintaining her selfhood—like "a map" (4) reminding her of a personal path of resistance and revision she must maintain through the outer constructions that seek to redefine her—it also documents the conditions of the nursing home. At first, Spencer believes that if the home were inspected by state authorities, witnesses who could "observe, and ... keep an outsider's eye on our keepers" (44), the abuses of power born of the home's isolation could be reversed. She hints to Thornhill, who does have the home inspected. The outside intervention does little to improve physical conditions and has a dire effect upon Spencer's status.[13] Blamed by the operators of the home for the subversive act of bringing in outside authorities, she suffers direct harassment and deteriorates in response.

Thornhill becomes the eventual heir to the secret texts that record the path of her disintegration.

Like Gilman's woman, Spencer is treated as a child, her opinions and efforts at self-exertion contradicted and demeaned. Placed under even closer surveillance and ridiculed before visitors, her authenticity is undermined, her own belief in herself shaken. She has nightmares of enclosure and entrapment, dreaming she is running along the sealed corridors of a ship, trying to reach open air, but instead reaching one locked door after another. As in *The Yellow Wallpaper* where the nursery is prison, crib, and cage, and passivity and compliance are rewarded, the nursing home in Spencer's journal encases people described as infants or animals. The old male inmates are compared to pigs, to "cattle, in a stupor" (40) or, worse, vegetative plant life, "amoebas" or seaweed, swaying in water (65 and 39)—not unlike the seaweedlike fungus women Gilman's heroine perceived in the wallpaper (Gilman 20).[14] Significantly, the keepers are also dehumanized. Harriet, the woman in charge, is variously described as brutish and beastly, as a "pig" (Sarton 41) or a "bloodhound" (58). Spencer studies Harriet in the way a former student of hers, who had been imprisoned in solitary confinement, once studied "spiders and mice" (9). In this environment of reduction, outer resistance gives way to adaptive paralysis; "One begins to feel like an animal in a cage," Spencer writes, "even if the door were open, one would not dare move" (16).[15]

While the isolated heroine of *The Yellow Wallpaper* begins making entries in her covert diary with a determined will to write "in spite of them," she soon finds the effort tiring. On one hand, she reports that confessing to the "dead paper" of her journal is "a great relief to my mind" (Gilman, 10). On the other hand, her attention is constantly divided; part of her mind must remain alert to the possibility of discovery and the need to revert to an appearance of innocent nonaction with little forewarning. She is attuned to the sound of footsteps approaching her room as she writes. She reports impending interruptions and notes the correlation drawn by those who watch over her between her writing and her subversion of normative mother-wife social roles.[16] Omissions and gaps in the chronology of her journal are telling; the unwritten spaces connote changes in the status of her confinement. Requests to get away or to receive visitors she can discuss her work with are rejected as unwise by husband-physician John, and she dissolves into tears at each thwarted effort. Self-doubt and disorientation weaken her ability to write; the sentences themselves become fragmented, truncated by the effort it takes to produce them ("I don't know why I should write this. / I don't want to. / I don't feel able. / . . . But I *must* say what I feel and think in some way—it is such a relief! / But the effort is getting to be greater than the relief") (21).[17] This feeling of the growing inability to create her own discourse on paper is associated with her increasing attention to interpreting the alternative text, the wallpaper. The interiority and fancy once directed to the journal is instead projected onto the papery boundaries that wall her in.

A similar disintegration of self-resolve and an increasing inability to keep the interiority of desires and emotions from being outwardly revealed is associated with Caro Spencer's writing in *As We Are Now*. While Gilman's character calls her diary "dead paper," Sarton's entitles her effort to keep herself whole *The Book of the Dead* (Sarton, 4).[18] Occasionally caught writing in her copybooks by the attendants, her private discourse is largely dismissed as a symptom of her strangeness as a woman who has eschewed domestic life for an intellectual profession, or as a sign of senile dementia, as if she has been discovered in an elaborate conversation with herself. Gaps in the text are also significant. When the state inspectors come and take away her friend, Standish, to an undignified death in an ambulance, she reacts violently and is physically restrained, sedated, and placed in solitary confinement. The hole created in the text by these events is later painfully filled in, like dirt shoveled into a grave. Similarly, she reports that "I have not been able to write for days" (21) after losing self-control during a disastrous visit with brother-incarcerator John. She broke into sobs while unsuccessfully trying to convince him to take her away—the operator of the home lurking in the corner of the room throughout the interchange, further restricting what she was able to say. While Gilman's woman is told by her husband to check her imagination and "habit of story-making," (Gilman, 15) Spencer's attendants increasingly attribute her verbal statements and observations to delusion, forcing her to question her own interpretations of reality. The journals that they see as part of her sickness are, to her, her hold on health. "It's very hard to write today," she records, "yet I must."

> This document is becoming in a very real sense my stay against confusion of mind. When I feel my mind slipping, I go back and rediscover what really happened. It must be true, I wrote it myself. (Sarton, 62–63)

Despite the effort it takes, Spencer still finds that "*expression* relieves the mind!" (75). Revitalized by the act of writing, she is temporarily transported out of her sense of entombment and self-doubt and granted transcendence over her physical limitations ("I feel quite lively and myself again" she notes, "just because I have managed to write two pages of dissent" on old age as deprivation [75]). She too begins to fear that her copybooks will be taken from her and guards against their discovery.

Unlike Gilman's heroine, Sarton's confined woman is temporarily arrested in the downward spiral of her condition. This stay against deterioration comes with the arrival of Anna Close, a Beatrix Potter figure of a farmwife who appears as if conjured from some fairy-tale portion of Caro Spencer's mind. Sarton's inclusion of the Close character allows room for exploration of the feminist dynamics of relation and individuation absent from *The Yellow Wallpaper*, where the only woman-to-woman bonds are more manacle-like than affective. In *The Yellow Wallpaper*, much of the day-to-day care of the heroine is provided by the husband's sister, Jennie, who is described as an ally of her brother, the physician, carrying out his orders and seeing through his prism of normalcy. She is herself the good house-keeper, the unquestioning domestic woman that the heroine is not. In *As We Are Now*, the authority of maintenance care comes completely in female form, indeed in a mother-daughter duo. While Caro Spencer occasionally allows some identification between herself and the mother and daughter who run the home where she is incarcerated—noting their long hours, the depressing aspects of their work, and realizing that they, too, were not always as they are now—she more typically erects self-protective barriers and attributes to them the animal-like characteristics that she feels they in turn impose upon her. The love relationship that Spencer forms with Anna Close causes her to lower the kinds of barriers she typically uses to define herself and instead to open herself to another. In doing so, she must reorient her sense of self from a position of identification with men and conventionally "male" choices and constructions of behavior to form the kinds of connections to women associated with cultural feminism.[19]

In becoming institutionalized, Spencer is forced to face the ramifications of the dominance of instrumental "male" values on many levels—those she recognizes and has valued in herself, those manifested in the organization of the nursing home that entraps her, and, by extension, in societal attitudes toward the aged and the health care of the aged. Spencer is an arch individualist whose nontraditional choices—becoming a mathematician, traveling alone, choosing not to marry—have set her apart. Her sense of personal authenticity is keenly connected to the firmness and impenetrability of her ego boundaries, which keep intact her interior self. "I'm myself alone," she

tells her journal, "there is some dignity in that" (17). She loves the aes-
thetically "stark, aloof" (24) and is attracted to men like Standish Flint,
whose tart bitterness she describes as "so authentic" (19). Indeed, she likes
Standish because he is a male double of herself. The two stay alive in the
home by sheer "tenacity, by passive resistance" made possible by calling on
a "deep, buried fire of anger that never goes out" (19).[20] She loves the
supposedly "male" constructions of the rational and the assertive, the sym-
metrical and tidy absolutes of perfect mathematical equations. She tells her
journal early on that she prefers boys, when noting that the younger attendant's children, all girls, play in the yard (10); the girls are never mentioned
again in the journal's pages. "I never liked women very much," she confesses,
"too intense . . . I like men much better" (18).[21] She recognizes that she has
held people at a distance with "arrogance and contempt" (69) and has
fostered a habit of actively imposing her will upon others in the name of
preserving her own integrity (36 and 87).

Mrs. Close is the personification of the very traits Spencer has spent
a lifetime avoiding and denying. A female figure of rescue, she is motherly
and a tender nurse, an empathetic and sensitive woman whose own boundaries
of self are fluid and encompassing. Her quiet love, her touch, her care, her
cognizance of beauty, allow a corresponding emotionalism and vulnerability
in Spencer. The correspondence Spencer feels with Anna Close is healing;
it reverses the damaging effects of dehumanization suffered in the normal
operation of the home.[22]

Spencer's feeling of merging with Anna is both a childlike need for
comfort and nurturing and an adult, physical, attraction. It is, in turn,
associated with a revitalization of her ability to write and with the outdoors.
Anna encourages her to "get outside in the warm sun . . . and do your
writing there" (88). Spencer's fingers "tingle with pleasure" (76) when she
describes Anna to her copybook and she allows herself to bask in sensuality
and sensation when she thinks of her. Anna, so earthbound and tied to the
human heart, is not a person of words. She is very different from Spencer,
whose identity is self-structured with words and dependent upon the transcendence of the here and now through music, mathematics, or verbal
abstractions. The difference is complementary, and Spencer's relationship
with Anna makes her feel whole. Anna's maternal "power and . . . healing
grace" (93) offer a cultural construction of mutual appreciation and empowerment that belies the construction of power as a model of dominance and
belittlement that normally shapes relationships in the home.

The curative respite of female love and connection comes to an end when the operator of the nursing home returns from vacation and Anna Close goes back to her own farm and family. Regression, born of the replacement of renewal and affirmation with repression, is quick and brutal. Spencer's immediate reaction to the returned attendant is to behave "like an animal that growls" with distrust at a stranger (96). Unsure of herself, she loses the power to write; her hand visibly shakes when she takes up the pen. She tries to keep intact her newfound powers of gentleness by thinking of Anna and contemplating "the wholesome world outdoors" that is associated with her (97). She appreciates her visits with Lisa Thornhill who, besides providing female companionship herself, is also the outside connection to Anna and another woman from Spencer's past and, thus, to a female world Spencer describes as like a "tonic" (94). Her ability to sustain her connection to this outside female world and to the health that her love for Anna has brought her is, however, cut short by the long-feared discovery of her subversive text.

Spencer writes a love letter to Anna in her copybook, then goes outside for a walk. Upon returning to the confines of the home, she finds Harriet, the operator of the home, reading the journal. Harriet informs her that she had "read what [she] had written," interpreted the text in homophobic terms, and would have her institutionalized in the state mental hospital if she should "dare send such a filthy letter" (100). Spencer is shocked by the violation of her interiority and the vehement denunciation of its most cherished content. In mute response, she "got up and walked out of the house" (100). The escape outside the home / outside herself is momentary. She is recaptured and locked up, reporting to her diary that "I am walled in" (105). The discovery of the diary reconstructs the dominant meaning of closeness. Whereas Spencer had succeeded temporarily in deconstructing the confines of the home and redefining closeness in human terms—in terms of Anna Close, "close to God? . . . close to me" (73 and 76)—the rapelike violation of self represented in the invasive and abusive reading of the text that embodies her inner self reverses the construction of the term and Spencer's long-defended authentic identity along with it. Closeness ceases to exist in its revised sense. It no longer means the emotional bonds and correspondence identified with the expressive aspects of discourse. Instead, its initial meaning—being enclosed, buried, claustrophic, watched, repressed—is reified. "The walls close in on every side" (109) Spencer writes, and with them comes the victory of sickness and death that Spencer's private text making had long been defying.[23]

The reading of Spencer's private writings is like a puncture wound through which the social constructions of debility and delusion that have been applied to her from without flow in and occupy her interior self. As she internalizes the constructions of sickness and decay Harriet has labeled her with, and that are, in turn, physically manifest in the walls/architectural limitations that restrict and isolate her, Spencer also reverses the focus of her journal. It remains a testament, but where it previously documented the countering of abuse with measures of self-preservation and sanity, it instead gives way to self-destruction and madness. Spencer subsumes the meanings of negative social worth applied to her, and, like Gilman's Victorian woman who projects her own oppression into the very walls of her cell-like room, she focuses those meanings in the physical structures that entomb her.

As Gilman's heroine comes to covertly identify with and project herself into (and eventually out of) the wallpaper, her outer demeanor seems to improve. "Life is very much more exciting now than it used to be. You see I have something more to expect, to look forward to" she writes in her journal (Gilman, 27). Where she previously begged to be released from her isolation, she instead becomes fearful that her husband will take her away before she has accomplished her plan to destroy the wallpaper. She thinks briefly of "burning the house—to reach the smell" (Gilman, 29) of the paper, which is by that time attached to her own person—smooched all over her clothes—but instead decides to strip it away to free the crawling woman behind it. She neglects her writing to concentrate on the changing movements of the woman/women caught in the walls of her enclosure.

Similarly, Caro Spencer writes less and shifts her attention to her own plan to destroy the entrapping walls of her interior space. "I am too tired now to go on writing—anyway why go on?" she records listlessly (Sarton, 103). Her power of deconstruction, of defiant renaming, erodes. She can no longer refer to Anna by name, feeling she contaminates the other woman's loveliness by the very act of writing the name with her contagious pen. After creating an almost-whole text that is an exercise in naming and defining herself, she also ceases to address herself by her own name, feeling the self she once was—and had, through the journal, strived to remain—had "ceased to exist. Someone else, mentally ill, tortured, hopeless, has taken over my body and my mind" (103). Feeling "stripped down to nothing" (120), and realizing that "everything here is twisted around into reverse" (108), she sets her mind on burning down the walls of the institution. Where in other Sarton works fire is associated with durable love, here it is a consuming conflagration born of inner anger.[24] The fire Spencer plans is an act of terrorist anarchy, a militant agentic action that will reverse the power of repression in an apocalyptic blaze.

The denouement of Sarton's plot shares elements with Gilman's. Spencer outwardly improves as she secretly stores combustibles. When Richard Thornhill offers to take her out of the home, she reacts with panic, wanting nothing to interfere with her secret purpose. While planning the logistics of the fire, the mutual regression suffered by the inmates of the home makes her note that the "room of old men had become a nursery in the middle of the night" (122). Snow comes and buries the house, further cutting it off from the outer world, and she stops reading the newspaper, her link of words with life outside. While Gilman's heroine physically reverses gender roles—her husband dropping to the floor in a womanly faint while she maintains her animal-like path, crawling across his prone body on all fours— so Spencer's final act is signaled by her knocking down Harriet, "like a wild animal" attacking a zoo keeper that has entered its cage (126). Her final defiance—and regression—is induced by finding Harriet reading her copybook a second time. Grabbing the journal from the attendant and pushing her to the floor in the process, Spencer flees and locks herself into the bathroom, where she makes a final entry. With great self-possession, she waits for quiet in the night and safeguards the copybooks in the refrigerator. The angry fire of the covert text then becomes overt action. She lights the flames that burn the home down, destroying herself, her fellow nursery mates, and her keeper in one violent, irreversible act of subversion.[25]

Like Gilman's heroine, Sarton's internalizes the labels of sickness thrust upon her, then projects them in a powerful and menacing way upon the structures that both literally confine her and metaphorically reflect the social constructions/constrictions that negate her inner identity. She expresses, and therefore maintains, her authentic self in her method of self-destruction, bringing others down with her in an inferno of her choosing. Both Sarton and Gilman's defiant, mad heroines succeed in wielding a power of redefined discourse. Theirs is a terrible triumph, the achievement of a macabre freedom that twists or disintegrates dominant restrictive patterns of normative behavior and social control. They ultimately exercise the questionably positive power of double negation. In their actions they fulfill the debilitating logic of constructions applied to them while simultaneously succeeding in penetrating and inverting those constructions with meanings supplied from their own subversive texts.[26]

NOTES

"Summer Oracle" appears in Audre Lorde, *The Black Unicorn* (New York: Norton, 1978). "Gestalt at Sixty" appears in May Sarton, *A Durable Fire* (New York: Norton, 1972), 11.

1. Charlotte Perkins Gilman, *The Yellow Wallpaper* (1892; reprint, Old Westbury, N.Y.: Feminist Press, 1973); May Sarton, *As We Are Now* (New York and London: Norton, 1973). References to *The Yellow Wallpaper* and *As We Are Now* will hereafter be cited in shortened versions as Gilman or Sarton; when the reference is supplied by context, the appropriate page numbers will be cited in parentheses within the text.

2. The concept of doubleness is central to this body of theory, which bases its foundation in (patriarchal) premises of binary constructions of culture and the idea of woman as second sex. As Mary Ann Doane has noted, in such configurations, "disease and the woman have something in common—they are both socially devalued or undesirable, marginalized elements which constantly threaten to infiltrate and contaminate that which is more central, health or masculinity" (Doane, "Clinical Eyes: The Medical Discourse," in *The Desire to Desire: The Woman's Film of the 1940s* [Bloomington: Indiana University Press, 1987], 38). Sandra Gilbert and Susan Gubar's *The Madwoman in the Attic: The Woman Writer and the Nineteenth-Century Literary Imagination* (New Haven: Yale University Press, 1979) has become the standard-bearer of this stage of theory. Gilbert and Gubar argue that, because patriarchal constructs define authorship as male, the female writer experiences anxiety of authorship, an internalized sense of "dis-ease" or freakishness that compels artistic duplicity and "infection in the sentence." They define feminist poetics as the creation of a double text, a kind of palimpsest "whose surface designs conceal or obscure deeper, less accessible [and less socially acceptable] levels of meaning" (73). While the overt story seemingly conforms to patriarchal standards, the underlying text in the double plot conveys a secret message of woman's subversive desires and quest for self-definition. This second plot is "the story of her attempt to make herself whole by healing her own infections and diseases" (76). The female writer's search for wholeness is structured, in part, by her expression of "covert authorial anger" (77), anger often projected onto a dark double, the quintessential madwoman, who is allowed the "power of self-articulation" and the luxury of interiority, the presentation of self "from the inside out" (79). Such a heroine is trapped and claustrophobic, literally and figuratively confined; her rebellion, in the form of rage and self-expression, which makes her monstrous, often results in an escape that is self-destructive. The paradigm of oppression and subversion is thus both gothic and fatalistic in its overtones, with emphasis on fear of entrapment and on escape and flight (common themes for male characters in American fiction). (See, for example, Ellen Moers, *Literary Women* [Garden City, N.Y.: Anchor/Doubleday, 1977], 185–213, 321–68; Leslie Fiedler, *Love and Death in the American Novel* [1960; reprint, New York: Stein and Day, 1982]; Nina Baym, "Melodramas of Beset Manhood:

How Theories of American Fiction Exclude Women Authors," *American Quarterly*
23 [Summer 1981]: 123–39.) The female version of the paradigm, elaborated by a
number of feminist critics in the 1970s, accepts an archetype of victimization in
which femininity itself is experienced as a kind of disability, described in medical
terms of inadequacy or violation. Patricia Meyer Spacks, for example, describes
Victorian womanhood as a "handicap" that occasionally can be "overcome" and
Annis Pratt identifies "rape-trauma" as a basic plot structure in women's fiction
(Spacks, *The Female Imagination* [New York: Discus/Avon, 1972], 70; Pratt, *Archetypal Patterns in Women's Fiction* [Bloomington: Indiana University Press, 1981]; see
also Elizabeth Hardwick, *Seduction and Betrayal: Women and Literature* [New York:
Vintage, 1974]). Carolyn Heilbrun and Catharine Stimpson describe the punishing
effect of struggling against sexual double standards, observing that "women in
literature who try to act or to exercise will, are by the book's denouement either
prisoners or paralytics" ("Theories of Feminist Criticism: A Dialogue," in *Feminist
Literary Criticism: Explorations in Theory,* ed. Josephine Donovan [Lexington: University Press of Kentucky, 1975], 62). Janet Todd chooses illness, madness, death
and failure as peculiarly female motifs (*Women's Friendship in Literature* [New York:
Columbia University Press, 1980]), and Joanna Russ, like Gilbert and Gubar, stresses
the internalization of female gender as inferiority or debilitation ("What Can a
Heroine Do: Or Why Women Can't Write," in *Images of Women in Fiction: Feminist
Perspectives,* ed. Susan K. Cornillon [Bowling Green, Ohio: Bowling Green University Popular Press, 1973], 4).

3. The development of the oppression-subversion paradigm in feminist literary
theory in the 1970s was paralleled by studies by feminist women's historians, who
explored the relationship between nineteenth-century bourgeois ideas of women's
"place" and medical theory and praxis, which posited a genderized womb-mind
opposition and defined exclusively female biological functions (menstruation, preg-
nancy, maternity, menopause) as diseases subject to medical intervention and as
deviations from the male physiological model of health. The functionalist definition
of the sick role, with its emphasis on the docility and compliance of the (female)
patient with (male) medical authority and diagnosis, translated the patriarchal prescriptive power of social construction into that of pseudoscientific, institutionalized,
social control. Women who failed to submit to such diagnosis, or to follow the
doctors' orders, were labeled noncompliant, "bad" patients, ill by the very virtue
of their subversion of the supposedly rational and objective medical process. Such
scholarship, published in the 1972–74 era, includes Nancy Cott, "Sexuality and
Gynecology in the Nineteenth Century," *Root of Bitterness: Documents of the Social
History of American Women* (New York: Dutton, 1972), 263–308; Ben Barker-Benfield,
"The Spermatic Economy: A Nineteenth-Century View of Sexuality," *Feminist Studies*
1 (1972): 45–74; Irving Zola, "Medicine as an Institution of Social Control," *Sociological Review* 20 (November 1972): 487–504; Carroll Smith-Rosenberg and Charles
Rosenberg, "The Female Animal: Medical and Biological Views of Women in

Nineteenth-Century America," *Journal of American History* 60 (1973): 332–56; Barbara Ehrenreich and Deirdre English, *Complaints and Disorders: The Sexual Politics of Sickness* (Old Westbury, N.Y.: Feminist Press, 1973); David J. Pivar, *Purity Crusade: Sexual Morality and Social Control, 1868–1900,* (Westport, Conn.: Greenwood Press, 1973); Ann Douglas Wood, "'The Fashionable Diseases': Women's Complaints and Their Treatment in Nineteenth-Century America," *Journal of Interdisciplinary History* 4 (Summer 1973): 25–52; Regina Morantz, "The Lady and Her Physician," in *Clio's Consciousness Raised: New Perspectives on the History of Women,* ed. Mary S. Hartman and Lois Banner (New York: Harper and Row, 1974), 38–53; John S. Haller, Jr., and Robin Haller, *The Physician and Sexuality in Victorian America* (Urbana: University of Illinois Press, 1974).

4. The narrator's name, spoken at the end of the story, may very well be Jane, a generic name for every/any woman, as in Jane Doe (Gilman, 36).

5. For accounts of Gilman's treatment, see Charlotte Perkins Gilman, *The Living of Charlotte Perkins Gilman* (New York: Appleton-Century, 1935), 95–96, 119–121; Elaine R. Hedges, Afterword, in *The Yellow Wallpaper,* by Charlotte Perkins Gilman (Old Westbury, N.Y.: Feminist Press, 1973), 37–63. See also Mary Hill, *Charlotte Perkins Gilman: The Making of a Radical Feminist* (Philadelphia: Temple University Press, 1980). It should be noted that Gilman's story of female debilitation and the "illness" of Victorian norms of gender is countered by the vigorous good health (physical strength, mental prowess, self-confidence, and self-government) of the short-haired and bloomer-attired women she created to populate her imaginative separatist utopia, *Herland* (1915).

6. Sarton's elderly retired woman, like Gilman's domesticated woman, is representative of a socially constructed caste of femininity. Gilman's heroine, suffering from partially postpartum-induced manic-depression, is marginalized by her failure to successfully internalize late nineteenth-century bourgeois norms. Sarton's heroine is marginalized by age and disability and by the negative self-worth assigned to the elderly. The issue of ageism is simultaneously an issue of sexism. In the mid-1970s, when Sarton wrote *As We Are Now,* the ratio of elderly women to elderly men was nearly two to one. While most men living into their seventies were married, with a surviving spouse, the majority of elderly women were widows. Eighty percent of men over the age of seventy-five lived in a family setting, while the same reality was true for only 34 percent of elderly women. For women, whose social worth has conventionally been concentrated in childbearing years, the life stage of family dissolution, retirement, and/or widowhood has become prolonged. And, while women constitute the majority of the aged, they also comprise a disproportionately large number of the poor. The subculture of age, then, is not only one of prescribed dysfunction, but of the devaluation of female experience, and one part of the feminization of poverty. See Herman Brotman, "The Fastest Growing Minority: The Aging," *American Journal of Public Health* 64 (March 1974): 249–52; Robert V. Wells, "Demographic Change and the Life Cycle of American

Families," in *The Family History: Interdisciplinary Essays*, ed. Theodore Rabb and Robert Rotberg (New York: Harper, 1971), 85–94; Claire Townsend, et. al., *Old Age: The Last Segregation* (New York: Grossman, 1971), 19.

7. See reviews in *Publisher's Weekly*, 13 August 1973, 44; *Christian Science Monitor*, 29 August 1973, 9; *Saturday Review*, 11 September 1973, 44; *New Republic*, 13 October 1973, 31; *New York Times Book Review*, 4 November 1973, 77; *Choice*, January 1974, 1722; *New Yorker*, 8 April 1974, 141–42; and *Spectator*, 27 July 1974, 119.

8. John also exclaims "Bless her little heart!" (Gilman, 24) and asks "What is it, little girl?" (23). Gilman's narrator is relieved, in the midst of the infantilization suffered at the hands of her husband, that her actual infant is not subject to a life in the nursery—"What a fortunate escape!" (22). William Veeder, sidestepping many feminist meanings in his intriguing psychoanalytic approach to Gilman's story, stresses the heroine's own culpability in the process of infantile regression, defined in part as movement away from an adult condition "where she must bear children and responsibilities" into one of security where she herself is cared for (Veeder, "Who is Jane? The Intricate Feminism of Charlotte Perkins Gilman," *Arizona Quarterly* 44 [Autumn 1988]: 46). Veeder observes that the yellow wallpaper, with its urinelike color and foul smell, is "among many other things—the saturated diaper of childhood" (48) and that the crawling woman's psychological retreat back into the womb is nearly complete by the end of the story, when she ties a rope around herself like an "umbilical cord" explaining that connection to it will keep her in the attic rather than "out in the road there" (63). See also Loralee MacPike, "Environment as Psychopathological Symbolism in *The Yellow Wallpaper*," *American Literary Realism* 8 (1975): 286–88.

9. As Veeder points out, there is some evidence that the "nursery" John places the protagonist in was actually inhabited by another madwoman before her, who has (as Gilman's heroine eventually does also) gnawed the bedstead and clawed at the walls. The narrator reports early on that the paper is "stripped off . . . in great patches all around the head of my bed, about as far as I can reach." It has either already been stripped by herself, or by another very like her, whose status she has inherited (12).

10. For analyses of the wallpaper as text, see Gilbert and Gubar, *Madwoman in the Attic*, 89–92, and Paula A. Treichler, "Escaping the Sentence: Diagnosis and Discourse in *The Yellow Wallpaper*," in *Feminist Issues in Literary Scholarship*, ed. Shari Benstock (Bloomington: Indiana University Press, 1987), 62–78. Gilbert and Gubar describe *The Yellow Wallpaper* (like *Jane Eyre*) as "*the* story that all literary women would tell if they could speak their 'speechless woe'" (*The Madwoman in the Attic*, 89).

11. Spencer later writes that Anna Close, the farmwife/nurse she has come to love, is "'outside,' safe. I am inside, in danger of despair and madness, in danger of appearing ridiculous—even to myself" (Sarton, 97).

12. For references to Spencer's lifeline relationship to the word, see Sarton, 4, 7, 8, 9, 14, 27, 30, 55, 58, 73, 75, 90–91, 92.

13. On the inefficacy of regulation and inspection policies and the need for an outside, watchdog presence within nursing homes, see Jane Lockwood Barney, "Community Presence as a Key to Quality of Life in Nursing Homes," *American Journal of Public Health* 64 (March 1974): 265–68; Townsend, et al., *Old Age,* 42–49.

14. Other references to infantilization and dehumanization include Sarton, 10, 55, 58, 74, 96. Spencer compares her incarcerators to child batterers in a conversation with Rev. Thornhill (84). Even brother John (like husband John in Gilman's story) addresses Caro in a tone of voice reserved for "children or the feeble-minded" (5). Spencer eventually prefers real animal company—Pansy the cat, the geese in the yard, or the old dog—to that of the dehumanized occupants of the home.

15. On the issue of the denial of patients' rights within medical institutions and the related processes of regression and dehumanization, see Sally Hart Wilson, "Nursing Home Patients' Rights: Are They Enforceable?" *Gerontologist* 18 (June 1978): 255–61; Nancy Quinn and Anne Somers, "The Patients' Bill of Rights," *Nursing Outlook* 22 (April 1974): 240–44; George Annas, *The Rights of Hospital Patients* (New York: Avon, 1975).

16. "There comes John, and I must put this away,—he hates to have me write a word"; "There comes John's sister [Jennie] . . . I must not let her find me writing . . . I verily believe she thinks it is the writing which made me sick!" (Gilman 13, 17–18).

17. Earlier she states that "if I were only well enough to write a little it would relieve the press of ideas and rest me. / But I find I get pretty tired when I try" (Gilman 16).

18. The title of the book, which is taken from the inscription on a New England tombstone that serves as the book's epigram ("As you are now, so once was I. / Prepare for death and follow me") carries with it the imagery of being buried or entombed alive. There is also a sense of warning (as in the macabre phrase "follow your leader" in Herman Melville's *Benito Cereno*) and of the mutuality of fate and responsibility (as in John Donnes's "ask not for whom the bell tolls, it tolls for thee") encapsulated in the title, which is furthered by Sarton in the concentration camp analogies used in the text.

19. On the sexual politics of difference and feminist relation theory, see Hester Eisenstein and Alice Jardine, eds. *The Future of Difference* (1980; reprint, New Brunswick, N.J.: Rutgers University Press, 1985); Nancy Chodorow, *The Reproduction of Mothering: Psychoanalysis and the Sociology of Gender* (Berkeley: University of California Press, 1978); Carol Gilligan, *In a Different Voice: Psychological Theory and Women's Development* (Cambridge, Mass.: Harvard University Press, 1982); Jean Baker Miller, *Toward a New Psychology of Women,* 2d ed. (Boston: Beacon Press, 1976).

20. Flint is like the stone that gives him his name, a very hard substance that creates sparks/fire when struck against steel. One of the important aspects of the relationship between Spencer and Flint is their mutual resistance to forced medication;

indeed, Spencer aids Flint in his resistance by routinely taking the pills he conceals and flushing them down the toilet. The use of major tranquilizers to ensure passive and manageable behavior, along with the maladministration of other medications, is a highly recognized form of abuse in nursing homes. The practice denies basic rights of self-control, weakens the capability for human interaction and the expression of an individual's unique identity, and hastens psychological death. On the use of drugs as a means of social control in institutional settings, see Mary Adelaide Mendelson, *Tender Loving Greed* (New York: Vintage, 1975), 177–81; Sharon R. Curtin, *Nobody Eved Died of Old Age* (Boston: Little, Brown, 1972); Raymond Glasscote et al., *Old Folks at Homes* (Washington, D.C.: American Psychiatric Association, 1976) 74–75; Townsend, *Old Age,* 111–21.

21. She likes some women very much, however; for example, her lesbian aunt, Isabel, the "black sheep" of the family who got a Ph.D. in political science, drank, smoked, and had women friends, becoming a role model for the younger Caro in the process (Sarton, 79). Spencer writes of feeling passionately attracted to "one or two" women in her life, but notes that such sexual interest "is different from liking" (18).

22. Harriet and Anna personify two extreme modes in health-care delivery that, in turn, relate to sameness/difference debates in feminist theory. Harriet's abrupt custodial care is an extension of the curative, instrumental bias of mainstream medical care, where the supposedly objective (conventionally "male") authority of the caregiver grants him or her diagnostic power over the passive patient. Anna Close, on the other hand, embodies the expressive values associated with female socialization, ethics, and primary care; values conventionally considered secondary, linked with nursing and subordinated within standard medical practice. The first situation is a "power over" model of domination and compliance; the second an interactive model in which the psychosocial health and needs of the patient are recognized as a key part of somatic well-being. On the division of the medical labor force by sex and value orientation (cure/control/science vs. care/support/humanism) see Jeane Quint Benoliel, "Care, Cure, and the Challenge of Voice," M. Vachon, et al., "The Nurse in Thanatology: What She Can Learn from the Women's Liberation Movement," and Nancy Proctor Greenleaf, "Stereotyped Sex-Role Ranking of Caregivers and Quality Care for Dying Patients," all in *The Nurse as Caregiver for the Terminal Patient and His Family,* ed. Ann M. Earle, Nina T. Argondizzo, and Austin H. Kutscher (New York: Columbia University Press, 1976) 9–27, 175–84, 185–93; Andrea O'Connor, *Dying and Grief: Nursing Interventions* (New York: American Journal of Nursing, 1976).

23. With institutionalization (coupled with the denunciation of her homosexual attraction to Anna Close), Spencer experiences what social scientists have called social death, which, in turn, leads to psychological death. Social death is a matter of devaluation partially expressed in physical and psychic segregation, a phenomenon that makes the experience of the institutionalized aged analogous in some ways to

the marginalized status of people of color. In turn, the cultural constructions of institutionalized aging—dependency, passivity, submissiveness—match those of femininity and of minority status. Social death, as Robert Kastenbaum has put it, is a "process of excommunication" from the body of humanity and isolation from the everyday interactions associated with "living." Institutionalization hastens social death, and the kind of treatment Spencer receives is the kind given to one who has "come to be classified as socially dead precisely because [s]he has *not* died." Chronic dehumanization reflects a social judgment, in short, that the aged person "should" be dead. The internalization of these values brings on psychological death, a form of "playing dead"—depression, lethargy, the symptoms of senility—as the elderly person completes the transition from "should be" to "is" dead (Robert Kastenbaum, "Psychological Death," in *Death and Dying*, ed. Leonard Pearson [Cleveland: Case Western Reserve University Press, 1969], 1–27; see also Kastenbaum, "While the Old Man Dies: Our Conflicting Attitudes Toward the Elderly," in *Psychosocial Aspects of Terminal Care*, ed. Bernard Schoenberg, Arthur C. Carr, David Peretz, and Austin H. Kutscher [New York: Columbia University Press, 1972], 116–25; Avery D. Weisman, *The Realization of Death: A Guide for the Psychological Autopsy* [New York: Jason Aronson, 1974]; Robert L. Fulton, ed., *Death and Identity* [Bowie, Md.: Charles Press, 1976]).

24. May Sarton, *A Durable Fire: New Poems* (New York: Norton, 1972). Sarton takes her title of the collection from Walter Raleigh: "But Love is a durable fire, / In the mind ever burning: / Never sick, never old, never dead / From itself never turning."

25. Institutionalization, as one critic has pointed out, is a matter of the submission to power, a surrendering of the self to a milieu where "the individual death no longer belongs to the individual life" (Melvin Krant, *Dying and Dignity: The Meaning and Control of a Personal Death* [Springfield, Ill.: Charles Thomas, 1974], 5). Spencer reverses this power dynamic through her terrorist action. "I see now," she tells the final pages of her notebook, "that death is not a vague prospect but something I hold in my hand" (Sarton, 119). She succeeds in making her death "something more like me than slow disintegration" (115).

26. A passage from the Sarton poem, "The Muse as Medusa," that Gilbert and Gubar use to illustrate the conversion of female power into self-hatred and a "deformed female creativity" in George Eliot's work, is appropriate also to the denouement of *As We Are Now:* "I turn your face around! It is my face. / That frozen rage is what I must explore— / Oh secret, self-enclosed, and ravaged place! / This is the gift I thank Medusa for" (quoted in Gilbert and Gubar, *Madwoman in the Attic*, 477). The negating "solutions" of internalized and asserted madness or holocaust, self-warping and suicide, represent the limitations of a singular focus on the oppression-subversion paradigm and lead one to alternative feminist texts in which female creation is depicted as positive and connective, rather than deformed, and constructive social transformation, rather than helplessly thwarted and monstrous rebellion, is posited.

Readers and Responses

Saving the Audience: Patterns of Reader Response to May Sarton's Work

Carol Virginia Pohli

For most of her long career as a writer, May Sarton's work has been viewed by literary critics as generally uninviting to analytical study or conceptual inquiry. Such misunderstanding is being dispelled, chiefly by feminist scholars. The development of reader-response theory invites further exploration of Sarton's literary achievement.[1] Positing a fluid relation between reader and text, reader-response theories are particularly appropriate tools for examining her work. This is so because Sarton offers bridges of connection to her readers that show the relational ground of both creativity and literary reputation.

The letters sent to Sarton by her readers over a fifty-year period provide evidence of common patterns of response as defined by such reader theorists as Wolfgang Iser, Stanley Fish, Norman Holland, and others. For example, Sarton's readers fulfill paradigms of the reader in affective relation with the text, the daydreaming reader and the peripatetic, implied reader.[2] My examination of letters in Sarton's private files uncovers something beyond this consistency. There is a pattern of response to Sarton's implied author and to her thematic repetitions (the instability of love; the difficulties of self-understanding and self-control; the provocative beauty of the natural world) showing "the common reader" as someone convinced of the intelligibility of experience and the validity of personal truth. In other words, recent pronouncements about the final indeterminacy of texts and interpretations contradict actual reader experience. Moreover, given the predominance of female readers among Sarton's respondents, their trust in the transactional features of literature and in the congruence of the actual and implied author may be identifiably female praxis, and it may indicate that many women resist indeterminacy.

A detailed survey of revived and refocused critical interest in the reader of literary texts lies beyond the purpose of this essay; still, highlights of the progress of affective poetics are important to any discussion of the reception of Sarton's work. Whether or not the text is *saved* in literary history (to borrow Geoffrey Hartman's term [1976]) as a determinate, formal, stable entity, its audience remains both permanently important to the text and hard to define. The recent audience-oriented or reader-response approach to literary study is not without precedent. Both classical and Renaissance criticism emphasized the text's impact on the audience, rather than its meaning. Homage to the moral purposes of literature during the eighteenth and nineteenth centuries, as well as the tenets of romanticism, implied the reader's importance; however, reader performance was not examined in theoretical terms. Within our own century, I. A. Richards's concern with response to poetry's moral/cultural meanings, as they are reflected in rhetorical "order" (1929), indirectly enhanced the reader's role by drawing attention to the differences between emotive and referential language. Although New Critics seemed to dismiss reader subjectivity along with psychological theorizing about literature, at the heart of New Criticism, according to Elizabeth Freund, was "an overwhelming but suppressed or rarely acknowledged concern with the reader. . . . Despite its ostensible endeavors to hypostatize the objectivity or autonomy of the literary work, the ghostly presence of 'readers' enacts a continuing resistance to its own dicta from within the project itself" (1987, 42). This uneasy relationship to the question of the reader's importance was sustained, perhaps casually, by William Empson's *Seven Types of Ambiguity* ([1930] 1961), which contributed to an awareness that verbal nuance permits alternative reactions to the text. Empson aside, close examination of Anglo-American criticism during the first few decades of this century reveals that literary discussions during those years say as much about the preferences and sympathies of the critics as about the texts being discussed or their readers' behavior. (This trend may persist.) As Hartman admits, the critical terminology (hence, literary concepts and ideologies) of the period became increasingly defensive and proprietary, betraying the anxiety of reductive principles of interpretation (1976, 218). In short, historically the reader's performance has been demeaned by privileged interest in the presumed objective authority of author or text and by literary critics' slowness to question their own performance.[3]

The present milieu of literary studies is one in which professional readers doubt the assumptions of formalism and New Criticism about the stability and integrity of the text.[4] Rather, such doubts co-create the text. This swerve to the reader, Freund argues, assumes that our relationship to reality is not a positive knowledge but a hermeneutic construct, that all perception is already an act of inter-pretation, that the notion of a "text-in-itself" is empty, that a [text] cannot be understood in isolation from its results, and that subject and object are indivisibly bound. (Freund 1987, 5)

Theorists of reader-response differ in their explanations of this bond or interaction between text and reader, but most discuss the complex perfor-mances of both author and reader by using labels that conflate function and identity. For example, Wolfgang Iser, a prominent German exponent of reader-response (or "reception") theory whose ideas build on those of Sartre and Roman Ingarden, uses the term *implied reader* to define the anticipated audience inevitably encoded within a literary text.[5] Iser argues that because a text defines its own reader by giving clues about expected response (requir-ing conformity with these clues, thus ensuring that the actual reader becomes the implied reader), the meaning of a literary work is prescribed but not fixed; rather, it is "a dynamic happening," the product of authorial intention and an actual reader's imaginative, subjective completion of limited inde-terminacies in the text. Still, Iser views reading as cognitive work, an activity of conscious selection. Norman Holland adapts Freudian concepts to explore how a literary text helps generate socially acceptable meanings for the fantasies, anxieties, and desires that it stimulates and to explain how a reader alters his or her self-image in the process of reading. Whereas Iser argues that meaning remains immanent (lodged in the text, waiting to be discovered and decoded), other theorists, among them Stanley Fish, deny this. Seeing language as indeterminate, Fish privileges the reader's experience as the locus of meaning and argues that all features of the text are interpretations.

To say that subjective response is the primary locus of textual value, that all contextual factors in reading are filtered through the reader's personal characteristics, is to challenge the premises on which the traditional literary canon is built. Thus, whether the reader's subjectivity can be understood in cognitive terms and whether subjective response necessarily conflates under-standing with feeling are now weighty critical questions.[6] They imply the importance of such contextual influences on the act of reading as race, gender, class, sexual orientation, ethnicity, and age. These unresolved ques-tions constitute the problematic relationship of feminist and reader-response theory.

We know too little about how women read, when and why they may read differently than men, and whether characteristics of female reading performance have salience that extends beyond the act of reading. Furthermore, since literary trends have been established by men, and since women and other deprecated groups have enjoyed only marginal participation in the literary enterprise, there is reason to suppose that some formulations of contemporary reader-response theory embody the same perceptual prejudices determining such trends and deprecations: neglect of gender as a positive factor in literary performance and resistance to those aspects of creative behavior that may be identifiably female. That is, the historic tendency to privilege cognitive modes of literary analysis whose abstract premises and taxonomic tastes have little relevance to the reader's material situation remains alive and well. It is evident in the theories to which I refer above, in spite of their increased acceptance of subjectivity as a governor of textual meaning. Reluctance to assess personal or emotive factors in the act of reading shows itself in the literary establishment's slowness to reach this place of concern for the reader, in the usual proliferation of theoretical difference, and (ironically) in a depersonalization of the discussion. To the extent that this is true, reader-response theory (like other abstract constructs, including those we prefer) may distance us from the text, author, or experience of reading even while explicating it. *If* such resistance and distance are characteristically male, it complicates the application of these theories to texts written by females or to the responses of female readers.

The neglect or disparagement of Sarton's work by many professional readers, contrasted with the sustained enthusiasm of a large readership (chiefly women), mirrors this problem, pointing to gaps in our understanding of literature's affect, as well as to the chauvinist critical tradition. Sarton's texts have an apparent simplicity misread by many critics as artistic failure.[7] However, continuing approval lavished on canonical writers of earlier periods whose style is similar makes such misreading suspect. Ironically it is also possible that Sarton's work has been neglected for interactive qualities that now provoke critical interest. Then too, recently legitimized bridges of connection with the reader evident in her work might receive more critical attention if her subject were not, persistently, woman's daily life. Sarton doggedly resists changing her vision of life or her creative formats to suit the intellectual fashions of the day. The focus of her work in several genres (poetry, fiction, memoirs, journals) is the power of passionate feelings to shape an individual's view of the world, self-image, relationships, and art. She explores several regions of this territory, working from the perspective of a writer's existential, solitary condition and within the context of ordinary domestic life. Most of her writing represents the self longing for escape from external constraints or from itself, wanting permanent, satisfying connection with someone else. Sarton's economic use of diction and her reliance on traditional prose or poetic forms to explore this longing in its many guises is a deliberate strategy, an attempt to capture elusive, fluid emotion within sturdy walls.

This is only to say that both stylistic simplicity and the apparent didactic tone of Sarton's work—her habit of raising meaning to the surface of the text, emphasizing what the image means, creating rounded closures that suggest completion or repletion—are methods appropriate to her purpose.[8] Such rhetorical strategies counterbalance Sarton's perception of lack. Contemporary critics frequently ascribe greater value to texts in which lack is represented as discontinuity, uncertainty, or meaninglessness, where textual ambiguities seem to present the reader with a variety of interpretive options. Sarton's work does not deny uncertainty, but displaces it from the level of narrative structure and authorial voice to that of phenomenological intention: a deliberately emphasized shared consciousness between author and reader, the place where doubts are mutual and consolable.[9] Like Stendahl, she limns sensibility. Like Faulkner, she insists upon human triumph. As my subsequent discussion affirms, her readers sense doubt and despair beneath her smooth textual surface, yet they also experience that benign surface as a powerful, affirmative aspect of the work. That is, they share her belief that metaphoric reach for what little is knowable or inevitable in life is an effective means of coping with what she calls "the lion's roar" of emotion and doubt. Their comments about her work also seem pertinent to our concern about the devaluation of literature by a cybernetic culture because those comments help define the personal nature of art. By doing so, they point to characteristics of female perspective and performance in the act of reading and to what Flynn and Schweickart call "the dialectic of conversation" between women readers and authors (1986, xiv).

In the next section, I extract quotations and infer patterns of reader response from letters by Sarton's readers sent to her in response to forty (of forty-seven) books she has published during the last half-century.[10] An actual reception study, this may contribute to our understanding of the relational basis of literary performance or help to assign the reader-as-person as much value as she or he enjoys as idealized construct.

Three prominent motifs emerge in the thousands of letters people from all walks of life have written to Sarton since the publication of her first book of poems (*Encounter in April*) in 1930.[11] Shock is common. Sarton's reader, typically, is so startled by his or her initial response to the work and by a discovery of shared values that he or she is compelled to write to her and to search for other Sarton books. Often, the reader claims an inability to understand or articulate this surprise; such confusion does not diminish the letter-writing urge. To describe their response, her readers choose words that convey their belief in Sarton as a kindred spirit and mediator able to limn human nature and open doors to its understanding: these frequently include "powerful," "scorching," "evocative," "awestruck," "enchanted," "it speaks," "it is luminous," "I was destined to read this." One reader's comment is representative: "I am stabbed by recognition and remembrance." This frequent, surprised recognition (that one's most private experience is shared, communicable, the stuff of art) and the compulsion to talk about it often arrives sheathed in self-effacing diffidence or its opposite—verbally unrestrained exhilaration. Claiming that the book at hand *demands* their response, Sarton's readers either apologize profusely for intruding on her time and privacy or create long, joyful paragraphs trying to describe the pleasures and benefits of reading her work: "You show me other sides of myself," "You give me courage," "You saved my life," "I am affirmed," "I felt like a plant being watered."

In effect, the experience of reading Sarton's work releases her readers' creative energy as well as a rush of complex feelings that, in turn, produce letters filled with reciprocal stories of her readers' ordinary delights, their personal crises or vocational problems. The letters are candid, emotive, and spontaneous, rather than reasoned attempts to explain the influence of Sarton's books. Trust that the book is a mode of exchange, of real contact with the author (and that the implied author is actual), often prompts the writing of letters to Sarton. Not surprisingly, letters of response (whether from men or women) are offered to her as evidence of affection. New readers address her as "Dear unmet friend," regular correspondents will use "Dearest May."[12] They admit to hugging her books, having a "love affair" with her work, "embracing" the thought of her, believing her "too big for us to contain." They persist in conflating author and text, or text and reader in ways that expose their most private vulnerabilities.

This brief sketch of responsive patterns outlines what my subsequent remarks will illustrate: that the typical reader of Sarton's work mirrors her own values and expressive methods. That is, her readers' behavior is implied or prescribed within the texts to which they respond; thus, reader partic-ipation in Sarton's work comprises a reinforcement of textual features and authorial purposes, making her books incrementally more readable for loyal readers. The work becomes a body of integrated and mutually reflexive parts. Furthermore, readers' affective relations with Sarton and her texts appear prompted by longings for intimacy that are denigrated by American culture at times. By modeling the intersubjective nature of literary performance, Sarton and her readers exemplify behavior that Iser, Holland, and Fish (among others) consider universal.[13]

As I have indicated, among the determinants of Sarton's readers' responses to her work are her own expectations of her books and their audience. Georges Poulet's model of reading suggests that

> a book is not only a book; it is a means by which an author actually preserves [her] ideas, [her] feelings, [her] modes of dreaming and living. It is a means of saving [her] identity from death.... To understand a literary work, then, is to let the individual who wrote it reveal [herself] to us *in* us. (Poulet, quoted in Flynn and Schweickart 1986, 52)

There is further theoretical comment relevant to Sarton's authorial role in Wolfgang Iser's view of reading as a dialectical process, a creative partnership between author and reader. Iser privileges the text and author by insisting that response has its roots in the written word and that the reader we discuss is hypothetical, not actual. *The Implied Reader* (1974) explains the term of its title as a construct; an author (also implied, as Wayne Booth has argued) uses devices such as narrative strategy, deliberately omitted information ("blanks") and value judgments ("negations") that require the reader to supply appropriate inferences. The text, Iser argues elsewhere, is thus "a structured indicator to guide the imagination of the reader" (1978, 9). Iser's theory is contradictory or at least puzzling because his hypothetical reader reflects the structure of the text, whereas it is a flesh-and-blood reader who peripatetically actualizes or "concretizes" the text—all meaning generated by the actual person's imaginative processing of the textual features shaping that act of imagination. Were the text as circularly determinate and the author as controlling as Iser claims, spontaneous written responses to a reading experience might display even greater uniformity than we see, for example, in our students' essays or in letters by Sarton's readers; moreover, such response might be quelled by belief that there is a single right way to read.

Whether or not meaning is as textually immanent as Iser suggests, the relationship between Sarton's work and her readers indicates a partnership that fulfills her inscribed expectations. The shock, recognition of shared perspectives, and affection exhibited by Sarton's readers in response to her work are effects of Sarton's choice of genres, fusion of personal and universal themes, and candor. It is Sarton's much-denigrated personal approach to literary creativity that enables our understanding of her work (and perhaps all literature) as a collaborative creation, an intercourse of desires. Paradoxically, since her work in each genre is characterized by narrative simplicity, by clarity of phrase, and by images that seem fully accessible, it might appear to require little of the inferential processing defined by Iser as reading. Still, it is the stylistic features I have mentioned that facilitate her readers' response. In addition, Sarton's work—particularly her lyric poems, memoirs, and journals—demonstrates the aesthetic uses of simplicity in the service of an exploratory and self-revealing creativity.

For example, her journal, *Plant Dreaming Deep* (1968), succeeds by disclosure, as journals do, as well as by its lyricism; but the width of its open door to Sarton's private life is also remarkable. Previous books of poems and her novel about a woman writer (*Mrs. Stevens Hears the Mermaids Singing*, 1965) were rooted in Sarton's personal experience as lover, writer, teacher, daughter, friend, gardener, observer of nature; but this journal gives literal access to the author's home life, describing her decision to live alone, her search for a house in rural New Hampshire, and her effort to make it and her life within it a reflection of her most cherished values. Although *Plant Dreaming Deep* is an evocation of place and the personalities of neighbors as well as a personal document, its drama is that of revelation, showing in anecdotes and meditative, often self-effacing passages how Sarton copes with difficulty. These inscriptions of mundane fortitude and the ordinariness of her self-imposed challenges prompt readers to write letters and tell friends about the book. Her literal struggles—at times serious, at times humorously told—to remodel the house, dig a new garden, sink a well during a drought, keep black flies away from herself while gardening, and scare woodchucks away from the phlox, all expose her personal vulnerability and consciousness of her faults. It is a narrative strategy that erases the distance between the implied narrator and reader, given a reader's willingness to see the journal as what Iser calls an unfolding, living event.[14]

Whatever distance remains is lessened by Sarton's working premise that both she and her reader are sensitive and trustworthy. One sign of this (illustrating Iser's belief that the reader confirms what the text holds) is the frequency with which her readers confess admiration for Sarton's ability to "express our deepest thoughts for us," especially as that skill is manifest

by her success in finding companionship in light and silence. Another is
their readiness to confess their most private feelings, sometimes eloquently;
one reader claims that *Plant Dreaming Deep* enabled her to believe that "I
have become the cause of my life, not the effect of it . . . a joyous thing. I
am an explorer [and your words] are my maps." The candor in Sarton's
writing elicits responsive disingenuousness: a woman admits reading the
book as if it were a film about her life, finding her own boring routine
transformed into newly fascinating adventure; a man writes in response to
the same journal, "How emotionally shallow we, as males, tend to
be . . . men fail to comprehend the true needs of human beings." Replicating
the quality of sensitivity and compassion in Sarton's text, many readers
write supportively, one claiming that Sarton writes "from a well of deep
subjectivity, but the result is universal. It will be years before it finds an
audience, but [the work itself] will build that audience." Another says,
"your way of life is itself a work of art, May, for the joy you have made
of it from discipline is a framework within which [even loneliness] has more
meaning."

Such comments mirror the traits of an implied author and indicate
Sarton's ability to write books that change color to reflect the reader's hue.
Although, as Iser might argue, such responses are implied by the text and
are the "discovery of an inner world of which [the reader] had hitherto not
been conscious," they seem to result from new scrutiny of what is familiar,
rather than from a processing of what Iser calls "alien" thoughts (1978,
158). Thus, if we credit her readers' testimonies, Sarton's work achieves what
Iser claims is requisite for a valuable work of literature; it offers new codes
for understanding reality. However, it does so differently than he predicts.
As her poems and stories dramatize her own and her reader's projected
selves, they enact repetitions of experience rather than the deconstructive
"disruption" of textual content that Iser identifies as the reading process.
The difference here between male theory and the actual reading experience
of women and men who write to Sarton indicates that when the reader is
not obliged to read against the text (needing to resist an author's androcentric
premises in order to avoid "immasculation," as Schweickart puts it), when
the reader does not perceive the author or implied reading self as different
or alien, but as peer, friend, beneficiary, then the act of reading becomes
dialectic. It becomes participatory, closely resembling a conversation with
the imaginable author—or, if you will, a marriage of true minds that Sarton's
readers attempt to consummate by mail. Their impulse to personalize her
authorial role supports Schweickart's notion of feminist reading as the tendency

to see the text not as an object, but as the manifestation of someone, the voice of a real speaker telling personally realized truth (Schweickart 1986, 47).

One formal product of Sarton's assumption that literature is an appropriate vehicle for personal experience is her strong thematic emphasis on existential isolation. Not surprisingly, some readers discover that reading Sarton's work is a painful experience. In Iser's terms, they intensify the "negations" of those portions of a text dealing with unrealized happiness (usually, in Sarton's case, the false promises of situational or material comforts), and they fill in the "blank" of what she does not or cannot say about psychic pain. One articulate reader writes to a third party in response to *Journal of a Solitude* (1973),

> When I first read [the book] I felt anger, anger that there was so much pain behind every word and . . . anger that such pain should be clothed so lyrically. There is nothing benign in my response to Sarton—it is total love/hate. But how can I say hate . . . [her work] says things to me of myself. . . . Why didn't she come sooner—she who was to tell my my own life? . . . To accept emptiness and call it full is [the power of] May's lyricism. She screams, she weeps, she rages, she loves, she writes, and the sound is rich and full—it is a kind of music. Within that lyricism is a dangerous place that smells of home to me. And I can't go there.

Still, female readers take courage from her texts because they are convinced that Sarton writes out of her actual experience as a woman who refuses to emulate behavior expected of women. They imbibe the courage her writing implies—in spite of her loneliness, financial worry, discouragement about critical rebuffs of her style and subjects. A well-known political figure writes to praise her "clear, radiant vision of life, presented unflinchingly. It encourages me." A feminist scholar writes, "you prove that a woman can be alone and *be* . . . you fill a great void in contemporary writing by daring to be yourself so openly . . . to reveal your loves in your work." A young lesbian describes how reading Sarton helped her make the decision "to come out of the closet." A woman physician writes, "I shall borrow courage from your power . . . to make my own journey. You remind me that woman's power and achievements are not won *from* men, they are won by her courage and from herself. I feel awe and joy in knowing that you . . . have written a woman's experiences of human connection."

Like Sarton, her readers often express a desire for both personal connection and "permanence"—the stability and security that some post-structuralist theorizing reminds us is merely wistful expectation of language or literary texts.[15] Norman Holland has examined the reading process using psychoanalytic tools to show how the reader and author unconsciously conspire to transform desire or fantasy into socially acceptable meanings. He argues that we intellectualize our desires by attempts to find coherence within the text and to extract from it a shared significance. The desire for connection expressed by Sarton's readers most often shows itself as a need for community and for relation to the natural world. Again in response to *Plant Dreaming Deep,* a reader models what Holland calls the search for coherence by saying, "You have made sense out of the tensions of being one's self and trying to be part of a community." This remark accurately describes the book, which (like *Journal of a Solitude*) unveils its author's struggles to accommodate seemingly incompatible desires for solitude, community participation, and friendship. That these are complex desires is evident in the confusion one reader admits: "reading your book I have come to feel . . . a longing for what I do not know . . . [it] moves me to express this to you for whom I feel a strange emotion." In the case of other books, too, as Sarton makes longing for intimacy a material component of her prose or poems, her work prompts letters that at once answer that longing—putting her in touch with appreciative professional or lay readers, caring strangers who may be potential friends—and confirm its presence in her readers' psyches. Thus, a man writes his thanks that Sarton's novel *A Reckoning* (1978) is "wise and polished and warm. . . . It makes me feel connected, as if I have known you forever or wanted to without realizing it." Holland's argument that a text is a personalized re-creation by its reader, reflecting the readers' psychological needs and "identity themes" (1975) suggests that readers who make equivalent comments about Sarton's work are prompted by fantasies of reunion with an omniscient, benevolent mother figure, at once heroic and protective. Letters to Sarton are a socially acceptable expression of these desires, while also embodying many readers' rebellion against dead social values and the need for identification with a figure who herself flouts convention. These psychosocial factors contributing to her readers' loyalty are partially explained by Holland's argument that we like best those books that maximize the opportunity to effect a pleasurable transformation of our desires, anxieties, or fears.

Her readers' desires to make a connection with Sarton herself are an analogue of the quality of relationship she has with her private thoughts, with people she loves, and with the earth. Such relationships do not always appear in her work as satisfying or safe (enhancing her sense of permanence), but her literary treatment of them is provocative for many readers. This is most evident in responses to the theme of nature in her work. Although letters to her contain fewer comments about nature, as such, than about other matters, the intensity of remarks about this subject implies that nature's role as a projection of human desires is as important to Sarton's readers as it is prominent in her work.

> Everything you write is *an evocation* of the living things all around us that matter so much.

> You show gardening as a sacrament.

> Here [in your work] is the sustaining power of nature . . . [it] creates the strength of the human spirit and the courage to endure.

> The poems in *Halfway to Silence* [1980] are not observation of nature, but absorption in it!

Comments like this hint of Sarton's ability to stir places in the human psyche that hold sensibilities attuned to the physical world, to conflate an image and her own strong feelings. It is a gift common to poets (and, as Elizabeth Evans observes, Sarton's strongest talent is lyric), but, with Sarton, the effect is enhanced by her candor, a deliberate strategy of "going naked" (to borrow her usual phrase) by choosing figurative language that neither hides nor restrains the emotion at hand. Recognizing this, a woman writes about Sarton's dark sonnet series, "A Divorce of Lovers," "you have made me like these painful poems because the comparisons [with nature] you use are so true in my experience and somehow reassuring."

In other words, the strong consciousness of affinity between Sarton and her women readers may derive from her skill in dramatizing the earth and its natural events as correlatives of human thought and female body life. In Sarton's hands, nature is minimally reified, never subject to her implied mastery or exploitation. Throughout her writing, Sarton relates herself to the elusive sea or solid earth with its predictable, cyclic movements. She also examines the qualities of woman's connection with the earth in ways that emphasize a universal, primitive longing for the harmonious fruitfulness she finds in nature. This desire is balanced by her awareness that natural forces themselves may undo their own fruitful rhythms.[16] Moreover, she is aware of the necessary risk and the sometimes questionable motives underlying the human desire for connection with the earth or with other people. Conversely, Sarton's natural world—actual and imaginative ever blended—may appear threatening or indifferent. Even the hopeful phoenix, her personal emblem, in one poem is a big bird with an angry neck "who never sings" (181). Yet he is mythical. Actual living things may appear strange to Sarton, but not fundamentally alien; where she inscribes otherness she emphasizes it as a mental projection. It may be that such tropes of nature woven through her work serve as the place where subjective and objective meet: in Holland's terms, the locus of "introjection" for the requisite transaction between self and other or text and desire. If so, Sarton's readers follow her lead; just as much of her work assigns to her own personality and experience the characteristics of what she observes in the physical world, so her readers, prompted by similar urgings, introject these "ties" to nature and Sarton's particular poetic vision of it. A reader of *As Does New Hampshire* (1967) says,

> I now always see the "small open parasols of Chinese green" on the trees in early Spring with your eyes and have come to respect and even love the outcroppings of rock in New England because they remind me of . . . the lines in your poems about how loss and pain can make us rock-strong.

These remarks and many others like it among the letters stuffed in Sarton's files constitute yet another instance of Iser's implied determinacy: the reader echoing / discovering what is already inscribed in the text. Those who read widely in Sarton's work find such discovery eased by her direct statements. For example, in her poem, "Composition," she asserts that the meaning of physical nature lies within the psyche: "we contain earth and water and the wind" (*Collected Poems*, 393).

Therefore, peaceable pictures of the natural world occurring in Sarton's work are not representations of escape from actual, brutal nature, nor from nasty humanity, but the creation of symbolic doors for author and reader into those regions of self where nostalgic desires are born. Although such figurations may indeed express the unconscious core of fantasy in Holland's transactive paradigm, for this author and her readers, natural images appear to promote conscious understanding and realization of desire. They are visual symbols that comprise a welcome or pursued body of feelings. This is implied by the impressive frequency with which readers praise Sarton's work as "luminous" or "exquisite" or "delicious." (I began by counting these occurrences and then gave it up.) It is more directly suggested by a reader who claims that poems such as "The Light Years" (*Collected Poems,* 194) and "Composition" (*Collected Poems,* 393) are "pictures of order and beauty in the midst of chaos . . . which help me see, be open to it all and feel part of the earth. It's a feeling I have wanted, but not had this way until reading your work."

For Stanley Fish, such a comment would be evidence for his argument that there is no text; rather, reading is a process of discovering the text's impact on the reader. Correspondingly, in his view, criticism of literary texts is a study of the structure of the reader's experience (affective poetics), because the text itself has no fixed, objective schema, as Iser claims. This is not a credo of pure indeterminacy because, Fish argues, readers bring to the act of reading some shared "interpretive strategies," along with linguistic or culturally produced meanings and uses of words that restrain and shape interpretation (1980). Since we as readers do not exist except as members of some "interpretive community," the meaning of a text is always at hand, a specific temporal event or encounter of text and mind. Although there are obscurities and contradictions in Fish's theories that I will bypass, his notion of a "rhetorical text" that mirrors reader expectations (in Freund's words, one that "presents for their approval the opinions they already hold," [1987, 98]) not only offers a flip-flop version of Iser's ideas about authorial intention, but also finds support in the way Sarton's readers read. Their testimony that her work enables the clarification of personal identity and transcendence of the personal aspects of experience seems to answer, as well as reflect the conundrum of difference between text/author and reader that Fish never resolves. Sarton's readers find her texts to be both therapeutic and transformative, bright lamp and beveled mirror. Many letters to Sarton indicate that her work provides new self-esteem by helping readers acknowledge formerly scorned aspects of personality, or unadmitted feelings.

> Always after reading your books I have felt more real, more human. I've been seized by a power I never fully understood before. . . . May, your books are magical.

> Reading your journals has been like looking deeply into myself.

> You show that feelings themselves are the essence of life.

An actress in conversation with one of Sarton's friends bursts out with, "May Sarton? My God! Oh you must tell her she changed my whole life when I discovered her [books] at fifty and needed her so desperately!" A seventy-year-old woman who worked in the anti-Nazi resistance during World War II writes, "Since then I have never shared my real thoughts with anyone. [Your journal] is more than a literary joy, it is a revelation . . . you give me the right to be myself, spelling mistakes and all." A professor of English in Nebraska writes to tell Sarton that *A Reckoning* elicited from her students

> more deeply felt emotional responses than anything we have read. One student writes in her journal that the book "motivated me to set things straight with my mother. It changed everything." So, May, the ripples from your books and your life widen.

Thus, Sarton's readers take from apparently "rhetorical texts" the type of "conversion" experience Fish claims is a product of the text's ability to induce uncertainty in the reader, then move her or him toward a visionary understanding that transcends language, where "the lines of demarcation between places and things fade in the light of an all-embracing unity" (1974, 3). It is an apotheosis encouraged by Sarton's deliberate reach for coherence; moreover, as Constance Hunting remarks, readers who explore Sarton's entire oeuvre find it to be an organic, unified vision of life, looming larger than any single book. Given the long-standing scorn of many professional critics for Sarton's allegedly naive, self-reflexive pursuit of wholeness, it is amusing to discover new literary theories providing a rationale for her readers' long-standing intuitive recognition of the dynamics of her art. Letters covering all periods of her career and her several genres are marked by reader insistence that her work enables their transcendence of personal circumstance or feelings. Their letters (and Sarton's texts) recognize the paradox implicit here; allegedly solipsistic preoccupation uncovers the relational origins of self-image and opens doors to a fuller realization of how dependent upon one another we are. Thus, writing about her marriage, a woman says: "Your books have changed our lives, although John hasn't read any. . . . I'm not afraid as I was to be myself or to ignore myself and see his needs as no odder than mine . . . and we understand and enjoy each other much more now." An elderly respondent writes, "You have helped me [recognize] a spiritual bond between myself and other women." A man comments that Sarton's books "show me that men too love one another, even though they won't admit it and only use the word *friend*.'' Fish's concept of the text as simultaneous intention, form, and reader-experience may beg the question of where we stand as critics when evaluating a book, but it also provides a theoretical construct more comprehensively bold than the ideas of Iser or Holland and, like theirs, undeniably useful in accounting for equivalences in Sarton's work and her readers' responses.

One product of that equity is the mingled awe and affection, respect and intimacy with which her readers address Sarton. They credit her with heroic courage, yet feel close to her. Unafraid to confide in her as if to a friend, they remain persuaded of the uniqueness of her literary gifts and her importance as a writer. One of the many who attend her public readings writes to say, "I sat and listened to you as though you were the oldest of friends, a Wise One, whispering secrets." Another remarks that

> I never realized that the big ideas are found in ordinary things that we usually look at with pedestrean [*sic*] eyes. . . . You are so young [in the spirit], so big yourself and you risk so much to write the truth as you see it. This book [of poems] is an album of difficult, beautiful pictures of you and me and everyone else . . . it amazes me.

Such comments testify to her readers' trust in the intelligibility of experience, the validity of personal truth. They also affirm that the transactive text is dependent on reader trust in authorial candor and in overlapped identities of author, narrator, and flesh-and-blood writer. In short, Sarton and her readers' letters posit different epistemological premises than most theorists of reader response. She strives for, and her readers credit, a transparency of style as well as an implied unguarded writing or reading self that expects a decipherable text and a readable response. These assumptions make the collaborative business of writing and reading literary texts a mimetic activity, essentially referential—rather than obliquely so, as reader-response theorists argue. Iser, Holland, Fish, and other serious investigators of reader behavior assume varying degrees of indeterminacy in both the text and the act of reading. They ascribe this to the illusory nature of language and to the gap (or "lag" as Paul de Man puts it) existing between text and interpreter. Fish implies that this gap, in turn, ensures that any discursive analysis of the act of reading (mine, theirs, yours; letters or theories) will never coincide with the reading experience. Rather, our commentaries comprise an infinitely regressive description of a deferred event, just as reading itself must be a repetitious reenactment of the text's strategies and linguistic vagaries.

Sarton's readers do not behave as if this is true; their letters do not sound as if their own tenuous consciousness were the only tentatively verifiable reality, nor do they posit an "ethics of deferral" (Miller 1986, 108) as the only possible evaluative stance. Readers whose letters I have examined look at Sarton's work as if they were New Critics in modest guise, convinced of the poem's or novel's ontological integrity. Unlike most professional readers of literature, they do not objectify the text in order to locate authority; they do not wrestle with the text, as some reader theorists propose (thereby revealing their own modus operandi). Sarton's correspondents trust the text's accessibility and its relevance. The readable correspondences between literary product and intention that both they and Sarton presume do not seem to limit insights (the old, feared "solipsistic trap"), but function as a springboard to fruitful understanding. In other words, Sarton's readers exemplify theoretical patterns of response by replicating what the author has inscribed in the text, thus, as implied readers, serving as its incarnation; the text mirrors expectations they bring to it. Still, the most significant feature of their praxis is an absence of belief that reading is complicated. Their untroubled acceptance of the text's stable function as a vehicle of revelation and their unquestioned assumption that we read the text with our beliefs and desires in this respect makes theoretical commentary almost redundant.

Self-reflexive or theoretical, all patterns of reader response may be related to gender. Neither authors, readers, nor critics escape the influence of their identity or the power of cultural forces shaping their perception of it. Therefore, it remains important that the most prominent theorists referred to previously are male, and equally noteworthy that none of their theories (with the partial exception of Holland's work)[17] accounts for any potential difference in female reading experience. Since the majority of Sarton's readers who respond in writing to her work are female, theories of reader behavior developed by Iser et al. may be inherently incapable of providing fully adequate, general explanations of the letter-writing behavior highlighted by actual reception studies like this one. What seems missing from the theories I have mentioned is a consideration of the idea that women may read with unique epistemological assumptions, as well as with different modes of comprehension. As the letters I have quoted illustrate and as the socioeconomic diversity of my sample implies, such differences characterize female readers of various ages and backgrounds. Feminist thought dealing with women's habitually different ways of apprehending or expressing the human need for meaning and for the intelligibility of experience (e.g., Gilligan 1982) points to the likelihood of gender-related differences in reader response as well. Sarton's readers conform to this hypothesis about femininity by writing letters that show them viewing the world through eyes and ears attuned to relationship and its associated values, rather than giving their primary attention to ideational structures. They also conform to the paradigms outlined by David Bleich's study of gender influence on reader response (1986). They immerse themselves in the textual world of her prose or lyrics; they do not exhibit what Bleich identifies as a typically male pattern of reading: remaining conscious of narrative voice and the constructed aspects of a text.[18] This raises the possibility that male theorists and nonprofessional male readers read "distrustingly." If Sarton's readers provide an adequate female model, women more often read with the eyes of faith. Flynn and Schweickart comment that women readers have "an immense appetite for texts that allow them to play out their characteristic identity themes. . . . Women [as readers] can cultivate and merge with fundamentally different— even hostile—texts, and often . . . do so at great cost to themselves" (1986, xxv). The degree to which such habits are innate or learned remains controversial, but their most interesting configurations appear related to gender— a fact pertinent to the neglect of women's writing and related issues of power and authority in academic discussions of such matters.

Sarton's marginal critical reputation owes some of its status to gender bias, to the regular denigration of patterns of response associated with women or writers and readers belonging to other minority groups of race or class. In other words, at times the author's or the common reader's imaginative freedom is restricted by academic critics of literature working to impose norms of correctness on texts and their interpretations. To label the work of marginalized writers "sentimental," "unsophisticated," "emotional," "overpersonalized," or "unmediated" without considering the origins of such valuations in the speaker's habits of mind is to imply, falsely, that nonwhite, nonmale or unprofessional readers shun or cannot see the world's actual complexity or lack the ability to invent subtle ways of representing it. It is to suggest that such authors or readers are like children in their praxis, unconscious of the impulses informing their manner of writing or reading. It is to presume that the judges of their habits regulate themselves as readers and writers by superior, different standards. Curiously, we now possess theoretical support elaborated by male readers (Iser, et al.) for understanding what are supposed to be normative processes of reading, yet without any discussion of the fact that these configurations of response and creativity have been manifest all along in women's performance. By idealizing the "informed reader," Fish and his colleagues sustain the illusion that meaning is so illusory and reading so "self-consuming" that only a theorist may grasp at its straws; but the persistent abstraction and unresolved complexities of their ideas suggest that these literary authorities strive for intellectual mastery as earnestly as Sarton's readers submerge themselves in her pages. Perhaps both professional and "common" readers yearn for monistic coherence, but professional readers who are male seem to displace or disguise that longing within the dogmatism of their convoluted theoretical disagreements. Whenever it ignores the actual behavior of readers or the concrete, social determinants of response, reader-response theory assumes the guise of formalism, attempting to direct and control the reader. The trend denotes a reluctance by many of us to examine whether and how a text's potentially determinate status makes it a vehicle of moral responsibility. This may persist as long as there is a disparity between the way we talk about literature and the way we read it.

Although females as such are not exempt from similar error, my study of Sarton's readers hints that femaleness may be advantageous to a reader; at least women who write to Sarton find little to obstruct their pleasure in the text. They grant its powers willingly, without denying their liberty to read into it what they will; they trust the meaning of words without presuming fixed definitions; and they see the transactional nature of reading as a fair exchange. In other words, Sarton's readers confirm the storytelling features of literature, its necessary trustworthiness as an expression of human creativity.[19] In this respect too, Sarton's work prefigures her audience; its thematic repetitions of material from her life story affirm the possibility of saying and hearing words whose meanings are inevitably personal, yet grounded in shared experience. That is, her work and its influence on readers indicate a need to go beyond Fish's idea of an interpretive community (characterized by dominance, emphasizing the controlling features of shared reading strategies) and to reconceptualize the family of readers more simply, as those who find ways of relating personally to the text and its author.

My study does not offer an exhaustive conceptual model for that project. Neither Sarton's readers nor her books provide more than an instance of female praxis in the work of creating and responding to literature.[20] Still, there may be exemplary patterns we shall identify more definitively someday as women's literary work. Certainly, the observable differences between what (female) readers of Sarton's work experience with book in hand and what most (male) theorists postulate seem to depend on a different sense of self.

As my use of their letters shows, one sign of this difference displayed by Sarton's readers is the persistent habit of reading in order to encounter the author and to recover the value of female experience. Sarton's constructed authorial self is similarly motivated; she insists on making self-disclosure the basis of her art. This is not to say that she lacks interest in other literary techniques, but that she writes in order to create a relationship with her reader by exploring the sources and effects of her own vulnerability. As I have explained, that Sarton's work is confessional may account for the replication of these patterns in her readers' letters, which indicates that her authorial influence is not by imposition of idea, but the benign manipulation of a storyteller who uncovers self or life's plots in order to share curiosity or delight or distress. In turn, her readers' responses to this strategy are largely intuitive rather than analytic, a fact that does not fit well with the theories of critics who view literature as a structured artifact, cognitively understood. For Sarton's readers, the seemingly mimetic features of her texts disclose what emotion recognizes, willy-nilly, as truth. By making this generalization I do not mean to beg the question of other complexities in the act of reading, but to record an observable pattern. Whatever we know of psychological projection, theories of reading do not yet fully explain what a typical reader of Sarton means in the letter that says, with some awe and puzzlement: "how is it that whenever I am dealing with something I can't understand, your next book writes about it?"

Sarton's work and her readers' letters not only locate women's subjectivity in relationships posited among author, reader, and text, but also raise the question of the value of modes of creativity or response that "overprivilege" private interiority. The number of correspondents who refer to measurable changes in their lives produced by an emotional response to her work suggests that Sarton has achieved a transformation of the sentimental, personalized mode of expression from one with implications of indulgence into a deliberately chosen means of studying and generating human response. It has precedent. Recent studies of folklore and tribal cultures uncover the uses and historic prevalence of stories that conflate private, existential, and sacred meanings. Although constrained by lyric form, by the conventions of narrative or of disciplined recollection (in journals and memoirs), the wildness of Sarton's feelings, along with the intensity of her disdain for rationalized experience, may stir her readers' collective, unconscious memories of the powers belonging to feeling and instinct. Moreover, female readers may possess unlabeled cognitive as well as intuitive receptors of these reverberations, nurtured and strengthened by the fact of female difference.

Their response to her writing supports my belief that Sarton's work is one coherent example of the attempt to speak "the wilderness" of female consciousness that Showalter, Ursula Le Guin, and others remind us is outside the pale of male understanding, women's consciousness having been excluded from the dominant culture and its arts. Ironically, for all its middle-class trimmings, Sarton's writing typifies what many class-biased intellectuals consider "primitive, undeveloped, unauthentic," to borrow Le Guin's words (1989, 163). Spontaneously and joyously, reader letters to Sarton provide evidence that she inscribes this wild country of women's experience truly: the experience that Le Guin claims "has not been spoken, and when spoken, has not been heard—what we are just beginning to find words for, our words, not their words" (163). There may exist many dialects of what Le Guin calls, in an address to young women, "the mother tongue," the language stories are told in.

> [R]epetitive . . . earthbound, housebound. . . . The mother tongue, spoken or written expects an answer. It is conversation, a word the root of which means "turning together." The mother tongue is language not as mere communication but as relation, relationship. It connects. It goes two ways, many ways, an exchange, a network. Its power is . . . in binding . . . in uniting . . . and we all know it by heart. (Le Guin 1989, 149–50)

Sarton's literary expressions are one version of this "tongue," now occasionally recognized beyond her readership as well adapted to what women have to say.

Turbulent feelings, given literary expression, producing turbulent response. Ironically, Sarton's work remains formally conventional, while its effects remain incompletely understood. As feminist studies of popular fiction and other "nonserious" genres are beginning to show, when the conventions of romanticism are used to convey women's experience, we lack consensus about methods of evaluation. Not revolutionary in overt content or form, Sarton's work has influenced many people in a way perhaps typical of women's writing—by helping to transform their thinking about themselves. Often this process involves anger about social constraints against expressing anger—another theme of Sarton's work, which may be more clearly and fairly valued when we know more about the causes and suppressions of women's anger. Her writing regularly displays the four patterns of women's conflict with culture that Catharine Stimpson describes: sublimated or terminated insubordination, self-contradiction, and fatalism (1988, 159). That is, although her books at times displace anger about women's predicaments or simultaneously affirm and reject traditional women's roles or overemphasize deterministic forces, Sarton's praxis is embattled and, in other ways as well, inherently feminist. Persisting for a half-century in making scenes of domestic life a field for the exploration of women's erotic and aesthetic consciousness, she has created texts that—at times, angrily—reconceive and valorize women's interests, modes of expression, and forms of relationship. Hers is a creative method that demythologizes art and beauty as elitist pleasures and reinvigorates mythic concepts of femaleness associated with the earth and with communal experience.

Letters to Sarton indicate that a common result of these practices is the enfranchisement of her readers' emotional, social, and intellectual capacities, including the power of speech. It is a benefit most evident in the tendency of self-confessedly shy readers to become Sarton's regular correspondents—an act that, for some, constitutes rebellion against culturally enjoined women's silence. "I have never written to an author before," writes a typical Sarton fan, "but your book [*Anger,* 1982] is such a gift. . . . It has broken down the wall of what keeps me afraid and alone." In subsequent letters, the same reader admits that she had signed a false name to her first note, fearful of too great a self-revelation. Like Sarton herself and many women writers, such readers devise "a series of strategies that simultaneously reveal and conceal their self-assertions through language" (Stimpson 1988, 158). Sarton, for example, waited until 1989 to publish a novel (*The Education of Harriet Hatfield*) dealing explicitly with lesbianism, an identity inseparable from much of her life's work. Yet, some letters show that reader enthusiasm for Sarton's poems or prose often includes embracing her values, even when the respondent does not share Sarton's sexual preference. A middle-class housewife writes, revealingly,

> I don't understand Lesbianism . . . or maybe I don't want to associate myself with a "radical fringe." . . . So many women who have women lovers seem to dislike women's biology as well as their social image as women. They try to make their bodies something other than female by dressing so strangely . . . or they hate men. Of course, most of those [women] are young. But you seem so whole, May, and your books for me are first and always a place where I can go to see the world sanely, to readjust my values. And my behavior! I want to have your kind of honesty and courage. Please understand that I do fully respect

your love for women. Sometimes I think it even makes your writing
more real for me. Once I was infatuated with an older woman, when
I was unmarried, and your poems remind me of that.

In spite of occasional coyness, like Sarton her readers generally shun irony
and thereby exhibit what may be a characteristically feminist point of view.
Her texts and their letters tend to be governed rhetorically by an assumption
that truth telling is feasible and preferable, an achievement not necessarily
enhanced by ironic distance. Thus, the author and her readers tacitly contradict the arguments of theorists who agree with Roland Barthes that
writing "is a negative space where all identity is lost," or that the reader
is "without history, biography, psychology" (1977, 142). In Sarton's world,
author and reader are live, interdependent, talking moral entities whose
mutual engagement with a clearly written work fertilizes a clearer sense of
identity.

   Still, author and readers in this study differ in an important way. Her
readers seldom mention the fact that Sarton's view of her subject—the self
in relationships—is fundamentally intellectual (although not abstracted). They
speak of her breadth of understanding, but do not classify it or note how
a remarkable insight depends upon some achieved distance from its subject;
they tend to overlook the artistic means by which Sarton conveys information
about incidents or issues having personal importance. Not many correspondents allude to what we might call the literariness of her texts. In other
words, most of her readers treat the formal aspects of literature as if they
were transparent or merely vehicular. Such assumptions (whether or not
they are definably female) may be deliberate or unconscious strategies, embraced because they facilitate the reader's sense of closeness to text and author
and the changes in thought and behavior that Sarton's readers claim her
books produce. Sarton, in contrast, writes with a keen awareness of her
formal choices and her connection with writers—male and female, canonical
and "minor"—whose work she admires. Her verse and prose style commonly
balance precise formal intention and turbulent feeling, building from her
conviction that specifically female experience can be successfully inscribed,
that it holds much that is universally important, that words are containers
of significance whose accessibility depends on one's trust in them. The
literary product of her beliefs is a disciplined, expressive form. It remains
likely that further study of her work will discover more about the importance
of emotion in the act of writing and that the responses of her growing

audience will continue to demonstrate the positive value of personal involvement in the act of reading.

NOTES

I am indebted to May Sarton for access to her private files, for the influence of
her life and work on my own, and for her generous responsiveness to readers who
write to her; all have helped to make this study possible.

1. In general, as well as in Sarton's case, professional readers have been slower
than "common" readers to recognize the subjective locations of literary value. The
ironies of this situation are obvious to admirers of Sarton's work and merit fuller
exploration than this essay can provide. Studies like mine may enlarge our understanding of the reader's role in the complex dynamic of reader response without
lessening our awareness that both writing and reading are products of personal
experience, historic factors, formal and generic precedents, as well as linguistic
indeterminacies.

2. For a useful summary of the many voices, methods, and definitions shaping
contemporary reader-response criticism, see Freund, 1987. She includes the following
personifications in her survey of the many different concepts of who the audience
or reader is: "the mock reader (Gibson), the implied reader (Booth, Iser), the model
reader (Eco), the super-reader (Rifaterre), the inscribed or encoded reader (Brooke-
Rose), the narratee (Prince), the ideal reader (Culler), the literent [fantasizing reader]
(Holland), the actual reader (Jauss), the informed reader or the interpretive community (Fish)" (7). I would add that Roland Barthes's *The Pleasure of the Text*
(1975) presents the reader as a neurotic anti-hero willing to accept any textual
inconsistencies in order to enjoy reading; his *Image, Music, Text* (1977) focuses on
the implied antagonism between reader and author, suggesting that its outcome is
the author's "death." Derrida and Lacan also suggest that the reader's identity is
merely an ephemeral locus of relationships, a "space" on which the text is written.
In Flynn and Schweickart's *Gender and Reading* (1986), feminist reader-response
theorists scrutinize the androcentric premises of such mainstream critical directions
and analyze how they obstruct the understanding of the interpersonal, interactive
features of women's reading.

3. Feminist critics have been less slow to notice these trends; see, among others,
Ellmann 1968; Fetterley 1978; Kolodny 1980. Ironically, their work has enhanced
the acceptability of reader-response theories, but the latter remain less engaged than
their feminist counterparts with ideological premises or the concrete realities of
reader experience.

4. Jane P. Tompkins's 1980 anthology of essays points to the gradual denial of
the objective status of the text. Suleiman and Crosman (1980), provide an excellent
review of the many interpretive approaches to reader response. Temma Berg (1987)

underscores Louise Rosenblatt's importance as one of the early theorists of reader response; Rosenblatt ([1938] 1976; 1978) offers anthropologically based models of reading as an aesthetic transaction in which reader purpose matters. Flynn and Schweickart's admirable volume (1986) demonstrates the variety of feminist perspectives among current reader-response theorists.

5. Iser relies specifically on Sartre (1965), who examines the question, "For whom does one write?" and poses the text's reception as constitutively determined as well as a matter of historic contingencies. Ingarden's philosophy insists on the ontological yet purely intentional status of a work of art, dependent on alert consciousness (an act of "concretization" by a reader) for its existence. Neither Ingarden nor Iser adequately explains how the text can remain an objective intentional structure and also a product of reader subjectivity.

6. Reader-response theorists hold widely differing views of the subjective features of reading. For example, in his 1981 *Diacritics* review of Wolfgang Iser's work, Stanley Fish rebukes the latter's acknowledgement of personalized reader subjectivity; Fish argues that a reader necessarily approaches the text carrying the values derived from his or her "membership" in various social groups. Thus, it is the "community" of readers who define a text, not an autonomous, individual reader.

7. Sarton's fiction and other prose swerve toward conventional, rather than experimental, narrative structures; she posits human thinking as sequential and works with easily recognized symbols. Her poetry (whether short lyrics or extended meditations) also relies on regularly patterned formal elements that tend to make her text accessible; it infrequently depends on complicated allusion. These qualities appeal to a wide readership, which in turn (by letters to Sarton) demonstrates the Iserian reader impulse to locate patterns of applicable meaning. At the same time, Sarton's dominant subject—the difficulty of understanding and expressing human emotion—is a complex one that receives serious treatment by her in several genres and prompts equivalent serious response by her readers. The subject of women's emotional experience is thus enhanced by Sarton's texts and by reader response to them. Ironically, the determinate, "predictable" features of Sarton's work that have elicited critical scorn now serve as topics for theoretical speculation.

8. Didactic purpose and unified structures characterize interpretive and theoretical texts, too, but there it is privileged, wearing the guise of objectivity. Nina Baym argues about Victorian literature, for example, that "'seriousness' as a criterion of literary merit . . . implies a profound . . . patriarchal didacticism and is often used to denigrate" women's writing that seems to lack artifice (1984, 46).

9. In the context of a phenomenology of reading, as Freund observes, intention does not signify overt desire or what the author aims at; rather, it "denotes the structure of an act by which the subject imagines or conceptualizes or is conscious of an object, thereby bringing the object into being; but the intuition of the object simultaneously constitutes the subject as a vessel of consciousness" (Freund 1987, 137).

10. I collected this data by examining Sarton's personal files, an opportunity

made possible by her invitation—evidence of her kind regard for the concerns of
her readers and the work of women scholars. Responsibility for the interpretation
of data is fully mine and unavoidably selective. First, my sample is limited: not all
of Sarton's readers write to her; of those who do, not all write in order to comment
directly on her work. Second, I have chosen the most articulate responses and ones
most pertinent to this study, taking care to omit irrelevant material without ignoring
comments that might be meaningfully contradictory. Although the sample contains
only the unsolicited comments of readers of one author's work, its scope (1930
through 1984) helps to ratify my claim that these data reflect some patterns of
response from the common reader. In the interests of privacy, fairness, and uniformity,
I do not cite names of letter writers; to do so would have required seeking the
writers' permissions, and, in many cases, the letters have no identifying address.
I use the phrase "Sarton's readers" to signify all those whose letters I have read,
whether or not I quote them. These usages will prove justified, or not, to the
extent that my arguments are persuasive. Works by Sarton not included in the
sample of response letters are those published since 1984.

11. Sarton's readers are a more diverse group than she acknowledges or her critics
assume. Commenting in a letter to me on the possibility that critical support for
her work might be forthcoming if she had a wider readership, she says, ruefully,
"I have a great appeal to non-intellectuals. About a fourth of the letters I get come
from near illiterates." This is somewhat misleading and, perhaps, a product of
Sarton's dejection about literary critics' failure to take her work seriously for so
many years. My research in her files shows that most of her readers belong to the
book-reading middle class, including those who might label themselves intellectuals.
Those who identify themselves by vocation in the sample used for this study include
cinematographers, painters, potters, aspiring novelists and poets, nuns, a banker,
an Episcopal bishop, a professional singer and other musicians, medical doctors,
nurses, actors and entertainers, an author, college professors and librarians, as well
as housewives and students.

12. One of the burdens of Sarton's life has been the weight of the self-imposed
responsibility to answer letters from her readers, her huge and regular volume of
mail making this project time-consuming and emotionally exhausting. It also indicates Sarton's capacity for genuine interest in the lives of many people, as well as
a desire for personalized connection; both attitudes relate to her use of a confiding
authorial voice.

13. In reviewing how patterns of reaction by Sarton's readers conform or prove
exceptions to the ideas of such reader theorists as Iser, Holland, and Fish, I summarize
and simplify. The complexity of their ideas remains important, but my chief objective
is not metacritical; it is a demonstration of how these ideas, complexly amorphous
as they are, help identify features of Sarton's work having relevance to any discussion
of reader interaction with the text. Because theories with similar premises intersect
with one another, my applications of the working premises of Iser, Holland, and

Fish also include some repetition and overlapping. This limited application of their ideas does not denote agreement with their full arguments. There is also some irony in my reference to these abstract systems of thought to demonstrate the empirical results of Sarton's work. It is not my purpose to "put the idea of woman before the experience of woman" (Todd 1988, 14). Rather, by using quotations and paraphrases of actual reader comments I hope to avoid one of the shortcomings of reader-response theory; namely, the substitution of a staged report of reader experience for its actuality.

14. The topic of the implied author or narrator is as complex and compelling as the evaluation of the reader's many roles. My discussion attempts to replicate the perceptions of Sarton's readers: considering her personal identity and authorial functions as identical or interchangeable.

15. Nancy K. Miller argues, however, that even Roland Barthes acknowledges "the persistence of the subject as the presence in the text of perhaps not some*one* to love in person, but the mark of the need to be loved . . . desire for connection" (Barthes, quoted in N. Miller 1986, 106).

16. For examples of Sarton's poetic treatment of nature's harmony and dangers see, respectively, the title poem of *Letters from Maine* (1984) and "The Waves," in *A Grain of Mustard Seed* (1971). Specific poems by Sarton referred to in this essay may be found in her *Collected Poems, 1930–1973* (1974), for which parenthetical page references are provided. Separate volumes of her poetry and other work are identified by title and date.

17. Holland has collaborated with Leona Sherman in a study of gender-differentiated responses to Gothic fiction printed in Flynn and Schweickart 1986 (215–33). However, his theory of reading discusses identity formation in terms of ego boundaries, control, and locus of authority, an approach that is more conventional than specifically feminist.

18. Letters from Sarton's male readers that conform to most of the paradigms of female response I have mentioned may be exceptions that prove the rule by illustrating either the psychological androgyny that Mary Daly (1978) equates with healthy wholeness and integrity, or each male correspondent's capacity to understand and empathize with women's experience, even when different from his own.

19. In this respect, Sarton is like Virginia Woolf, whom Janet Todd describes as "literary through and through, tending towards narrative or story at every turn. She makes ideas into a particular biography and criticism into a kind of life history" (1988, 19). Also like Woolf, Sarton is "essentialist," accused of being "too individualistic," inclined to "private martyrdom and self-effacement" (19), yet alert to causes of women's dependencies and silence. (A point of difference: Sarton makes gardening more integral to her creation of life history and to her poetics.)

20. Among the useful studies of women's performance as writers and readers not referred to elsewhere in this essay are Mary Jacobus's *Reading Woman* (1986), which looks at how the play of linguistic difference influences gender, identity, and

meaning, and Elaine Showalter's "Toward a Feminist Poetic" (1985). The latter's definition of "feminist critique" as literary study focusing on how the reader's female identity may determine understanding of a text is pertinent here, although studies like mine expand the notion of "feminist critique," allowing it to include literal response from readers as well as hypothetical conclusions about their reading methods.

A Decade of Creativity
and Critical Reception:
A May Sarton Bibliography

Nancy S. Weyant

The decade of the 1980s represents a period of both prodigious creativity for May Sarton and a significant turning point in the critical reception of her writings. As Lenora P. Blouin observed in her 1978 annotated bibliography of writings by and about Sarton, "With the exception of a critical book and a few major articles, serious criticism of Sarton's work was scarce."[1] Even the most superficial analysis of the entries in that foundational bibliography dramatically substantiates Blouin's statement. Out of 207 pages of citations, 136 list books and individual poems by Sarton, 65 list book reviews, and only 5½ pages lead the scholar to critical articles. In her introductory remarks to her 1982 supplement to this compendium, Blouin noted that the intervening years had "witnessed a new and more intense interest in May Sarton, both as a woman and as a writer."[2] This trend not only has continued but has intensified during the rest of the decade. This bibliography focuses on the decade of the 1980s and serves as a supplement to the solid foundation laid by Lenora Blouin. It was developed by using the broad range of traditional and computer research sources available to most scholars. It carries the usual disclaimer of all bibliographies. Although I have strived for completeness, I am certain there are sources I have missed. I have included numerous sources that only briefly discuss Sarton or her works, but I have excluded the growing number of works focused on other authors or themes that merely name Sarton by comparison in the text.

A review of May Sarton's works published during the 1980s documents three distinct patterns. Sarton has continued to publish works written in the genres for which she had become well known: novels such as *The Magnificent Spinster* and *The Education of Harriet Hatfield,* and poetry collections such as *Halfway to Silence, Letters from Maine,* and *The Silence Now.* She firmly established her reputation with the genre through which she began to speak during the previous decade, the journal. The critical reception of her sensitive treatment of her experiences with illness, aging, and death brought her to the attention of a new population of readers. At the same time, earlier works were reprinted in either paperback or large print editions, with the latter clearly directed to the market of the visually impaired. Last, a series of individual poems or small collections of poems were issued as broadsides in limited, signed editions. These fine editions, printed on special papers and designated for private distribution, are certain to command the attention of future bibliophiles. In all, May Sarton published some nineteen new or revised works during the 1980s, the decade in which she celebrated her seventy-fifth birthday.

May Sarton's "voice" has not found expression just on the printed page. In an age characterized by an inclination to hear the written word spoken, there is strong interest in preserving authors' works (especially poems) on audio- or videotapes. May Sarton has read selections of her prose and poems for several well-established producers of spoken-word tapes. In fact, a *Washington Post* article on the *Watershed Foundation* entitled, "Play It Again, Poet," identifies May Sarton's recording as one of their three most popular.[3]

In addition to such preserved readings of May Sarton's poems and prose, the bibliographic record of the 1980s documents her stature as an established author in other ways. Newspaper accounts track her appearances at poetry readings from Boston to Sacramento. She is listed as a "best-selling author," lending her support to such political and social causes as animal rights and AIDS relief. Her books are included routinely on lists for summer reading and Christmas gift suggestions. New editions of standard reference sources have added entries on Sarton or significantly expanded what previously had been only a brief biographical note. Her writing has provided the inspiration for musical compositions. Interviews published in newspapers, popular magazines, and scholarly journals combine to further testify to the broad recognition of May Sarton as one of America's most eminent women authors.

The most significant measure of Sarton's stature as an author, however, rests not in accounts of her personal appearances or headlines labeling her as a "famous woman poet." Rather, it is the dramatic increase in the number of serious critical studies of Sarton's writings that speaks most effectively to her importance as a poet, novelist, and essayist. In 1982, when Lenora Blouin commented on the increase in critical attention being accorded Sarton, she appropriately ascribed the change to the emergence of feminist literary criticism. Certainly the intervening years have seen a strengthening and expansion of feminist discourse on the writings of May Sarton. Doctoral dissertations and master's theses focusing on Sarton (a new development in the 1980s) have addressed such topics as the myth of Medusa and a feminist vision, female heroism, female friendships, cultural construction of gender in American women's fiction, and sources and images of female creativity. Journal articles and monographs on the female muse have repeatedly explored the writings of May Sarton as a context for understanding female creativity, female friendships, and female spirituality. Critical discourse on Sarton, however, has not been limited to the feminist perspective. Authors of scholarly studies on such varied topics as the literary treatment of aging and death, spirituality, friendships, and solitude either have integrated a brief discussion of Sarton's writings into a broad discussion of these themes or focused exclusively on the writings of Sarton. Additionally, gerontologists have discussed the value of reading the novels and journals of May Sarton as a means of developing a greater understanding of and sensitivity to the aging process, while psychologists have examined her journal writings as a virtual model for self-renewal following extreme trauma. Although May Sarton continues to speak eloquently to the feminist mind, clearly her voice is being heard by a diverse, rapidly expanding audience. It is this reality, documented by her critical reception and her continuing creativity during the 1980s that attests to her achievements as a major American literary figure.

NOTES

1. Lenora P. Blouin, "A Revised Bibliography" in *May Sarton: Woman and Poet,* ed. Constance Hunting (Orono: National Poetry Foundation and University of Maine at Orono, 1982), 283.

2. Blouin, "Revised Bibliography," 283.

3. Victoria Dawson, "Play It Again, Poet," *Washington Post,* December 17, 1985.

Primary Works, Including Broadsides, Recordings, and Reprints (1980–1992)

Absence.
Concord, N.H.: William B. Ewert, 1984.
(Broadside . . . "Limited to 336 copies for private distribution. Of these, 36 copies have been numbered and signed by the author.")
After the Stroke: A Journal.
New York: Norton, 1988.

Anger.
New York: Norton, 1982.
As Does New Hampshire, and Other Poems.
Dublin, N.H.: W.L. Bauhan, 1987. Reissue of the 1967 ed. with additional
material.
As Fresh, As Always New.
Concord, N.H.: William B. Ewert, 1985.
(Broadside ... "336 copies were printed ... for private distribution. Of these, 36
copies have been numbered and signed by the author.")
As We Are Now.
New York: Norton, 1982, ©1973.
At Seventy: A Journal.
New York: Norton, 1984.
The Birth of a Grandfather.
New York: Norton, 1989, ©1957.
Blizzard.
Concord, N.H.: William B. Ewert, 1986.
("186 copies were printed ... of these 50 copies are on special paper and signed
by the author.")
The Bridge of Years.
New York: Norton, 1985, ©1971.
Christmas Light.
Concord, N.H.: William B. Ewert, 1987.
("Calligraphy by R. P. Hale ... It is limited to 350 copies. Of these 50 numbered
copies were printed on special paper and signed by the author and calligrapher.")
Crucial Conversations.
New York: Norton, 1980, ©1975.
December Moon.
Concord, N.H.: William B. Ewert, 1988.
(Broadside ... "limited to 436 copies.")
The Education of Harriet Hatfield.
New York: Norton, 1989.
Endgame: A Journal of the Seventy-Ninth Year.
New York: Norton, 1992.
Faithful Are the Wounds.
New York: Norton, 1983.
Faithful Are the Wounds, reprint.
New York: Norton, 1985, ©1983.
Friendship and Illness.
Concord, N.H.: William B. Ewert, 1990.
(Broadside ... "limited to 536 copies. Original woodcut by Mary Azarian.")

The Fur Person.
  Boston, Mass.: G. K. Hall, 1980, ©1978.
  ("Published in large print.")
Halfway to Silence: New Poems.
  New York: Norton, 1980.
Honey in the Hive: Judith Matlack, 1898–1982.
  Boston, Mass.: Warren Publishing, 1988.
The House by the Sea: A Journal.
  New York: Norton, 1981, ©1977.
Interview.
  Columbia, Mo.: American Audio Prose Library, 1982. Sound recording.
Joanna and Ulysses: A Tale.
  New York: Norton, 1987, ©1963.
Journal of a Solitude.
  London: Women's Press, 1985, ©1973.
Kinds of Love.
  New York: Norton, 1980, ©1970.
Letters from Maine: New Poems.
  New York: Norton, 1984.
Letters to May. [by Eleanor Mabel Sarton, 1878–1950].
  Selected and edited with an introduction by May Sarton.
  Orono, Me.: Puckerbrush Press, 1986.
The Magnificent Spinster.
  New York: Norton, 1985.
May Sarton.
  Columbia, Mo.: American Prose Library, 1982. Sound recording.
  (May Sarton reads from *As We Are Now* and *Journal of a Solitude;* Interview)
May Sarton: A Self Portrait. Edited by Marita Simpson and Martha Wheelock. New
  York: Norton, 1986, ©1982. (Rev. ed. of *World of Light.*)
May Sarton Hears the Mermaids Singing.
  Los Angeles: Pacifica Tape Library, 1983. Sound recording.
  (May Sarton reads from the poems and speaks of her motivations, her muse,
  her loves, and the rigors of being a poet.)
May Sarton: Writing in the Upward Years.
  Fla.: Florida Media Arts Center, 1990. Videocassette.
My Sister, O My Sisters.
  Washington, D.C.: Watershed Tapes., 1984. Sound recording.
Now I Become Myself.
  Burlington, Vt.: Rumble Press, 1992.
  (A volume of poetry on the theme of self-actualization. Hand-printed and hand
  set by Bruce Conklin.)

Old Trees.
  by *Barbara Hirsch,* 1981. Musical score.
  (Chorus for mixed voices with piano.)
The Phoenix Again.
  Concord, N.H.: William B. Ewert, 1987.
  ("Seventy-five copies of this broadside, designed by John Kristensen . . . were
  printed . . . to honor May Sarton on her seventy-fifth birthday, May 3, 1987.")
The Phoenix Again: New Poems.
  Concord, N.H.: W. B. Ewert, 1987.
  ("Of a total of 150 copies signed by the author and the artist, this is one of
  125 handsewn in wrappers.")
The Phoenix: Ordeals and Rebirth.
  Bloomington: Indiana University. Sound recording.
  (Patten Foundation Lectures: "Ms. Sarton reads selections of her poetry relating
  to the theme of ordeals and rebirths.")
Plant Dreaming Deep.
  New York: Norton, 1983, ©1968.
The Poet and the Donkey.
  New York: Norton, 1984, ©1969.
A Reckoning.
  New York: Norton, 1981, ©1978.
A Reckoning.
  London: Women's Press, 1984, ©1978.
A Reckoning. Large type ed.
  South Yarmouth, Mass.: J. Curley and Association, 1985, ©1978.
Recovering: A Journal.
  New York: Norton, 1980.
Sarton Selected: An Anthology of the Journals, Novels, and Poetry of May Sarton. Edited
  and with an introduction and notes by Bradford Dudley Daziel. New York and
  London: Norton, 1991.
Seven Holiday Greetings from 1985.
  Concord, N.H.: William B. Ewert, 1985.
  ("Fifty sets of cards have been issued by the publisher. Of these, the cards in
  36 sets have been printed on special papers and are numbered and signed by their
  authors.")
Shadow of a Man.
  New York: Norton, 1982, ©1950.
Shell.
  Lincoln, Mass.: Penmaen Press, 1982.
  ("Wood engraving by Michael McCurdy. One hundred copies were made . . . all
  copies are signed by the author and artist.")
The Silence Now: New and Uncollected Earlier Poems.
  New York: Norton, 1988.

Small Joys.
    Concord, N.H.: William B. Ewert, 1989.
    (Broadside ... "Original woodcut illustration ... by Mary Azarian ... 436 copies of this first edition were printed at Firefly Press in December, 1989 for private distribution.")
The Smile: After a Painting by Stefano Sasetta [ca. 1400–1450].
    (A broadside ... "printed letterpress at the Firefly Press, Somerville, Massachusetts, during August, 1987. It is limited to 70 copies.")
The Values We Have to Keep.
    Cambridge, Mass.: Cambridge Forum, 1982. Sound recording.
    ("The poet and playwright quotes her poetry to illustrate social values which are worth keeping: love of the arts.")
A Winter Garland: New Poems.
    Concord, N.H.: William B. Ewert, 1982.
    ("One hundred fifty numbered copies ... all copies are signed by author.")
Wo Pu Yao Teng Ssu.
    Taipei: Ssing Kuany, 1988.
    (Chinese translation: *As We Are Now*)
The Work of Happiness.
    Concord, N.H.: William B. Ewert, 1991.
    (Broadside ... "limited to 136 copies ... to honor May Sarton on her 79th birthday.")
World of Light: A Portrait of May Sarton With Additional Poems and Comments.
    New York: Two Lip Art, 1982.
World of Light: A Portrait of May Sarton; and Poems and Comments Sarton Reads Sarton.
    New York: Ishtar, 1982. Sound recording.
A World of Light: Portraits and Celebrations.
    New York: Norton, 1988, ©1976.
Writing in the Upward Years.
    Chicago: Terra Nova Films, 1990. Videocassette.
    (May Sarton talks about the role of aging in her poetry.)
Writings on Writing.
    Orono, Me.: Puckerbrush Press, 1980.

Critical Analysis

Books, Articles, and Essays

Atwood, Margaret. "That Certain Thing Called the Girlfriend." *New York Times Book Review,* 11 May 1986, 1ff.

Bainlin, George. "A Shining in the Dark: May Sarton's Accomplishment." In *May*

Sarton: Woman and Poet, edited by Constance Hunting, 264–80. Orono: National Poetry Foundation and University of Maine at Orono, 1982.

Bakerman, Jane S. "May Sarton's The Small Room: A Comparison and an Analysis." In *May Sarton: Woman and Poet,* edited by Constance Hunting, 123–32. Orono: National Poetry Foundation and University of Maine at Orono, 1982.

———. "Patterns of Love and Friendship: Five Novels by May Sarton." In *May Sarton: Woman and Poet,* edited by Constance Hunting, 113–22. Orono: National Poetry Foundation and University of Maine at Orono, 1982.

———. "Perimeters of Power: An Examination of *As We Are Now.*" In *May Sarton: Woman and Poet,* edited by Constance Hunting, 145–56. Orono: National Poetry Foundation and University of Maine at Orono, 1982.

Bennett, Paula. *My Life A Loaded Gun: Female Creativity and Feminist Poetics.* Boston: Beacon Press, 1986.

Blouin, Lenora P. "A Revised Bibliography." In *May Sarton: Woman and Poet,* edited by Constance Hunting, 283–319. Orono: National Poetry Foundation and University of Maine at Orono, 1982.

Bryan, Mary. "Rage for Justice: Political, Social and Moral Conscience in Selected Novels of May Sarton." In *May Sarton: Woman and Poet,* edited by Constance Hunting, 133–44. Orono: National Poetry Foundation and University of Maine at Orono, 1982.

Code, Lorraine, and Dianne Romaine. "Persons and Others." In *Power, Gender, Values,* edited by Judith Genova, 143–71. Edmonton, Alberta: Academic Printing and Publishing, 1987.

Coldwell, Joan. "The Beauty of the Medusa—20th Century." *English Studies in Canada* 11 (1985): 422–37.

Connelly, Maurene. "Metaphor in Five Garden Poems by May Sarton." In *May Sarton: Woman and Poet,* edited by Constance Hunting, 187–92. Orono: National Poetry Foundation and University of Maine at Orono, 1982.

Contemporary Literary Criticism 14:480–82. Detroit: Gale Research, 1980.

Contemporary Literary Criticism 49:306–23. Detroit: Gale Research, 1988.

Cooper, Joanne E. "Shaping Meaning: Women's Diaries, Journals, and Letters—The Old and the New." *Women's Studies International Forum* 10 (1987): 95–99.

Creange, René. "The Country of the Imagination." In *May Sarton: Woman and Poet,* edited by Constance Hunting, 85–99. Orono: National Poetry Foundation and University of Maine at Orono, 1982.

Cruickshank, Margaret. "A Note on May Sarton." In *Historical, Literary, and Erotic Aspects of Lesbianism,* edited by Monica Kehoe, 153–55. New York: Harrington Park Press, 1986.

DeShazer, Mary K. "Towards Durable Fire: The Solitary Muse of May Sarton." In *Inspiring Women: Reimagining the Muse,* by Mary K. DeShazer, 111–34. New York: Pergamon Press, 1987.

Drake, William. "The Passion of Friendship." In *The First Wave: American Poets in America 1915–1945,* edited by William Drake, 239–65. New York: Macmillan, 1987.

Eagleton, Sandra. *Women in Literature: Life Stages Through Stories, Poems and Plays.* Englewood Cliffs, N.J.: Prentice-Hall, 1988.

Eddy, Darlene Mathis. "The Sculptor and the Rock: Some Uses of Myth in the Poetry of May Sarton." In *May Sarton: Woman and Poet,* edited by Constance Hunting, 179–88. Orono: National Poetry Foundation and University of Maine at Orono, 1982.

Evans, Elizabeth. *May Sarton, Revisited.* Boston: Twayne Publishers, 1989.

Farwell, Marilyn R. "Toward a Definition of the Lesbian Literary Imagination." *Signs* 14 (1988): 100–118.

Fowler, Sigrid H. "A Note on May Sarton's Use of Form." In *May Sarton: Woman and Poet,* edited by Constance Hunting, 173–78. Orono: National Poetry Foundation and University of Maine at Orono, 1982.

Frank, Charles E. "May Sarton: Approaches to Autobiography." In *May Sarton: Woman and Poet,* edited by Constance Hunting, 33–41. Orono: National Poetry Foundation and University of Maine at Orono, 1982.

Friedman, Melvin J. "Recent New England Fiction: Outsiders and Insiders." In *American Literature: The New England Heritage,* edited by John Nagel and Richard Astio, 167–82. New London, Conn.: Garland Press, 1981.

Gaskill, Gayle. "The Mystery of the Mother and the Muse in May Sarton's *Mrs. Stevens Hears the Mermaids Singing.*" *Notes on Modern American Literature* 8, no. 1 (1984): Item 7.

———. "Redefinitions of Traditional Christmas Emblems and Outlooks in May Sarton's Novels of 1970–1975." In *May Sarton: Woman and Poet,* edited by Constance Hunting, 157–69. Orono: National Poetry Foundation and University of Maine at Orono, 1982.

Gilbert, Sandra M., and Susan Gubar. *The War of the Words.* Vol. 1, *No Man's Land: The Place of the Woman Writer in the Twentieth Century.* New Haven: Yale University Press, 1988.

Gubar, Susan D. "Sapphistries." *Signs* 10, no. 1 (1984): 43–62.

Heilbrun, Carolyn G. "May Sarton's Memoirs." In *May Sarton: Woman and Poet,* edited by Constance Hunting, 43–52. Orono: National Poetry Foundation and University of Maine at Orono, 1982.

———. "May Sarton's Memoirs." In *Hamlet's Mother and Other Women,* by Caroline G. Heilbrun, 160–69. New York: Columbia University Press, 1990.

———. "May Sarton's *Mrs. Stevens Hears the Mermaids Singing.*" In *Hamlet's Mother and Other Women,* by Caroline G. Heilbrun, 148–59. New York: Columbia University Press, 1990.

Hunting, Constance, ed. *May Sarton: Woman and Poet.* Orono: National Poetry Foundation and University of Maine at Orono, 1982.

————. "'The Risk is Very Great': The Poetry of May Sarton." In *May Sarton: Woman and Poet,* edited by Constance Hunting, 201–9. Orono: National Poetry Foundation and University of Maine at Orono, 1982.

Hyde, Lewis. "The Commerce of the Creative Spirit." *American Poetry Review* 12, no. 2 (1983): 7–13.

Jaffe, Dennis T. "Self-Renewal: Personal Transformation Following Extreme Trauma." *Journal of Humanistic Psychology* 25 (1985): 99–124.

Jensen, Marvin D. "Helical Thought Development and Chronology Revision: Intrapersonal Communication Processes Reflected in Memoirs." *Kentucky Journal of Communication Arts* 11, no. 1 (1985): 11–13.

————. "Introspective Writings as Reflections of Intrapersonal Communications." In *Intrapersonal Communication Process,* edited by Kittie W. Watson and Charles V. Roberts, 111–34. Scottsdale, Ariz.: Gorsuch Scarisbirck, 1989.

Kehl, D. G. "The Distaff and the Staff—Stereotypes and Archetypes of the Older Woman in Representative Modern Literature." *International Journal of Aging and Human Development* 2 (1988): 1–12.

————. "Thalia Meets Tithonus: Gerontological Wit and Humor in Literature." *Gerontologist* 25 (1985): 539–44.

Klein, Kathleen Gregory. "Aging and Dying in the Novels of May Sarton." *Critique: Studies in Modern Fiction* 24 (1983): 150–57.

LeBar, Barbara. "The Subject Is Marriage." *Journal of Evolutionary Psychology* 9 (1988): 264–69.

Lydon, Mary. "A French View of May Sarton." In *May Sarton: Woman and Poet,* edited by Constance Hunting, 71–77. Orono: National Poetry Foundation and University of Maine at Orono, 1982.

Manning, Gerald F. "Fiction and Aging—Ripeness Is All." *Canadian Journal on Aging* 8, no. 2 (1989): 157–63.

Nett, Emily M. "The Naked Soul Comes Closer to the Surface, Old-Age in the Gender Mirror of Contemporary Novels." *Women's Studies: An Interdisciplinary Journal* 18, nos. 2–3 (1990): 177–90.

Ostriker, Alicia Suskin. *Stealing the Language: The Emergence of Women's Poetry in America.* Boston: Beacon Press, 1986.

————. "The Thieves of Language—Women Poets and Revisionist Mythmaking." *Signs* 8 (1982): 68–90.

Otis, Danielle. "Sarton's 'Because What I Want Most Is Permanence.'" *Explicator* 47 (1989): 55–57.

Owens, Suzanne. "House, Home and Solitude: Memoirs and Journals of May Sarton." In *May Sarton: Woman and Poet,* edited by Constance Hunting, 53–68. Orono: National Poetry Foundation and University of Maine at Orono, 1982.

Ross-Bryant, Lynn. "Imagination and the Re-valorization of the Feminine." *Journal of the American Academy of Religion: Thematic Studies* 48, no. 2 (1981): 105–17.

Rule, Jane. "May Sarton." In *Lesbian Images,* by Jane Rule, 164–74. New York: Doubleday, 1975. Reprint. New York: Crossing Press, 1982.

Shaw, Sheila. "Living Rooms: Amity in the Novels of May Sarton." In *May Sarton: Woman and Poet,* edited by Constance Hunting, 101–11. Orono: National Poetry Foundation and University of Maine at Orono, 1982.

Springer, Marlene. "As We Shall Be: May Sarton and Aging." *Frontiers: A Journal of Women's Studies* 5 (Fall 1980): 46–49.

Taylor, Henry. "The Singing Wound: Intensifying Paradoxes in May Sarton's 'A Divorce of Lovers.'" In *May Sarton: Woman and Poet,* edited by Constance Hunting, 193–200. Orono: National Poetry Foundation and University of Maine at Orono, 1982.

Thyng, Deborah. "'The Action of the Beautiful': The Concept of Balance in the Writings of May Sarton." In *May Sarton: Woman and Poet,* edited by Constance Hunting, 79–84. Orono: National Poetry Foundation and University of Maine at Orono, 1982.

Waxman, Barbara Frey. "Caro Spencer's Struggle to Know Reality and Achieve Wholeness in a 'Place of Punishment.'" Chap. 4 in *From the Hearth to the Open Road: A Feminist Study of Aging in Contemporary Literature.* Westport, Conn.: Greenwood Press, 1990.

Wheelock, Martha. *A Resource Guide and Bibliography to Accompany the Film* World of Light, A Portrait of May Sarton. New York: Ishtar, 1980.

Wolf, Mary A. "Human Development, Gerontology, and Self-Development through the Writings of May Sarton." *Educational Gerontology* 13 (1987): 289–95.

Woodward, Kathleen. "May Sarton and Fictions of Old-Age." In *Women and Literature: Gender and Literary Voice,* edited by Janet Todd, 108–27. New York: Holmes and Meier, 1980.

Wyatt-Brown, Ann M. "The Coming of Age of Literary Gerontology." *Journal of Aging Studies* 4, no. 3 (1990): 299–315.

Dissertations

Bair, Barbara. "Ties of Blood and Bonds of Fortune: The Cultural Construction of Gender in American Women's Fiction—An Interdisciplinary Analysis." Ph.D. diss., Brown University, 1984.

Barker-Nunn, Jeanne Beverly. "A More Adequate Conception: American Women Writers' Quest for a Female Ethic." Ph.D. diss., University of Minnesota, 1985. (Chap. 7 examines the moral summing up that comes with old age and approaching death as illustrated by the novels of May Sarton.)

Clewett, Barbara Jane. "Creativity and the Demonic in Mann's *Dr. Faustus* and Two Sarton Novels." Ph.D. diss., Northwestern University, 1982.

DeShazer, Mary Kirk. "The Woman Poet and Her Muse: Sources and Images of Female Creativity in the Poetry of H.D., Louise Bogan, May Sarton and Adrienne Rich." Ph.D. diss., University of Oregon, 1982.

Flug, Christine Margaret. "The Journey Inward: An Examination of the Non-Fictional Prose of May Sarton." Ph.D. diss., Harvard University, 1986.

Funck, Susana Borneo. "The Finely Woven Web of Interaction: Human Relationships in the Novels of May Sarton." Ph.D. diss., University of Texas at Arlington, 1982.

Owens, Eloise Suzanne. "The Phoenix and the Unicorn: A Study of the Published Private Writing of May Sarton and Anne Morrow Lindbergh." Ph.D. diss., Ohio State University, 1982.

Palumbo, Kathryn Ellen. "Psyche Revisited: Images of Female Heroism in American Literature." Ph.D. diss., Emory University, 1989.

St. Germain, Sheryl Ann. "Medusa and the Struggle Toward a Feminist Vision in Twentieth-Century American Women's Poetry: Evolving Patterns and Visual Responses to Medusa." Ph.D. diss., University of Texas at Dallas, 1986.

Sobal, Nancy Lee. "Curing and Caring: A Literary View of Professional Medical Women." Ph.D. diss., University of Cincinnati, 1984.

Master's and Honors Theses

Allison, Terri M. "A Manner of Life and Death: Analysis and Performance of May Sarton's *As We Are Now.*" Master's thesis, University of North Carolina at Chapel Hill, 1986.

Chadwell, Faye Ann. "Female Friendships in Three Novels by May Sarton." Master's thesis, Appalachian State University, 1987.

Chang, Marilee Laine. "Of Painted Floors and Planted Dreams: May Sarton's Sense of Place." Honors thesis, Harvard University, 1989.

Savage, Terry Lynn. "Solitude: The Richness of Self: An Analysis of Selected Works by May Sarton." Master's thesis, George Washington University, 1980.

Whyte, Patricia M. "'Friends of the Work'—May Sarton and William Heyen: A Descriptive Bibliography of the Heyen Collection of Sarton's Work and Correspondence." Master's thesis, SUNY College at Brockport, 1988.

Biographies and Interviews

Bakerman, Jane S. "May Sarton." In *American Women Authors* 4:20–21. New York: Frederick Ungar, 1982.

———. "May Sarton." In *Dictionary of Literary Biography Yearbook: 1981*, 233–40. Detroit: Gale Research, 1982.

———. "May Sarton." In *Contemporary Novelists*, 4th ed., 574–75. New York: St. Martin's Press, 1982.

Benet's Reader's Encyclopedia. 3rd ed., 866. New York: Harper and Row, 1987.

Bonetti, Kay. *May Sarton: Interview.* Columbia, Mo.: American Audio Prose Library, 1983. Sound recording.

Bray, Rosemary L. "When Everything is a Gift." *New York Times Book Review,* 27 March 1988, 30.

Christy, Marian. "May Sarton: Alone, Not Lonely." *Boston Globe,* 14 January 1987, 34.

Contemporary Authors, New Revision Series 1 (1981): 566–67.

Dawson, Victoria. "May Sarton's Crowded Solitude." *Washington Post,* 29 September 1985.

Hammond, Karla. "To Be Reborn." In *May Sarton: Woman and Poet,* edited by Constance Hunting, 227–38. Orono: National Poetry Foundation and University of Maine at Orono, 1982.

———. "A Further Interview with May Sarton." In *May Sarton: Woman and Poet,* edited by Constance Hunting, 239–48. Orono: National Poetry Foundation and University of Maine at Orono, 1982.

Hershman, Marcie. "May Sarton at 70: 'A Viable Life Against the Odds.'" *Ms.* 11, no. 4 (1982): 23–26.

Hunting, Constance. "May Sarton." In *Dictionary of Literary Biography.* Vol. 48, *American Poets, 1880–1945,* 376–86. Detroit: Gale Research, 1986.

Ingersoll, Earl G., ed. *Conversations with May Sarton.* Jackson, Miss.: University Press of Mississippi, 1991.

Kaplan, Robin, and Shelly Neiderbach. "'I Live Alone in a Very Beautiful Space': An Interview with May Sarton." In *May Sarton: Woman and Poet,* edited by Constance Hunting, 249–60. Orono: National Poetry Foundation and University of Maine at Orono, 1982.

Kendle, Burton. "Sarton, (Eleanor) May." In *Contemporary Poets,* 3rd ed., 744–45. New York: St. Martin's Press, 1985.

Moffatt, Penelope. "Poet May Sarton Recalls Forty Years with Her Muse." *Los Angeles Times,* 29 April, 1987.

Nemy, Enid. "May Sarton: Creative Solitude at 71." *New York Times,* 20 November 1983.

Oxford Companion to American Literature. 5th ed. Edited by James D. Hart, 670. New York and Oxford: Oxford University Press, 1983.

Rosenthal, Lois. "May Sarton (Novelist and Poet)." *Writer's Digest* 69, no. 3 (1989): 44–45.

Putney, Paula G. "Sister of the Mirage and Echo." In *May Sarton: Woman and Poet,* edited by Constance Hunting, 213–25. Orono: National Poetry Foundation and University of Maine at Orono, 1982.

Saum, Karen. "May Sarton." In *Writers at Work: The Paris Review Interviews.* Seventh Series. Edited by George Plimpton, 71–98. New York: Viking, 1984.

Something About the Author 36:159–66. Detroit: Gale Research, 1984.

Springer, Marlene. "May Sarton." In *Encyclopedia of World Literature in the 20th Century.* 2nd ed., 4:152–54. New York: Frederick Ungar, 1984.

Straw, Deborah. "Interview." *Belles Lettres* 6 (Winter 1991): 34–38.

Swartzlander, Susan, and Marilyn Mumford. "May Sarton." In *Cyclopedia of World Authors II* 4:1313–14. Englewood Cliffs, N.J.: Magill, 1990.

Todd, Janet. "May Sarton." In *Women Writers Talking,* edited by Janet Todd, 3–19. New York and London: Holmes and Meier, 1983.

Wheelock, Martha. "May Sarton: A Metaphor for My Life, My Work and My Art." In *Between Women: Biographers, Novelists, Critics, Teachers, and Artists Write About Their Work on Women,* edited by Carol Ascher, Louise DeSalvo, and Sara Ruddick, 413–29. Boston: Beacon Press, 1984.

Works Cited

Abel, Elizabeth, Marianne Hirsch, and Elizabeth Langland, eds. *The Voyage In: Fictions of Female Development.* Hanover, N.H.: University Press of New England, 1983.

Adams, Léonie. *Poems: A Selection.* New York: Funk and Wagnalls, 1954.

Allen, Paula Gunn. *The Woman Who Owned the Shadows.* San Francisco: Spinsters/ Aunt Lute, 1983.

Alloway, Lawrence. Introduction to *Audrey Flack on Painting* by Audrey Flack. New York: Abrams, 1981.

Angus, Ian, and Sut Jhally, eds. *Cultural Politics in Contemporary America.* New York: Routledge, 1989.

Annas, George J. *The Rights of Hospital Patients.* New York: Avon, 1975.

Ascher, Carol, Louise DeSalvo, and Sara Ruddick, eds. *Between Women.* Boston: Beacon Press, 1984.

Bannon, Barbara. "May Sarton." *Publishers Weekly* 205 (June 24, 1974): 16–17.

Barker-Benfield, Ben. "The Spermatic Economy: A Nineteenth-Century View of Sexuality." *Feminist Studies* 1 (1972): 45–74.

Barney, Jane Lockwood. "Community Presence as a Key to Quality of Life in Nursing Homes." *American Journal of Public Health* 64 (March 1974): 265–68.

Barthes, Roland. *Image, Music, Text.* Selected and translated by Stephen Heath. New York: Hill and Wang, 1977.

———. *The Pleasure of the Text.* Translated by Richard Miller. New York: Hill and Wang, 1975.

Bateson, Mary Catherine. *Composing a Life.* New York: Atlantic Monthly Press, 1989.

Baym, Nina. "The Madwoman and Her Languages: Why I Don't Do Feminist Literary Theory." *Tulsa Studies in Women's Literature* 3 (1984): 45–59.

———. "Melodramas of Beset Manhood: How Theories of American Fiction Exclude Women Authors." *American Quarterly* 33 (Summer 1981): 123–39.

Belenky, Mary Field, Blythe McVicker Clinchy, Nancy Rule Goldberger, and Jill Mattuck Tarule. *Women's Ways of Knowing: The Development of Self, Voice, and Mind.* New York: Basic Books, 1986.

Bellow, Saul. *Dangling Man.* New York: Vanguard Press, 1944.

Benoliel, Jean Quint. "Care, Cure, and the Challenge of Voice." In *The Nurse as Caregiver for the Terminal Patient and His Family,* edited by Ann M. Earle, Nina T. Argondizzo, and Austin H. Kutscher, 9–27. New York: Columbia University Press, 1976.

Benstock, Shari, ed. *The Private Self: Theory and Practice of Women's Autobiographical Writings.* Chapel Hill: University of North Carolina Press, 1988.

Berg, Temma F. "Psychologies of Reading." In *Tracing Literary Theory,* edited by Joseph Natoli. Chicago: University of Illinois Press, 1987.

Berlo, J. C. "Beyond *Bricolage:* Women and Aesthetic Strategies in Latin American Textiles." In *Textile Traditions of Mesoamerica and the Andes,* edited by M. B. Schevill, J. C. Berlo, and E. Dwyer. New York: Garland, 1991.

———. "Directions for a Performance Piece Upon the Death of Georgia O'Keeffe." *Women Artists News* 11, no. 4 (September 1986): 33.

Berzon, Betty. *Permanent Partners: Building Gay and Lesbian Relationships That Last.* New York: Dutton, 1988.

Bleich, David. "Gender Interests in Reading and Language." In *Gender and Reading: Essays on Readers, Texts, and Contexts,* edited by Elizabeth A. Flynn and Patrocinio P. Schweikart, 234–66. Baltimore: Johns Hopkins University Press, 1986.

Bogan, Louise. *The Blue Estuaries: Poems, 1923–1968.* New York: Ecco Press, 1977.

———. *Collected Poems, 1923–1953.* New York: Noonday Press, 1954.

———. *Journey Around My Room: The Autobiography of Louise Bogan: A Mosaic.* Assembled by Ruth Limmer. New York: Viking, 1980.

———. *Selected Criticism: Poetry and Prose.* New York: Noonday Press, 1955.

———. *What the Woman Lived: Selected Letters of Louise Bogan, 1920–1970.* Edited by Ruth Limmer. New York: Harcourt Brace Jovanovich, 1973.

Booth, Wayne C. *The Rhetoric of Fiction.* Chicago: University of Chicago Press, 1961.

Bowen, Elizabeth. *Bowen's Court.* New York: Knopf, 1942.

Brodzki, Bella, and Celeste Schenck. *Life/Lines: Theorizing Women's Autobiography.* Ithaca, N.Y.: Cornell University Press, 1988.

Brotman, Herman. "The Fastest Growing Minority: The Aging." *American Journal of Public Health* 64 (March 1974): 249–52.

Bullett, Gerald William, ed. *The English Galaxy of Shorter Poems.* London: J. M. Dent & Sons, 1933.

Burch, Beverly. "Barriers to Intimacy: Conflicts over Power, Dependency, and Nurturing in Lesbian Relationships." In *Lesbian Psychologies: Explorations and Challenges,* edited by Boston Lesbian Psychologies Collective. Urbana: University of Illinois Press, 1987.

Cass, Vivienne. "Homosexual Identity Formation: A Theoretical Model." *Journal of Homosexuality* 4, no. 3 (Spring 1979): 219–35.

Chodorow, Nancy. *The Reproduction of Mothering: Psychoanalysis and the Sociology of Gender.* Berkeley: University of California Press, 1978.

Cooper, Patricia, and Norma Bradley Buford. *The Quilters: Women and Domestic Art.* New York: Doubleday, 1978.

Cornillon, Susan Koppelman, ed. *Images of Women in Fiction: Feminist Perspectives.* Bowling Green, Ohio: Bowling Green University Popular Press, 1972.

Cott, Nancy. *Root of Bitterness: Documents of the Social History of American Women.* New York: Dutton, 1972.

Cruikshank, Margaret. "A Note on May Sarton." *Journal of Homosexuality* 12, nos. 3–4 (1986): 154.

Culler, Jonathan. *On Deconstruction: Theory and Criticism after Structuralism.* Ithaca, N.Y.: Cornell University Press, 1982.

Curtin, Sharon R. *Nobody Ever Died of Old Age.* Boston: Little, Brown, 1972.

Curtius, Ernst. *European Literature and the Latin Middle Ages,* translated by Willard R. Trask. New York: Harper and Row, 1963.

Daly, Mary. *Beyond God the Father: Toward a Philosophy of Women's Liberation.* Boston: Beacon Press, 1973.

———. *The Church and the Second Sex.* New York: Harper and Row, 1968.

———. *Gyn/Ecology: The Metaethics of Radical Feminism.* Boston: Beacon Press, 1978.

———. *Pure Lust: Elemental Feminist Philosophy.* Boston: Beacon Press, 1984.

DeShazer, Mary K. *Inspiring Women: Reimagining the Muse.* New York: Pergamon Press, 1987.

Dinnerstein, Dorothy. *The Mermaid and the Minotaur: Sexual Arrangements and Human Malaise.* New York: Harper and Row, 1976.

Doane, Mary Ann. *The Desire to Desire: The Woman's Film of the 1940s.* Bloomington: Indiana University Press, 1987.

Donovan, Josephine, ed. *Feminist Literary Criticism: Explorations in Theory.* Lexington: University Press of Kentucky, 1975.

Drake, William. *The First Wave: Women Poets in America, 1915–1945.* New York: Macmillan, 1987.

Drewes, Caroline. "A Radical Feminist with a Quiet Voice." *San Francisco Examiner,* 29 November 1976.

DuBay, William H. *Gay Identity: The Self under Ban.* Jefferson, N.C.: McFarland, 1987.

Dunker, Buffy. "Aging Lesbians: Observations and Speculations." In *Lesbian Psychologies: Explorations and Challenges,* edited by Boston Lesbian Psychologies Collective. Urbana: University of Illinois Press, 1987.

DuPlessis, Rachel Blau. "For the Etruscans." In *The New Feminist Criticism: Essays on Women, Literature, and Theory,* edited by Elaine Showalter. New York: Pantheon Books, 1985.

———. *Writing Beyond the Ending: Narrative Strategies of Twentieth-Century Women Writers.* Bloomington: Indiana University Press, 1985.

Eagleton, Sandra. *Women in Literature: Life Stages through Stories, Poems, and Plays.* Englewood Cliffs, N.J.: Prentice-Hall, 1988.

Earle, Ann, Nina T. Argondizzo, and Austin M. Kutscher, eds. *The Nurse as Caregiver for the Terminal Patient and His Family.* New York: Columbia University Press, 1976.

Ehrenreich, Barbara, and Deirdre English. *Complaints and Disorders: The Sexual Politics of Sickness.* Old Westbury, N.Y.: Feminist Press, 1973.

Eisenstein, Hester, and Alice Jardine, eds. *The Future of Difference.* 1980. Reprint. New Brunswick, N.J.: Rutgers University Press, 1985.

Ellmann, Mary. *Thinking about Women.* New York: Harcourt, 1968.

Empson, William. *Seven Types of Ambiguity.* 1930. Reprint. Harmondsworth: Penguin, 1961.

Evans, Elizabeth. *May Sarton, Revisited.* Twayne's United States Authors Series 551. Boston: Twayne/G. K. Hall, 1989.

Faderman, Lillian. *Surpassing the Love of Men: Romantic Friendship and Love between Women from the Renaissance to the Present.* New York: William Morrow, 1981.

Fairbrother, Nan. *An English Year.* New York: Knopf, 1954.

Ferguson, Ann. "Patriarchy, Sexual Identity, and the Sexual Revolution." In "On 'Compulsory Heterosexuality and Lesbian Existence': Defining the Issues," by Ann Ferguson, Jacquelyn N. Zita, and Kathryn Pyne Adelson. *Signs* 7 (1981): 158–72.

Fetterley, Judith. *The Resisting Reader: A Feminist Approach to American Fiction.* Bloomington: Indiana University Press, 1978.

Fiedler, Leslie. *Love and Death in the American Novel.* 1960. Reprint. New York: Stein and Day, 1982.

Fish, Stanley. *Is There a Text in This Class? The Authority of Interpretive Communities.* Cambridge, Mass.: Harvard University Press, 1980.

——. *Self-Consuming Artifacts: The Experience of Seventeenth-Century Literature.* Berkeley: University of California Press, 1972.

——. "Why No One's Afraid of Wolfgang Iser." *Diacritics* 11, no. 1 (1981): 2–13.

Flack, Audrey. *Art and Soul: Notes on Creating.* New York: Dutton, 1986.

——. *Audrey Flack on Painting.* New York: Abrams, 1981.

Flynn, Elizabeth A., and Patrocinio P. Schweickart, eds. *Gender and Reading: Essays on Readers, Texts, and Contexts.* Baltimore: Johns Hopkins University Press, 1986.

Frank, Elizabeth. *Louise Bogan: A Portrait.* New York: Knopf, 1985.

Freund, Elizabeth. *The Return of the Reader: Reader-Response Criticism.* New York: Methuen, 1987.

Friday, Nancy. *My Mother/My Self: The Daughter's Search for Identity.* New York: Delacorte Press, 1977.

Friedman, Susan Stanford. "Women's Autobiographical Selves." In *The Private Self: Theory and Practice of Women's Autobiographical Writings,* edited by Shari Benstock, 34–62. Chapel Hill: University of North Carolina Press, 1988.

Fulton, Robert L., ed. *Death and Identity.* Bowie, Md.: Charles Press, 1976.

Galford, Ellen. *The Fires of Bride.* 1986. Reprint. New York: Firebrand Books, 1988.

Gearhart, Sally Miller. *The Wanderground: Stories of the Hill Women.* Watertown, Mass.: Persephone Press, 1979.

Gelfant, Blanche. *Women Writing in America.* Hanover, N.H.: University Press of New England, 1984.

Gérin, Winifred. *Charlotte Brontë: The Evolution of Genius.* Oxford: Oxford University Press, 1967.

Gilbert, Sandra, and Susan Gubar. *The Madwoman in the Attic: The Woman Writer and the Nineteenth-Century Literary Imagination.* New Haven: Yale University Press, 1979.

―――. *No Man's Land: The Place of the Woman Writer in the Twentieth Century.* Vol. 1: *The War of the Words.* New Haven: Yale University Press, 1988.

―――, eds. *The Norton Anthology of Literature by Women: The Tradition in English.* New York: Norton, 1985.

Gilligan, Carol. *In a Different Voice: Psychological Theory and Women's Development.* Cambridge, Mass.: Harvard University Press, 1982.

Gilligan, Carol, Janie Victoria Ward, and Jill McLean Taylor, eds., with Betty Bardige. *Mapping the Moral Domain: A Contribution of Women's Thinking to Psychological Theory and Education.* Cambridge, Mass.: Harvard University Press, 1988.

Gillmore, Inez Haynes. *Angel Island.* 1914. Reprint. New York: New American Library, 1988.

Gilman, Charlotte Perkins. *Herland.* 1915. Reprint. New York: Pantheon Books, 1979.

―――. *The Living of Charlotte Perkins Gilman: An Autobiography.* New York: Appleton-Century, 1935.

―――. *The Yellow Wallpaper.* 1892. Reprint. Old Westbury, N.Y.: Feminist Press, 1973.

Glasscote, Raymond, et al. *Old Folks at Homes.* Washington, D.C.: American Psychiatric Association, 1976.

Glendinning, Victoria. *Elizabeth Bowen, A Biography.* New York: Avon, 1979.

Golden, Carla. "Diversity and Variability in Women's Sexual Identities." In *Lesbian Psychologies: Explorations and Challenges,* edited by Boston Lesbian Psychologies Collective, 18–34. Urbana: University of Illinois Press, 1987.

Gouma-Peterson, Thalia, ed. *Miriam Schapiro: A Retrospective, 1953–1980.* Wooster, Ohio: The College of Wooster, 1980.

Graves, Robert. "In Dedication," prologue to *The White Goddess.* New York: Farrar, Straus, and Giroux, 1975.

Greenleaf, Nancy Proctor. "Stereotyped Sex-Role Ranking of Caregivers and Quality Care for Patients." In *The Nurse as Caregiver for the Terminal Patient and His Family,* edited by Ann M. Earle, Nina T. Argondizzo, and Austin H. Kutscher, 185–93. New York: Columbia University Press, 1976.

Gubar, Susan. "'The Blank Page' and the Issues of Female Creativity." *Critical Inquiry* 8 (1981): 243–63.

Haller, John S., Jr., and Robin Haller. *The Physician and Sexuality in Victorian America.* Urbana: University of Illinois Press, 1974.

Hardwick, Elizabeth. *Seduction and Betrayal: Women and Literature.* New York: Vintage, 1974.

Hartman, Geoffrey H. "Literary Criticism and Its Discontents." *Critical Inquiry* 3 (1976): 203–20.

H. D. [Hilda Doolittle]. *End to Torment: A Memoir of Ezra Pound.* New York: New Directions, 1979.

Hedges, Elaine R. Afterword to *The Yellow Wallpaper* by Charlotte Perkins Gilman. Old Westbury, N.Y.: Feminist Press, 1973.

Heilbrun, Carolyn G. *Writing a Woman's Life.* New York: Norton, 1988.

Heilbrun, Carolyn, and Catharine Stimpson. "Theories of Feminist Criticism: A Dialogue." In *Feminist Literary Criticism: Explorations in Theory,* edited by Josephine Donovan, 61–73. Lexington: University Press of Kentucky, 1975.

Hill, Mary A. *Charlotte Perkins Gilman: The Making of a Radical Feminist, 1860–1896.* Philadelphia: Temple University Press, 1981.

———, ed. *Endure: The Diaries of Charles Walter Stetson.* Philadelphia: Temple University Press, 1985.

Hoagland, Sarah Lucia. *Lesbian Ethics: Toward New Value.* Palo Alto, Calif.: Institute of Lesbian Studies, 1988.

Holland, Norman. *5 Readers Reading.* New Haven: Yale University Press, 1975.

Howe, Irving. *Decline of the New.* New York: Harcourt, Brace, and World, 1963.

Howe, Mark DeWolfe, ed. *Holmes-Laski Letters: The Correspondence of Mr. Justice Holmes and Harold J. Laski, 1916–1935.* 2 vols. Cambridge, Mass.: Harvard University Press, 1953.

Huf, Linda. *A Portrait of the Artist as a Young Woman: The Writer as Heroine in American Literature.* New York: Frederick Ungar, 1983.

Hunting, Constance, ed. *May Sarton: Woman and Poet.* Orono, Maine: National Poetry Foundation and University of Maine Press, 1982.

Ingarden, Roman. *The Literary Work of Art: An Investigation on the Borderlines of Ontology, Logic, and the Theory of Literature.* Translated by George G. Grabowicz. Evanston, Ill.: Northwestern University Press, 1973.

Iser, Wolfgang. *The Act of Reading: A Theory of Aesthetic Response.* Baltimore: Johns Hopkins University Press, 1978.

———. *The Implied Reader: Patterns of Communication in Prose Fiction from Bunyan to Beckett.* Baltimore: Johns Hopkins University Press, 1974.

Jacobus, Mary. *Reading Woman: Essays in Feminist Criticism.* New York: Columbia University Press, 1986.

Kaplan, Deborah. "Representing Two Cultures: Jane Austen's Letters." In *The Private Self: Theory and Practice of Women's Autobiographical Writings,* edited by Shari Benstock, 211–29. Chapel Hill: University of North Carolina Press, 1988.

Kastenbaum, Robert. "Psychological Death." In *Death and Dying: Current Issues in the Treatment of the Dying Person,* edited by Leonard Pearson, 1–27. Cleveland: Case Western Reserve University Press, 1969.

———. "While the Old Man Dies: Our Conflicting Attitudes toward the Elderly." In *Psychosocial Aspects of Terminal Care,* edited by Bernard Schoenberg, Arthur C. Carr, David Peretz, and Austin H. Kutscher, 116–25. New York: Columbia University Press, 1972.

Kearns, Martha. *Käthe Kollwitz: Woman and Artist.* Old Westbury, N.Y.: Feminist Press, 1976.

Kinsey, Alfred, W. B. Pomeroy, C. E. Martin, and P. H. Gebhard. *Sexual Behavior in the Human Female.* Philadelphia: Saunders, 1953.

Kinsey, Alfred, Wardell B. Pomeroy, and Clyde E. Martin. *Sexual Behavior in the Human Male.* Philadelphia: Saunders, 1948.

Kizer, Carolyn. *Mermaids in the Basement.* Port Townsend, Wash.: Copper Canyon Press, 1963.

Kolodny, Annette. "A Map for Rereading: or, Gender and the Interpretation of Literary Texts." *New Literary History* 11 (1980): 451–67.

Krant, Melvin J. *Dying and Dignity: The Meaning and Control of a Personal Death.* Springfield, Ill.: Charles Thomas, 1974.

Kumin, Maxine. *In Deep: Country Essays.* New York: Viking, 1987.

Lane, Ann J. Introduction to *Herland,* by Charlotte Perkins Gilman. New York: Pantheon Books, 1979.

Lavelle, Louis. *Le Mal et la Souffrance.* Paris: Plon, 1940.

Le Guin, Ursula K. *Dancing at the Edge of the World: Thoughts on Words, Women, Places.* New York: Grove Press, 1989.

Levertov, Denise. *Poems 1960–1967.* New York: New Directions, 1967.

———. *The Poet in the World.* New York: New Directions, 1973.

Lewis, C. Day. *An Italian Visit.* London: Jonathan Cape, 1953.

Lorde, Audre. *The Black Unicorn.* New York: Norton, 1978.

MacPike, Loralee. "Environment as Psychopathological Symbolism in 'The Yellow Wallpaper'." *American Literary Realism, 1870–1910* 8, no. 3 (1975): 286–88.

Marcus, Jane. "Invincible Mediocrity: The Private Selves of Public Women." In *The Private Self: Theory and the Practice of Women's Autobiographical Writings,* edited by Shari Benstock, 114–46. Chapel Hill: University of North Carolina Press, 1988.

Mason, Mary G. "The Other Voice: Autobiographies of Women Writers." In *Life/Lines: Theorizing Women's Autobiography,* edited by Bella Brodzki and Celeste Schenk, 22. Ithaca, N.Y.: Cornell University Press, 1988.

Mendelson, Mary Adelaide. *Tender Loving Greed.* New York: Vintage, 1975.

Meszaros, Patricia K. "Woman as Artist: The Fiction of Mary Lavin." *Critique* 24 (1982): 39–54.

Meynell, Viola. *A Girl Adoring.* London: E. Arnold, 1927.

Miller, Jean Baker. *Toward a New Psychology of Women.* 2d ed. Boston: Beacon Press, 1976.

Miller, Nancy K. "Changing the Subject: Authorship, Writing, and the Reader."

In *Feminist Studies, Critical Studies*, edited by Teresa de Lauretis, 102–20. Bloomington: Indiana University Press, 1986.

Moers, Ellen. *Literary Women*. Garden City, N.Y: Anchor/Doubleday, 1977.

Moffat, Mary Jane, and Charlotte Painter, eds. *Revelations: Diaries of Women*. New York: Vintage, 1975.

Moore, Marianne, trans. *The Fables of La Fontaine*. New York: Viking, 1954.

Morantz, Regina. "The Lady and Her Physician." In *Clio's Consciousness Raised: New Perspectives on the History of Women*, edited by Mary S. Hartman and Lois Banner, 38–53. New York: Harper and Row, 1974.

Morrison, Toni. *Sula*. New York: Knopf, 1973.

Nemser, Cindy. *Art Talk: Conversations with Twelve Women Artists*. New York: Charles Scribner's Sons, 1975.

Neumann, Erich. *The Great Mother: An Analysis of the Archetype*. Translated by Ralph Manheim. 1955. Reprint. Princeton, N.J.: Princeton University Press, 1972.

O'Connor, Andrea. *Dying and Grief: Nursing Interventions*. New York: American Journal of Nursing, 1976.

Pagels, Elaine. *Adam, Eve, and the Serpent*. New York: Random House, 1988.

Pitter, Ruth. *The Ermine: Poems, 1942–1952*. London: Cresset Press, 1953.

Pivar, David J. *Purity Crusade: Sexual Morality and Social Control, 1868–1900*. Westport, Conn.: Greenwood Press, 1973.

Pound, Ezra. Introduction to *The Natural Philosophy of Love*, by Rémy de Gourmont. London: Spearman, 1957.

Pratt, Annis. *Archetypal Patterns in Women's Fiction*. Bloomington: Indiana University Press, 1981.

Quinn, Nancy, and Anne Somers. "The Patients' Bill of Rights." *Nursing Outlook* 22 (April 1974): 240–44.

Rich, Adrienne. "Compulsory Heterosexuality and Lesbian Existence." In *Women-Identified Women*, edited by Trudy E. Darty and Sandra J. Potter. Palo Alto, Calif.: Mayfield Publishing, 1984.

———. *Of Woman Born: Motherhood as Experience and Institution*. New York: Norton, 1976.

———. *On Lies, Secrets, and Silence: Selected Prose, 1966–1978*. New York: Norton, 1979.

———. "Poetry, Personality, and Wholeness: A Response to Galway Kinnell." *Field: Contemporary Poetry and Poetics* 7 (1972): 14.

Richards, I. A. *Practical Criticism: A Study of Literary Judgment*. 1929. Reprint. New York: Harcourt, Brace, 1935.

Rosenblatt, Louise. *Literature as Exploration*. 3d ed. New York: Noble and Noble, 1976.

———. *The Reader, The Text, The Poem: The Transactional Theory of the Literary Work*. Carbondale: Southern Illinois University Press, 1978.

Ross-Bryant, Lynn. "Imagination and the Re-Valorization of the Feminine." *Journal of the American Academy of Religion. Thematic Studies* 48, no. 2 (1981): 105–17.

Rule, Jane. "May Sarton." In *Lesbian Images.* New York: Doubleday, 1975.

Russ, Joanna. "What Can a Heroine Do: Or Why Women Can't Write." In *Images of Women in Fiction: Feminist Perspectives,* edited by Susan Koppelman Cornillon. Bowling Green, Ohio: Bowling Green University Popular Press, 1973.

Sarton, Eleanor Mabel. *Letters to May, by Eleanor Mabel Sarton, 1878–1950.* Selected and edited with an introduction by May Sarton. Orono, Maine: Puckerbrush Press, 1986.

Sartre, Jean-Paul. *What Is Literature?* Translated by Bernard Frechtman. New York: Harper and Row, 1965.

Saum, Karen. "The Art of Poetry XXXII: May Sarton." *Paris Review* 89 (1983): 80–110.

Schapiro, Miriam. "The Education of Women as Artists: Project Womanhouse." In *Feminist Collage,* edited by Judy Loeb 247–53. New York: Teacher's College Press, 1979.

———. *Femmages, 1971–1985.* St. Louis, Mo.: Brentwood Gallery, 1985.

———. "Notes from a Conversation on Art, Feminism, and Work." In *Working It Out,* edited by Sara Ruddick and Pamela Daniels, 283–305. New York: Pantheon Books, 1977.

Schapiro, Miriam, and Melissa Meyer. "Femmage." *Heresies* 4 (1978): 66–69.

Schweickart, Patrocinio P. "Reading Ourselves: Toward a Feminist Theory of Reading." In *Gender and Reading: Essays on Readers, Texts, and Contexts,* edited by Elizabeth A. Flynn and Patrocinio Schweickart, 31–62. Baltimore: Johns Hopkins University Press, 1986.

Shelley, Dolores. "A Conversation with May Sarton." *Women and Literature* 7 (1979): 33–41.

Showalter, Elaine. "Toward a Feminist Poetic." In *The New Feminist Criticism: Essays on Women, Literature, and Theory,* edited by Elaine Showalter. New York: Pantheon, 1985.

———, ed. *The New Feminist Criticism: Essays on Women, Literature, and Theory.* New York: Pantheon, 1985.

Sibley, Agnes. *May Sarton.* Twayne's United States Author Series 213. New York: Twayne Publishers, 1972.

Slonczewski, Joan. *A Door into Ocean.* 1986. Reprint. New York: Avon, 1987.

Simpson, Marita, and Martha Wheelock, eds. *May Sarton: A Self-Portrait.* New York: Norton, 1982.

Smith-Rosenberg, Carroll, and Charles Rosenberg. "The Female Animal: Medical and Biological Views of Women in Nineteenth-Century America." *Journal of American History* 60 (1973): 332–56.

Spacks, Patricia Meyer. *The Female Imagination.* New York: Discus/Avon, 1972.

Spencer, Sharon. "'Femininity' and the Woman Writer." *Women's Studies* 1, no. 3 (1973): 247–57.

Stetson, Erlene, ed. *Black Sister: Poetry by Black American Women, 1746–1980.* Bloomington: Indiana University Press, 1981.

Stimpson, Catharine R. "Female Insubordination and the Text." *Where the Meanings Are: Feminism and Cultural Spaces,* 155–64. New York: Methuen, 1988.

Suleiman, Susan R., and Inge Crosman, eds. *The Reader in the Text: Essays on Audience and Interpretation.* Princeton, N.J.: Princeton University Press, 1980.

Todd, Janet. *Feminist Literary History.* New York: Routledge, 1988.

———, ed. *Women Writers Talking.* New York: Holmes and Meier, 1983.

———. *Women's Friendship in Literature.* New York: Columbia University Press, 1980.

Tompkins, Jane P. *Sensational Designs: The Cultural Work of American Fiction, 1790– 1860.* London: Oxford University Press, 1985.

———, ed. *Reader-Response Criticism: From Formalism to Post-Structuralism.* Baltimore: Johns Hopkins University Press, 1980.

Townsend, Claire, et al. *Old Age: The Last Segregation.* New York: Grossman, 1971.

Treichler, Paula. "Escaping the Sentence: Diagnosis and Discourse in *The Yellow Wallpaper.*" In *Feminist Issues in Literary Scholarship,* edited by Shari Benstock. Bloomington: Indiana University Press, 1987.

Vachon, M., et al. "The Nurse in Thanatology: What She Can Learn from the Women's Liberation Movement." In *The Nurse as Caregiver for the Terminal Patient and His Family,* edited by Ann M. Earle, Nina T. Argondizzo, and Austin H. Kutscher, 175–84. New York: Columbia University Press, 1976.

Valéry, Paul. *Collected Works of Paul Valéry.* Edited by Jackson Mathews. Princeton: Princeton University Press, 1989.

Veeder, William. "Who Is Jane? The Intricate Feminism of Charlotte Perkins Gilman." *Arizona Quarterly* 44, no. 3 (1988): 40–79.

Walker, Alice. *In Search of Our Mothers' Gardens: Womanist Prose.* New York: Harcourt Brace Jovanovich, 1983.

Weisman, Avery D. *The Realization of Death: A Guide for the Psychological Autopsy.* New York: Jason Aronson, 1974.

Wells, Robert V. "Demographic Change and the Life Cycle of American Families." In *The Family in History: Interdisciplinary Essays,* edited by Theodore Rabb and Robert Rotberg. New York: Harper, 1971.

Whitehead, Alfred North. *Dialogues of Alfred North Whitehead.* Boston: Little, Brown, 1954.

Wilson, Sally Hart. 'Nursing Home Patients' Rights: Are They Enforceable?" *Gerontologist* 18 (June 1978): 255–61.

Winterson, Jeanette. *Oranges Are Not the Only Fruit.* 1985. Reprint. New York: Atlantic Monthly Press, 1987.

Wittig, Monique. *Les Guérrillères*. Translated by David Le Vay. New York: Avon, 1973.

Wood, Ann Douglas. "'The Fashionable Diseases': Women's Complaints and Their Treatment in Nineteenth-Century America." *Journal of Interdisciplinary History* 4 (1973): 25–52.

Zola, Irving. "Medicine as an Institution of Social Control." *Sociological Review* 20 (November 1972): 487–504.

A Selected Bibliography of Works by May Sarton

Volumes of Poetry

As Does New Hampshire. Peterborough, N.H.: Richard R. Smith, 1967.
As Does New Hampshire, and Other Poems. Dublin, N.H.: W. L. Bauhan, 1987.
Cloud, Stone, Sun, Vine: Poems Selected and New. New York: Norton, 1961.
Collected Poems, 1930–1973. New York: Norton, 1974.
A Durable Fire. New York: Norton, 1972.
Encounter in April. Boston: Houghton Mifflin, 1937.
A Grain of Mustard Seed. New York: Norton, 1971.
Halfway to Silence: New Poems. New York: Norton, 1980.
Inner Landscape. Boston: Houghton Mifflin, 1939.
In Time Like Air. New York: Rinehart, 1958.
Land of Silence and Other Poems. New York: Rinehart, 1953.
The Leaves of the Tree. Mount Vernon, Iowa: Cornell College Chapbooks, 1950.
Letters from Maine: New Poems. New York: Norton, 1984.
The Lion and the Rose. New York: Rinehart, 1948.
The Phoenix Again: New Poems. Concord, N.H.: W. B. Ewert, 1987.
A Private Mythology. New York: Norton, 1966.
Selected Poems of May Sarton, edited by Serena Sue Hilsinger and Lois Byrnes. New York: Norton, 1978.
The Silence Now: New and Uncollected Earlier Poems. New York: Norton, 1988.

Fiction

As We Are Now. New York: Norton, 1973.
The Birth of a Grandfather. New York: Rinehart, 1957.
The Bridge of Years. New York: Doubleday, 1946.
Crucial Conversations. New York: Norton, 1975.
The Education of Harriet Hatfield. New York: Norton, 1989.
Faithful Are the Wounds. New York: Rinehart, 1955.
The Fur Person. New York: Rinehart, 1957.
Joanna and Ulysses. New York: Norton, 1963.
Kinds of Love. New York: Norton, 1970.
The Magnificent Spinster. New York: Norton, 1985.

Miss Pickthorn and Mr. Hare: A Fable. New York: Norton, 1966.
Mrs. Stevens Hears the Mermaids Singing. New York: Norton, 1965.
The Poet and the Donkey. New York: Norton, 1969.
Punch's Secret. New York: Harper and Row, 1974.
A Reckoning. New York: Norton, 1978.
Shadow of a Man. New York: Rinehart, 1950.
A Shower of Summer Days. New York: Rinehart, 1952.
The Single Hound. Boston: Houghton Mifflin, 1938.
The Small Room. New York: Norton, 1961.
A Walk through the Woods. New York: Harper and Row, 1976.

Nonfiction

After the Stroke: A Journal. New York: Norton, 1982.
Anger. New York: Norton, 1982.
At Seventy: A Journal. New York: Norton, 1984.
Endgame: A Journal of the Seventy-Ninth Year. New York: Norton, 1992.
Honey in the Hive; Judith Matlack, 1899–1982. Boston: Warren Publishing Co., 1988.
The House by the Sea: A Journal. New York: Norton, 1977.
I Knew a Phoenix: Sketches for an Autobiography. New York: Holt, Rinehart and Winston, 1959.
Journal of a Solitude. New York: Norton, 1973.
Plant Dreaming Deep. New York: Norton, 1968.
Recovering: A Journal. New York: Norton, 1980.
A World of Light: Portraits and Celebrations. New York: Norton, 1976.
Writings on Writing. Orono, Me.: Puckerbrush Press, 1980.

Anthologies

Sarton Selected: An Anthology of the Journals, Novels, and Poems of May Sarton. Edited, with an introduction and notes, by Bradford Dudley Daziel. New York: Norton, 1991.

Contributors

BARBARA BAIR is a Fellow at the Virginia Center for the Humanities in Charlottesville. She has been affiliated with the James B. Coleman African Studies Center, University of California at Los Angeles. She received her Ph.D. in American Civilization at Brown University, where she taught courses in women's studies, including American women's literature. She has been a Rockefeller Humanist-in-Residence at the Institute for Research on Women, Rutgers University. She is currently working on two books, one on gender and the Garvey movement, the other an anthology, edited with Susan Cayleff, on women of color and health.

JANET CATHERINE BERLO is Professor of Art History at the University of Missouri–St. Louis. She has also taught at Yale and the Rhode Island School of Design. She has published extensively on pre-Columbian art and archaeology, native American art, and women's studies. At present, she is completing a book entitled *Dreaming of Double Woman: Reflections on Native American Women and Art.*

JEANNE BRAHAM is a poet and the founding editor of Heatherstone Press. She teaches creative writing at Clark University in Massachusetts. She has also taught at Allegheny College, Smith College, and the University of New Hampshire. She has published a full-length study of Saul Bellow's fiction, *A Sort of Columbus,* and is currently completing a study of women's autobiographies. Most recently, she was selected as a Research Associate of the Five College Women's Studies Research Center at Mount Holyoke College.

MARY K. DESHAZER is Associate Professor of Women's Studies in English and Coordinator of Women's Studies at Wake Forest University. She is the author of *Inspiring Women: Reimagining the Muse* and of a book in progress, tentatively entitled *A Poetics of Resistance: Women Writing from El Salvador, South Africa, and the United States.* Articles from her work-in-progress appear in the Summer (1990), and Summer (1992), issues of the *NWSA Journal.*

WILLIAM DRAKE, Emeritus Professor and former chair of the English Department, State University of New York at Oswego, presently lives in San Francisco. He is the author of *Sara Teasdale: Woman and Poet* and of *The First Wave: Women Poets in America, 1915–1945,* as well as editor of *Mirror of the Heart,* selected poems of Sara Teasdale. He is currently working on a study of Africa in the Western imagination.

ELIZABETH EVANS is Professor Emerita at the Georgia Institute of Technology, where she taught from 1964–90, serving as department head from 1986–89. She has published monographs on Ring Lardner, Thomas Wolfe, and Eudora Welty. Her book *May Sarton, Revisited* appeared in the fall of 1989.

K. GRAEHME HALL is Director of the Sexual Offense Prevention and Survivors' Advocacy Program at Antioch College, Ohio. She will complete her doctoral program in English at Michigan State University. She has an M.A. in creative writing; her poems may be found in *The Centennial Reveiw* and other journals. Her most recent article appeared in *Charlotte Perkins Gilman: The Woman and Her Work*. She is presently conducting research on violence against women in twentieth-century American literature.

MAUREEN TERESA MCCARTHY is a former contributing editor in American Studies at Harcourt Brace Jovanovich. She is a native of central New York, currently completing an M.A. in American literature at Syracuse University. She teaches at Onondaga Community College. Her research interests include nineteenth-century American women writers; her current focus is Elizabeth Stoddard. May Sarton's journals have had a profound influence on her life.

MARILYN R. MUMFORD is Professor of English at Bucknell University, where she is also co-director of the Race / Gender Resource Center. She teaches medieval literature, women's studies, and gay and lesbian literature. She received her Ph.D. from the Pennsylvania State University. Her publications include articles on *Beowulf*, Robert Henryson, medieval romance, Hildegard of Bingen, Anne Cameron, feminist pedagogy, and May Sarton. An occasional poet, she has published work most recently in *Sinister Wisdom*.

CAROL VIRGINIA POHLI has been reading the works of May Sarton since 1979, when *A Reckoning* changed her life. A Ph.D. candidate at Ohio State University, she has published several articles about women in literature and a research poll of the public-issue views of evangelical women.

SUSAN SWARTZLANDER received her Ph.D. from the Pennsylvania State University in 1988. She is an Assistant Professor of English at Grand Valley State University in Michigan. Her publications include articles on Joyce, Hemingway, Hawthorne, Faulkner, Durrell, Shaw, Pynchon, Hoult, and Sarton. She is currently at work on a critical biography of the Irish writer Norah Hoult.

NANCY S. WEYANT earned her B.A. from American University, her M.S.L.S. from Wayne State University, and her M.A. in English from Bucknell University. She has taught library science at Williamsport Area Community College and Clarion University. For the past sixteen years she has been a reference librarian at Bucknell University. Her M.A. thesis is an annotated bibliography of criticism of Elizabeth Gaskell published between 1976 and 1991.

Index